Yesterday...

CAME SUDDENLY

All My best,
Bob Cebrian

Yesterday...
CAME SUDDENLY

The Definitive History
of the Beatles

Bob Cepican
AND
Waleed Ali

ARBOR HOUSE   **NEW YORK**

Manufactured in the United States of America

10 9 8 7 6 5 4 3 2 1

This book is printed on acid-free paper. The paper in this book meets the guidelines for permanence and durability of the Committee on Production Guidelines for Book Longevity of the Council on Library Resources.

Library of Congress Cataloging in Publication Data

Cepican, Robert, 1956–
  Yesterday—came suddenly.

  Bibliography: p.
  1. Beatles. 2. Rock musicians—England—Biography.
I. Ali, Waleed, 1950–   II. Title.
ML421.B4C49 1985   784.5′4′00922 [B]   84-24536
ISBN: 0-87795-620-0

CONTENTS

ACKNOWLEDGMENTS

In Europe: Steve Aldo, Arthur Ballard, Tony Barrow, Billy Butler, Tony Carricker, Paddy Chambers, Rod Davis, Geoffrey Ellis, Clive Epstein, Mike Evans, Eric Griffiths, Colin Hanton, George Harrison (*Liverpool Echo*), Bill Harry, Arthur Howes, Liz Hughes, Barry Humphries, Dick James, Brian Kelly, Vic Lewis, Tommy Moore, Rod Murray, William Pobjoy, Dick Rowe, Mike Smith, Mimi Smith, Victor Spinetti, Brian Sommerville, Chris Walley, Alan Williams, Len Wood, Lord Woodbine, and Bob Wooler.

In North America: Lester Bangs, Jo Bergman, Sid Bernstein, Bob Bonis, Al Brodax, Peter Brown, Tommy Charles, Dave Dexter, Jr., Ian Dove, Voyle Gilmore, Walter Hofer, Tony King, Ed Lefler, Nancy Lewis, Alan Livingston, Larry Lujack, Geoff McKuen, Paul Marshall, Brown Meggs, Joe O'Brien, Vidal Sassoon, Red Schwartz, Walter Shenson, Klaus Voorman, Norman Weiss, and Vicky Whitcombe.

And special thanks to: Joel Selvin of the *San Francisco Chronicle*; David Pritchard of Sonic Workshop, Toronto; Johnny Beerling of the BBC, London; Walter Shenson of Walter Shenson Films; and Bob Bonis.

GROWING UP IN
LIVERPOOL

Since the 1960s, the city of Liverpool has been a shrine to the Beatles. Indeed, the enduring popularity of the group has forced this English seaport to live up to the public's picturesque visions of the Liverpool where the Beatles were raised: sea gulls flying from building to building, quaint townsfolk exchanging witticisms all day, weathered sailors sitting in pubs spinning yarns about the sea. Those who remember the Beatles' Liverpool, however, have an appreciably different memory of the city. Although much attention has been focused on the musical influences that helped shape the group, the environment of Liverpool was one of the major influences that inspired John Lennon, Paul McCartney, George Harrison, and Ringo Starr to pursue careers in music.

The Beatles belonged to the generation of war babies that grew up in the austerity that engulfed England following World War II. The economic hardship that the country en-

9

dured in the 1940s and 1950s was intensified in Liverpool, which was devastated by widespread unemployment. A majority of Scouse—as Liverpudlians are called in Britain—then lived either on the dole, in tenement flats (as Ringo Starr's family did), or in subsidized government housing called "council estates" (like the families of Paul McCartney and George Harrison). Liverpool was an impoverished city whose people might well have simply wallowed in despair had they been so inclined. Liverpudlians, however, had distinguished themselves from the rest of the country by their scathing sense of humor. In fact, the city produced many of England's most famous comics, prompting the well-known London quip "So many comedians come from Liverpool because you've gotta be a comedian to live there."

The emotional anxieties brought on by the city's economic plight were heightened by the general attitude that Liverpudlians were an inferior people—a prejudice similar to the one directed toward black Americans then. Liverpudlians were set apart by their poverty, their lack of power, and by the contempt in which Londoners held them. This prejudice made it almost impossible for the Beatles to secure a recording contract and, later, to obtain national coverage in the media.

England's social structure rarely permitted those from the lower classes to rise above their position in life. Thus by the time Liverpool's male generation of war babies reached their late teens, they were conditioned to believe that there was no way a guy with a Scouse accent could achieve the kind of success he read about in the press. Teenagers from working-class backgrounds were expected to follow in the footsteps of their fathers, while those from middle-class families were advised to excel in school if they were to have any hope of a decent life.

There were not many alternatives for the thousands of young men who, upon leaving high school, found themselves unemployed and on the dole. Some turned to boxing, hoping to fight their way out of this environment. Others chose the merchant navy, which had been a way of life for generations of young Liverpudlians. (John Lennon considered joining the merchant navy after leaving high school.) The military had been eliminated as a source of involuntary employment when the British government ended conscription with males born in 1939. Subsequently, many of England's premier musicians of the 1960s grew to manhood holding a guitar or a pair of drumsticks rather than a rifle. This interest in performing music began in the mid-1950s when a popular new musical form called "skiffle" inspired thousands of English high-school boys to play the guitar or drums. They were not encouraged to pursue music as a career then, but playing in a band kept thousands of unemployed Liverpool boys off the streets at night and out of trouble.

Throughout the late 1950s and early 1960s, Liverpool's unemployment rate remained a dark spot in England's economic picture. By this time skiffle bands were performing rock 'n' roll in cellar clubs and dance halls all over the city. Playing in a band was often the sole source of income for many Liverpool teenagers; beat groups with four- or five-man lineups were earning between £6 and £8 a night (about $16 to $20). Most of these bands saw no point in trying to secure a recording contract. Since London controlled the British music industry and rarely signed acts from the provinces, the chances of a Liverpool group achieving more than local fame were less than remote.

A few Liverpudlian musicians nevertheless saw their music as the only way out of a depressed and impoverished environment. One such musician was John Lennon; it was through him that the Beatles were formed.

PART 1

THE BIRTH OF THE BEATLES

Circa 1940 to 1960

1

Throughout the Beatles' seven-year history as a recording band, John Lennon was the most controversial and harshly criticized member of the group. In the early 1960s, the press claimed that his strong personality was "the soul of the Beatles," but by the end of the decade, Lennon's outrageous public behavior had earned him the label "the weird Beatle."

John often said that whenever he was depressed, the memories of the emotional traumas he experienced as a child and teenager came back to haunt him. The rock opera *Tommy* was rumored to be loosely based on Lennon's childhood, which he believed shaped his rebellious character. John had been abandoned by his parents when he was only two years old, and had been on his own from the time he was a teenager; he was responsible to no one but himself. His father, Fred Lennon, was a seaman. John's mother, Julia Stanley, was the black sheep of a proper middle-class family. They dated for ten years before marrying in 1938 as a practical joke on Julia's parents, who had previously warned their daughter that Lennon was too irresponsible to take care of her. Following a brief wedding ceremony at a Liverpool registrar's office, the bride, who was twenty-four, returned to her parents' house at 9 Newcastle Road in Wavertree, Liverpool, and the groom, who was twenty-six, returned to his job as a steward in the merchant navy. On the morning of October 9, 1940, during a Luftwaffe assault on Liverpool, Fred was somewhere at sea when his wife gave birth to their only child. Julia's eldest sister, Mimi, named the boy John (after her father) Winston (after Prime Minister Churchill) Lennon.

Fred Lennon learned about his son's birth three months later. He had arranged for his wife to receive two-thirds of his wages each week from the shipping line's Liverpool office to support herself and their child. In the spring of 1942, however, when John was a year and a half old, the office informed Julia that her husband had deserted his ship, thus terminating the weekly payments. Fred's desertion abruptly ended the Lennons' marriage.

Although their prophecy about Fred Lennon had come true, the Stanley family rallied around Julia and her child. Mimi was particularly attentive to the boy; she was at Julia's side when John was born and fell in love with her nephew the moment she saw him. In the months that followed Fred Lennon's disappearance, the Stanleys realized that Julia could not cope with the responsibility of raising her son. The situation was further complicated when Julia met and fell in love with a man named John Dykins. She wanted to marry him, but he did not want to raise another man's child. Forced to choose between her son and a man who offered her happiness, Julia decided to live with John Dykins in Allerton, Liverpool, and passed on to Mimi and her husband, George Smith, the responsibility of raising John, who was then two years old.

George and Mimi raised John as their son, intending to give him a proper upbringing and education. Their home, at 251 Menlove Avenue in Woolton, Liverpool, provided John with a comfortable and stable environment. The area was suburban, quiet and middle-class. There was a playground nearby to which Mimi brought him after the long walks they often took together, and a golf course where a youthful Lennon and his childhood friends played, sometimes hunting for lost golf balls to sell back to the golfers. The Smiths did their best to give John a happy and undisturbed homelife, and though he knew that Mimi and George were not his natural parents, he accepted them as his guardians.

When John was five, however, his natural father suddenly entered his life. Fred Lennon had returned to England after the war, having spent the duration in a maritime brig on Ellis Island, New York. He settled in Blackpool (thirty miles north of Liverpool) and lived a prosperous life through the black market. One day in 1945, Fred's curiosity to see the child he had fathered brought him to Menlove Avenue, where he persuaded the Smiths to let him have his son for an afternoon. Fred, however, absconded with John to Blackpool, and father and son spent several days together, during which time Fred decided not to return John to Mimi and George. A friend who was planning to immigrate to New Zealand persuaded Lennon to come along, but before he could leave England with John, Julia appeared at his flat.

This was the first time John had seen his parents together, and the reunion was not a happy one. The couple argued over who should have custody of the boy. Fred told Julia that he was determined to take his son with him to New Zealand, and at one point suggested that the three of them go there together as a family again. Julia refused this offer of reconciliation and was determined to leave Blackpool with her son. They continued to argue until Fred finally asked John to decide with whom he wanted to live. The boy ran to his father and sat on his lap. Julia watched for a moment, then left the flat in tears. When Fred told his son that he would never see his mother again, John jumped from his father's hold and ran after his mother.

John's guilt at choosing his father over his mother was compounded by a feeling that his mother was punishing him when, having led him to believe that he was going home to live with her, she returned him to Mimi and George. Actually, she had no intention of raising John, but she knew that Fred could not provide him with a proper home. Fred Lennon disappeared from John's life as suddenly as he had entered. He did not return until his son was rich and famous. John suppressed the memory of these events and expressed the anguish he felt then twenty-five years later in the song "Mother."

From the age of five, John's life with the Smiths grew more settled. He played games; took part in such sports as soccer, cricket, and basketball; and got into mischief like any youngster. He displayed his creative talents by filling dozens of notebooks with poems and fairy tales, which he illustrated with humorous cartoons. "He always loved reading, but only the classics," said Mimi. "I never saw him look at a comic book or novel. His favorite books were about painting and painters, like John Ruskin's *Book of Beauty*."

The mystique of music had captured John's attention at an early age and he fell in love with it; he often sang nursery songs to himself until he fell asleep. The first instrument he learned to play was the harmonica, acquired from one of the college students who rented a room from the Smiths. If John could learn a tune, the student would buy him a harmonica. John learned two.

Throughout John's childhood and adolescence, his contact with his mother was limited to her occasional visits to Menlove Avenue, and these visits only added to his confusion. He loved Julia and could not understand why he was living with relatives and not with her. Mimi never told him the truth about his parents' separation except that they had fallen out of love, and she was careful not to reveal to him that Julia did not want to raise her child. As he grew older, John's confusion increased, particularly when his parents agreed that he should be adopted by the Smiths. In the end, however, Fred and Julia could not be persuaded to appear together to finalize the adoption.

John's belief that his mother and father no longer loved him, his foster childhood and the death in 1953 of Uncle George (the only father figure John had known), coalesced to create a brash, unruly, and often rude teenager, free from the stricture of parents, but inwardly miserable.

John said that the awareness he acquired from not being with his parents made him feel different from his friends, who had at least a mother or a father. He also believed that his childhood fantasies inspired his rebellion. John's friends remember him as a boy who was always in trouble with the neighbors, a boy in a constant state of delinquency, continually fighting and rebeling. By the time he entered Quarry Bank High School in 1952, he was a clever, incorrigible, strong-willed youth; no one could force him to do anything. "Like a lot of us, he was very anti toward school," says Chris Walley, a close childhood and teenage friend of Lennon's. "I hated school, John hated school, and quite frankly we'd do anything to upset the system without it being criminal, if you know what I mean. But I think with his father disappearing when he was a child, living with his mother now and again and then living with his auntie, it made a disjointed life for him."

At fourteen, John was a highly imaginative and intelligent young man, but he was bored with schoolwork and uninterested in the curriculum. At Quarry Bank his teachers, whom he felt did not understand him, tried to mold him into a proper student by beating him with a cane, but this only encouraged his rebellion. On countless occasions, teachers enraged by his impudence stormed into the headmaster's office and vehemently complained about his latest prank.

In early 1955, as American teenagers were embracing a musical craze called "rock 'n' roll," English teenagers were captivated by a musical mania of their own—skiffle, a fast shuffle, up-tempo folk music.

Prior to the skiffle craze, many high-school boys felt they could never achieve sufficient skill to reproduce a recorded song on a musical instrument, and many parents, particularly in Liverpool, discouraged their children's musical interest because they could not afford to purchase or lease an instrument and pay for lessons. Skiffle music, however, could be performed with minimal talent, no formal training, and the simplest instruments. Sparked by the Scotch-born jazz musician Lonnie Donegan and his recording of Huddy Ledbetter's "Rock Island Line," boys rushed to acquire guitars, banjos, and drums. If they could not afford to buy a cheap guitar or a set of drums, they used crude, homemade instruments, such as a washboard, an old tea chest fashioned into an upright bass—anything capable of making "musical" sounds. As a result, thousands of high-school boys learned to play chords and rhythm patterns nearly a year before the advent of rock 'n' roll in England. Though many youngsters lost interest in playing an instrument once the skiffle fervor waned, the popularity of rock 'n' roll fired the enthusiasm of those who continued.

The skiffle influence was felt strongly in predominantly working-class cities such as Liverpool. Teenage boys practiced feverishly on their instruments, trying to produce sounds that sounded faintly melodic. Their enthusiasm was heightened when they talked about music and guitars with friends and classmates. These discussions often led to group practice sessions.

John Lennon did not express a desire to play the guitar until the skiffle craze began. During one of Julia's visits to Menlove Avenue, he told her about his interest in the guitar, and she bought him one for £10.

John recalled that the appearance of the guitar in his life made high school "bearable." Since nearly all the students around him were affected by the craze, he decided to form a skiffle group. The original lineup featured John Lennon (guitar), Eric Griffiths (guitar), Rod Davis (banjo), Pete Shotton (washboard), Colin Hanton (drums), and Bill Smith (tea-chest bass). Smith was replaced by Len Garry, a student from the Liverpool Institute High School. The group was known by several names then, as Rod Davis recalls: "We were the Blackjacks for a time, but I think we got rather fed up with that. Then there was our school song. The first line went: 'Quarrymen strong before our birth.' We weren't too serious when we sang the school song. Quarrymen seemed to be a joke at the school song's expense, but it also tied in with the Woolton Quarries and we all did go to Quarry Bank, so we became the Quarrymen."

The Quarrymen were heavily influenced by Lonnie Donegan, and with the help of Julia Lennon—who taught John, Eric, and Rod three-finger banjo chords—they learned to play the songs Donegan popularized in England: "Rock Island Line," "John Henry," "Midnight Special," "Don't You Rock Me Daddy-O," and "Alabamie Bound." They quickly built a repertoire by adapting pop or blues tunes to a skiffle rhythm. One of the Quarrymen's earliest public performances was in May 1955 at a garden fete celebrating the crowning of the May

Queen at the St. Peter's Youth Club, to which most of the members of the group belonged. "It started out as a procession around Woolton Village with decorated floats on lorries," says Colin Hanton. "We were placed on the back of one of these lorries, where we played from." The boys were not paid for this booking, nor for any other booking during their first year. All the skiffle groups on Merseyside played for their enjoyment and were given a meal for their time.

The group had few opportunities to perform in public following the St. Peter's fete and had to wait three to four weeks between each engagement. They used this time to rehearse, usually at Eric Griffiths' house, at the home of a classmate, or wherever they could without causing complaints about the noise. At most of these practices, the boys listened to the radio or played records, trying to learn the words and chords to the songs they liked. "John would figure out the tunes first," says Eric Griffiths. "He had a better ear for music than anyone in the group." The Quarrymen occasionally practiced at Menlove Avenue, but Mimi did not care for John's involvement with a skiffle band nor his interest in the guitar, feeling that it would interfere with his schoolwork. As soon as her ears detected the faint sounds of a guitar being strummed behind a closed bedroom door, a familiar cry reverberated through the house: "Pack up that guitar and get down to work!"

Aunt Mimi was a disciplinarian who tried to steer her nephew away from the wrong influences, including some of his friends, but this only inspired John to rebel against her. "John was like the Artful Dodger," says Chris Walley. "He was always one step ahead of Mimi because in many ways she was an older parent. At that age I pictured Uncle George, before he died, to be in his fifties and Mimi quite possibly to be the same age. You often find that kids become brighter because they're brought on much quicker with older people and in the end they outwit them."

Mimi wanted John to grow into a responsible young man, unlike his father, but she could see that her efforts were failing. He was smoking cigarettes and drinking himself into a stupor wherever the Quarrymen performed, and had affected the appearance of a Teddy boy, which she feared would bring trouble. (The Teddy-boy image had begun in London as a fashion craze for Edwardian clothing. By the time the fad reached Liverpool, it had become synonymous with juvenile delinquents attacking elderly people with bicycle chains and razor blades.) John was failing at Quarry Bank and was constantly getting himself into trouble. His waywardness at home and in school was running parallel with another influence that further encouraged Lennon's rebellion—rock 'n' roll.

The release of the film *Blackboard Jungle* in late 1955 linked teenage rebelliousness to the emerging sounds of rock 'n' roll by featuring "Rock Around the Clock" by Bill Haley and the Comets in the opening sequence. The record had been released in Britain earlier that year as a single and was moderately successful, but when used as the theme song for a movie about teenagers in revolt, "Rock Around the Clock" became the anthem for the teenage generation growing up in the 1950s.

As popular as Bill Haley was in England then, he did not initiate the Quarrymen's transition from skiffle to rock, because the group considered his music too complicated for them to perform. Moreover, John said that Bill Haley made only a mild impression on him; rock 'n' roll did not have a real impact on Lennon until May 1956 when Elvis Presley's "Heartbreak Hotel" made its English debut. John imitated Elvis when he sang, and tried to look like him by combing his hair in Presley's style.

The sole source for rock music in England then was Radio Luxembourg, Europe's only commercial radio station. All the major British record labels sponsored programs on Radio Luxembourg to promote their releases. Decca Records, in particular, aired a two-hour program called the "Decca Radio Show," which was largely responsible for establishing rock 'n' roll in England. Decca was the British distributor for Atlantic, Chess, Cadet, Specialty, and Imperial—the American independent record companies considered to be the backbone of the rock revolution. On Saturday night, Radio Luxembourg broadcast a program hosted by Alan Freed called the "Moondog House Rock 'n' Roll Party Show," which featured recordings by Chuck Berry, Little Richard, Fats Domino, Bo Diddley, Jerry Lee Lewis, Carl Perkins, and Gene Vincent. All these performers had an influence on John Lennon and drew him closer to rock 'n' roll, transforming his life.

The Quarrymen played whatever songs John wanted to sing—at least, as many as their talent would allow. "John was the lead singer," says Rod Davis. "He was the only singer of any note. The rest of us were hopeless. We used to join in on the chorus, but we didn't sing. Musically, what John said went." It was important to Lennon's ego to be the undisputed leader of the group and among his friends, but stories about his forcing members to leave the Quarrymen if they did not fall in line are not true. "I'm quite sure we all disagreed at times," says Eric Griffiths, "but I can't recall John ever giving anyone an ultimatum where he said, 'We do it this way or you're out of the group!' If you weren't one of John's friends or in the group, it was very hard to know him. He didn't react the same way toward you, but he would test your friendship. John would call the bluff: 'If you still want to go with me, we'll do it this way.' John would only move against those he knew would back down, but with someone who stood up to him and posed a challenge, he was careful." Rod Davis adds: "There really didn't seem to be any need for leading, although if there was a leader at all, then it was John. The only way he was forceful was the way he played. John played so strongly that hardly an evening went by when he didn't break a string on his guitar."

By autumn 1956 the Quarrymen were performing once a week and were occasionally paid several shillings for their work. The boys appeared in numerous talent and skiffle competitions throughout Liverpool but never won. They received one steady booking from a promoter named Charlie McBain, who ran the Wilson Hall in Garston, Liverpool, and paid them £2.50 a night—enough for their bus fare back to Woolton and a bottle of beer for each of the boys. The knowledge that he could earn money by playing his guitar delighted Lennon, despite the advice of Rod Davis's father, who jokingly told him, "Look, John, take my word for it. If you start getting money for it, it'll ruin you!" As a teenager, Lennon would do anything to make money as long as it did not involve physical labor. "When John was fourteen he joined the Saint Peter's Church choir," says Mimi, "but I think he joined for the money—he thought he was going to get paid. After he realized that there was no money in it, he left!"

During the eight weeks that the Quarrymen played at Wilson Hall, the group found that they were unpopular with the local Teddy boys. "We always had to run for our lives at the end of the night," says Eric. "Garston was a pretty tough area and some of the locals liked to have a go at us afterwards because their girlfriends turned their attention on us and not on them. We used to have to time our run to get onto the bus just as it drove off. There were quite large gangs and there was one gang who we knew were after us—getting us as a group. There would be thirty Teds to a gang, so you made sure you avoided them. We never got into a fight, although one time they almost caught up with us, but we managed to split up and go in different directions to get away from them."

There was a streak of arrogance in John's personality that annoyed people. He'd stand onstage squinting, looking cocky, cool, and confident while he performed. The tough-guy squint was actually due to his refusal to wear his eyeglasses onstage; since he was farsighted and virtually blind without them, he had to squint to see if any friends or classmates were in the audience. Still, he enjoyed giving people the impression that he was a tough guy, though he admitted it was a pretense to make others think twice about challenging him to a fight. He also enjoyed imitating tough rebels like Elvis and Marlon Brando.

Faced with the possibility of a fight in which he suspected he might not fare very well, John would either run away or, as Colin Hanton remembers, "he'd just talk and talk and talk until the other bloke felt it was time to go home." At age sixteen he was not physically impressive, but he could take care of himself in the schoolyard. "John would stand there and take the punches if he knew he was going to win," says Chris Walley. "This was the sort of guy he was. John would act first before any talking was done, punch the other fella in the nose and get the initiative over him. John would not stand there and wait for the other guy to move first. John'd steam in, whack him one while the other guy was thinking about it."

In July 1957 the Quarrymen were booked to peform at a garden fete at the Woolton Parish Church. Ivan Vaughan, a close friend of John's and a student at the Liverpool Institute High School, had talked about the group to a fifteen-year-old schoolmate named Paul McCartney, who was equally enthusiastic about the guitar and rock 'n' roll.

Paul arrived at the church eager to impress Ivan's friends, his impeccable Teddy-boy outfit accentuated by his Elvis Presley hairstyle. He stood in the audience watching the Quarrymen until his attention became focused on John Lennon, who was singing an ad-libbed version of Del Viking's "Come Go with Me," which John said was the first set of lyrics he wrote for a song. Paul was impressed.

John rarely knew the correct lyrics to the songs the Quarrymen played, so he sang any words that popped into his head. "We really couldn't afford to buy much in the way of records to learn words from," says Rod Davis. "So while we knew the melody, John would write words to the songs. One was called 'Long Black Train' and another was 'Come Go with Me,' [for] which he rewrote the lyrics 'Come, come, come, come/Come go with me/Down, down, down, down/Down to the penitentiary.' "

The entertainment moved inside the church, where the Quarrymen played once more. By then Paul knew that his ability on the guitar exceeded Lennon's, and he borrowed a guitar from someone and began to show off. "Paul did 'Long Tall Sally,' which went down quite well," remembers Eric Griffiths. "John was impressed with Paul's playing. For a start he played guitar chords, not banjo chords, and he appeared to have a good grasp of music, compared to ourselves." The clincher was Paul's ability to tune a guitar, which the others did not know how to do.

Lennon began to talk to Paul about rock 'n' roll, and Paul gave him the words to 'Twenty Flight Rock' and a few others, impressing John, who was a bit drunk.

During the 1960s Paul McCartney was regarded as the romantic idol of the Beatles. He enjoyed this image and made sure that his appearance—hairstyle, clothing, and personality—reflected it when he stepped out in public. Paul hadn't changed much since 1957. Even as a teenager, he'd been confident of his talent and his looks, but was careful not to be too obvious with his affectations. Raised in a conservative environment, he grew to be a polite, well-behaved, respectful youth.

Paul was the eldest son of two loving and hardworking parents, Jim and Mary McCartney. Jim's position as a salesman at the Cotton Exchange in Liverpool and Mary's work as a hospital nurse enabled the family to live in middle-class comfort during the austerity of postwar England. The couple had met in the summer of 1940 in the basement of a house during a Luftwaffe air strike and were married the following year. Jim was then thirty-nine and Mary thirty-one. James Paul McCartney was born in Walton Hospital on June 18, 1942, in a state of asphyxia and had to be resuscitated. After Paul's birth, Mary quit nursing to become a midwife and the family moved from their first home in Anfield (Liverpool) to Wallasey, then to a bungalow in Knowsley Estate (Liverpool), where Jim and Mary's second child, Michael, was born in January 1944. The McCartneys moved three more times before settling in a council estate at 20 Forthlin Road in Allerton when Paul was thirteen.

Aside from these moves, Paul's childhood was largely undisturbed; indeed, it was close to idyllic. While John Lennon could recall only the pain and trauma of his early years, McCartney could sentimentally reminisce about a family who went away on holiday each year to the vacation camps and farms of north Wales; about growing up on the outskirts of a big industrial city where there were spacious parks and green fields in which to play with his brother and his pet sheep dog, Prince; and about a mother and father who never let their children forget how much they were loved. Jim and Mary took an interest in whatever interested Paul and Mike, and they encouraged their sons' boyhood dreams. They instilled in both boys the confidence that they could do or be anything they wanted so long as they worked hard and respected the values that the family regarded highly. Jim McCartney blended sternness with humor and love. He was a gentle father, quick to praise his sons' achievements, but just as quick to punish them for misbehaving. Mary McCartney was a soft-spoken woman dedicated to her husband and sons. The demands of her job as a midwife and her determination to raise Paul and Mike in a healthy environment were the reasons for the family's frequent moves. Mary paid careful attention to her sons' appearance and stressed the importance of good manners. She was a perfectionist and a stickler for detail—traits she passed on to the boys. Mike says he was closer to his mother while Paul, an independent child, was closer to his father.

As children the McCartney brothers were inseparable—wherever one went, the other followed. The family's frequent moves made it difficult for them to establish any lasting friendships with other children their age. They were mischievous and occasionally got into serious trouble. Once they were badly stung by bees after throwing rocks at some hives. Another time they fell into a pond and Paul nearly drowned.

The bond between the boys strengthened as they grew older, even though, like all brothers, they frequently quarreled. Mike found that one sure way to get to Paul was by teasing him about his weight when Paul was going through a chubby stage from age ten to thirteen and was sensitive about it.

Paul remembers his days in the Boy Scouts as the most exciting part of his boyhood. He spent one summer in the country, cooking over an open fire, enjoying the outdoors during the day and sitting around a campfire at night, wrapped in a blanket, singing songs and telling ghost stories. While attending Joseph Williams Primary School in Gateacre, Liverpool, Paul became convinced that his left-handedness placed him at a disadvantage, often feeling so disoriented he would do things like riding a bike backward.

Despite this evident disability, Paul qualified for the best high school in the city, the Liverpool Institute, which accepted only the top students from the educational system. During his first year, he maintained high marks and applied himself to his studies, taking an interest in English literature and foreign languages. The lord mayor of Liverpool presented him with a copy of Geoffrey Trease's book *The Seven Queens of England* as a Coronation Day prize for the best-written essay in his class.

Jim and Mary were proud of Paul's achievements and began making plans for him to become an English teacher. But after a year at the institute, Paul suddenly lost interest in school. He realized he had no idea why he was being educated or where an education would lead him. His feelings about school were shared by many other teenagers in the working-class area where Paul's family lived. He was one of the few boys living near Ardwick Road who attended the institute, and his neighborhood friends teased him, calling him a "college puddin'."

Music had always been an important part of Paul's life. His father had once played piano and trumpet in a jazz band, and Paul loved the ballads and melodic tunes of the Thirties and Forties that his father played and sang—songs like "White Christmas" and "Stairway to Paradise." Paul and Mike would sing along with their father, who frequently paused to explain a few principles of music theory such as harmony. When Paul, at eleven, expressed a desire to play the piano, his father sent him to a piano teacher living near Ardwick Road. After three or four lessons, however, he tired of the discipline required to learn the instrument and dropped it. Jim then tried to persuade him to join a church choir, but Paul purposely failed his audition.

On his thirteenth birthday, in June 1955, Paul was given a trumpet, and like his father he learned to play by ear. With the trumpet too, however, his fascination was short-lived. The problem this time was that he failed to develop an embouchure. And anyway, if he played the trumpet he couldn't sing. The guitar was by now the rage, so Paul started playing. The guitar proved even tougher for McCartney because it was strung for a right-handed person and he thought it had to be played that way. Once he figured it out though he was on his way.

Paul's first guitar was a Rosetti Lucky Seven, which he describes as "a plank of wood with strings." He began by learning his favorite skiffle and pop tunes with the aid of an instruction book—but here again his left-handedness was a problem, since the chord diagrams were designed for a right-handed person. After some experimenting he overcame the handicap by propping the book in front of a mirror so that the chords were reflected in reverse.

During his summer holiday away from school, Paul practiced the guitar as much as he could. His interest was inflamed when classes resumed in September and he discovered that many of his schoolmates affected by the craze now owned guitars. They would meet during their lunch hour each day and talk about music. Eager to learn as much about the guitar as possible, McCartney was drawn to those who played better than he. One afternoon during his lunch hour, he attended a Lonnie Donegan concert at the Pavilion Theatre in Lodge Lane—a decisive event for him. His father had suggested that being a musician was a sure way to become popular, but the enthusiasm with which the audience greeted Donegan was a revelation. Visions of stardom danced in Paul's head and inspired him to practice with renewed diligence. He devoted all his spare time to playing the guitar or listening to the radio, memorizing the words and figuring out the chords to the pop tunes he liked.

Like John Lennon, Paul was mildly influenced by Bill Haley and learned to play the songs that he had popularized, but didn't get really caught up in rock 'n' roll until he heard Elvis Presley. Teenage boys everywhere fell under Presley's influence, and Paul was no exception. Geoff McKuen, a friend and classmate of Mike McCartney's, remembers that "Paul never had a lot to say for himself, even when we sat down. He was always off in another world, either strumming his guitar or tinkering on the piano. He was one of these lads who was filled with ideas. Paul was going to be a star one way or another because he looked like Elvis or whatever. He was brimming with talent and vanity. My God, he took a long time combing his hair!"

By the age of fourteen, Paul had outgrown his chubbiness and was aware that he was better looking than many of his classmates. He was too baby-faced to have a tough-guy image, but he did flaunt his good looks and became one of the most sexually precocious boys in his class. He lectured his friends on sex and produced detailed drawings of nude women, which convinced the other boys that he had firsthand experience (though McCartney says that he did not lose his virginity until age fifteen). By then totally immersed in the world of music, he spent his free time listening to contemporary songs on the BBC and religiously tuned in to Radio Luxembourg to hear their rock broadcasts. In addition to his increasing skill on the guitar, he had a good, clear singing voice that he demonstrated for classmates at school or with his brother whenever they performed for their parents and relatives. The first time he ever sang onstage was for a holiday camp, and he did 'Long Tall Sally.' Jim McCartney was understanding about his son's interest in rock 'n' roll, but felt that it was not as good as the music he himself had played when his band was touring the Liverpool dance halls.

* * *

The serenity of Paul's homelife was shattered one month after he began his fourth year at the institute. He and Mike returned home from school one day and found their mother weeping. Mary did not tell the boys that she was crying from a severe pain in her chest, but her years as a nurse led her to believe that her condition was serious. She was right. Only one month passed from the first twinge of pain until her death from breast cancer on October 31, 1956, at the age of forty-seven. Paul and Mike stayed with relatives during Mary's wake and interment in the Yew Tree Cemetery.

Though devastated by his wife's death, Jim McCartney proved to be a remarkable father and man, taking good care of the boys and not drowning himself in drink and women. Jim McCartney's grief was compounded by the financial dilemma in which he suddenly found himself. He was drawing from the Cotton Exchange a weekly salary of £8 on which he was to support two sons, ages fourteen and twelve. He was on the verge of a promotion when Mary died, but he decided to turn it down because it would have required long hours and would have meant neglecting Paul and Mike at a time when they needed him. Instead, he decided to be both father *and* mother to his sons, which was not an easy task.

After the death of his mother, Paul withdrew more deeply into his music. Without Mary's guidance, Paul became less concerned about his proper schoolboy appearance. He began smoking cigarettes and gradually affected the image of a well-dressed Teddy boy.

Throughout the spring and early summer of 1957, Paul spent most of his time with a schoolmate named Ian James, who also played the guitar. On weekends Paul and Ian either dressed up and went looking for girls or played their guitars, playing Elvis and Little Richard. Ian taught Paul several of the songs that Paul eventually played for John Lennon at the Woolton Parish Church fete.

In the days that followed Paul's performance at the church, John could not decide whether or not he should ask him to join the Quarrymen. Lennon was torn between wanting to improve the group and his reluctance to share the limelight with someone not only good-looking but more musically adept than himself. He also thought about the influence McCartney would have on the other Quarrymen, who, like himself, were impressed by his knowledge of chords, his skill on the guitar, and his Elvis-like appearance and singing voice.

His decision to invite Paul to join the group was one of the first signs of professionalism on his part. A week after the church fete, Pete Shotton, who was a member of the Quarrymen and Lennon's best friend, told Paul the news, who accepted happily.

Paul joined the Quarrymen as their lead guitarist and made his first appearance with the group at the Conservative Club in Broadway, Liverpool, in August 1957. He had a big solo, which he totally botched, due he says to "sticky fingers." So he was put on rhythm guitar.

Despite his sticky fingers, the Quarrymen were glad to have someone of McCartney's talent in the band. His presence, however, brought a strong feeling of insecurity to John, who knew then that it was not going to be easy keeping McCartney in line. "Paul was proving to be a very talented person and he obviously wanted to make decisions that John was making all the time," says Chris Walley. "John was always the leader of the group, but at the same time Paul was trying to be just as powerful. There was always going to be a rift there because one's talent was pushing the other out, and John wouldn't let that be."

Paul was the smoothest character John had ever encountered. Part of his insecurity about McCartney came from trying to figure him out. Paul had a stylish manner of easing his way into a situation and dealing with people. He was clever and thought things out, in contrast to Lennon, who, though clever, steamed into a situation without thinking. McCartney was also a persuasive talker and, according to Eric Griffiths, was often successful in persuading Lennon to do things his way. "There was one occasion where John realized what was happening," says Eric. "John and I were walking together one day and the rest of the group, including Paul, were walking some ways behind us. John suggested to me that we should split up from them. What he really meant was to split up from Paul."

The other Quarrymen recall that there was a difficult period before John became comfortable with Paul, who described their clash of egos in the 1983 song "Here Today," in which he said that they were both playing hard to get. "Paul was not as strong a character as John," says Eric Griffiths. "He wouldn't have drawn the others from the group toward him. If there was any decision to go along with John or Paul, it would have been John. Paul was the newcomer to the group and he had to prove himself and try and fit in. He had to work at it rather than John."

John Lennon later said that the day he met Paul McCartney was the turning point for the group, and though the nucleus of the Beatles had been born, the significance of their meeting then was in the fact that two teenagers with a common interest had crossed paths.

2

In the summer of 1957, John Lennon left Quarry Bank High School, unconcerned about his future. For a while he contemplated a life on the sea, as Chris Walley recalls: "John and I decided that we'd go into the merchant navy. We actually sent away for our railway warrants to go on a course to be stewards aboard a ship. When the warrants arrived in the mail, we said, 'Oh, no thanks, it's not for us.'"

Headmaster Pobjoy, who *was* concerned about Lennon's future, called Mimi to Quarry Bank one day and asked her, "What are you going to do with him?" But she placed the problem back in his hands, replying, "You've had him for five years, what are *you* going to do with him?" Pobjoy knew that the answer to that question was enigmatic. John had failed every subject in school and his irresponsible behavior did little to convince the headmaster that he was capable of anything more than manual labor, which John adamantly detested.

The only subject that interested John was art. He frequently displayed his artistic talents by designing posters for school dances and contributing line drawings to the school magazine. So art school seemed the natural place for him.

The Liverpool Art School, located on Hope Street in the City Centre, was then *the* major art college in the north of England. In September 1957 John entered the school at the intermediate level, which was a two-year preparatory course that gave students a basic grounding in art. He arrived there thinking that the next five years were going to be easy, but after attending several classes he found that his line drawings had no place in the school's curriculum, nor could he grasp the aesthetics of his subjects. In class he was the least prepared. Instead of being enrolled in a graphic-arts course, he was placed in lettering, which he could not comprehend.

During his first week at art school, John became friends with a first-year student from Widnes named Tony Carricker, who remembers meeting Lennon in lettering class. "The teacher did his little bits on the blackboard and John sat on the window ledge because art school, being different from an ordinary school, was slightly informal. The window was open, with a sash hanging from the shade, and every time the teacher's back was turned, John'd push the sash away. As it moved back and forth, he'd hold his hands out in front of him and stare at it intensely and pretend to be controlling its movement. The teacher turned around, saw what he was doing, and threw him out of the classroom. John walked out with a swagger. That's the first time I noticed him and *everybody* noticed him, because that was very noticeable—deliberately noticeable, whatever you'd like to call it in retrospect, like 'rebellious.' But he didn't give a shit and he was getting off on it."

The art school was part of the same complex that housed the Liverpool Institute (the doors joining the two schools had been sealed with bricks sixty years before), where Paul McCartney had begun his fifth year. Over their summer holiday, John and Paul had spent time getting acquainted and had gradually become better friends. They frequently returned to Paul's house to play their guitars, listen to records, or raid Jim McCartney's refrigerator while he was away at work. The first time Jim met his son's new friend, he did not approve of him.

Recognizing John as a troublemaker, Jim warned Paul, "He'll get you in trouble, son."

Once their honeymoon period passed, John and Paul's relationship was characterized by a siblinglike rivalry that would underline their friendship until the breakup of the Beatles. Lennon and McCartney did not verbally challenge each other to do better, but each was motivated by pride and ego to keep pace or excel in something that one could do as well as the other. In the years to come, their rivalry would cause both of them to improve their musical and songwriting skills.

During the first year of their friendship, each had made a noticeable impression on the other. Before he met Paul, John was not serious about improving his guitar playing, because music was still a hobby; in fact, though he'd been playing the guitar for two years, he still used three-finger banjo chords. When John suddenly found himself competing with someone—a challenge to which he was unaccustomed—Paul's skill inspired him to practice diligently and learn the proper fingerings, although left-handed ones when Paul taught them! McCartney made sure that he maintained an edge over Lennon and stayed two chords ahead of him.

Paul claims to have been initially intimidated by John's presence—he'd never met such an outgoing and forceful personality. Most of Paul's friends were schoolboys who expressed their rebellion in harmless pranks. Paul considered John a street kid—a Ted. As their friendship developed, Paul became stronger and bolder, almost as a defense against Lennon's brashness. John also fueled Paul's rebelliousness. He had planned to remain in school for two more years and take the examinations for admittance to a teachers' college as his parents had urged so he'd have some security, but because John had given up his education, Paul halfheartedly decided to do the same.

By autumn 1957 the Quarrymen had become a quartet. After graduating high school, Pete Shotton, Rod Davis, and Len Garry left the group, but Eric Griffiths and Colin Hanton stayed with John and Paul for another year. "I don't think any of us believed there would be anything at the end of the rainbow, as it were," says Colin. "Eventually, we all got a year or two older and a bit fed up with the whole routine of lugging our equipment around." With the departure of the washboard, banjo, and tea-chest bass, the Quarrymen affected the appearance of a rock 'n' roll band. "The difference in the group at this time," says Eric, "was the types of music we were trying to play, and also wanting to be a little more professional."

There were now two lead singers in the group. Besides the Elvis Presley and Little Richard tunes they liked, John and Paul began harmonizing to songs like the Everly Brothers' "Bye Bye, Love" and "Wake Up, Little Susie." They spent more time practicing together than with Eric and Colin, getting together with the other two only to rehearse for a booking. Two traits in McCartney, which surfaced while he was a member of the Beatles, were evident at this time: Paul strove for perfection whenever the Quarrymen practiced; and, struggling to achieve the right sound for the songs he sang, he badgered Eric and Colin about their playing. "The difference between John and Paul then was John didn't give a shit," says Geoff McKuen. "He was going to sing a song his way. He wasn't copying everybody else, but he was singing it his way. It didn't matter if he was off-key. Paul was always very much aware of *Paul*. If he sang a song, it always had to be the exact copy of the original."

McCartney also wanted to be center stage because he felt that he had a better voice than Lennon. Paul would mimic the vocal styles of his rock 'n' roll idols—Elvis Presley, Little Richard, Fats Domino, and Eddie Cochran. After years of imitating these different singing styles, he explains, "you would level out into your own voice."

John's social life at the art school centered on his friendships with Tony Carricker and an Arab-Italian student named Geoff Mohammed. They hung out afternoons and evenings in a pub on Rice Street called the Crack, a popular gathering place for students. After a few pints of beer, John often made a nuisance of himself, and was barred from the pub numerous times for such antics as dancing on a table. "John used to get incredibly drunk," says Tony, "and when he got drunk and laughed, he went hysterical and couldn't stop. He'd do this hiccuping laugh and just go higher and higher and he'd slide up the side of the wall in the pub. He'd go berserk laughing. There's a lot of spirit and ebullience in that kind of laughter, and he'd just cackle at the top of his voice. To be seventeen years old, not having to work, and you've got mates to get drunk with, to have good times with—it was that period of our lives when we were totally irresponsible and carefree."

Even without dancing on tables, John's personality and wit made him the center of attention among his school friends and the other art students who patronized the Crack. Says Rod Murray, a friend and schoolmate of Lennon's, "John would tell very amusing stories or make up things about the people who came into the Crack—absolutely ridiculous things that would have us rolling all over the place. John needed an audience. He was either telling stories or being funny, and you can't do that by yourself! I found him really amusing for the first hour or so, and it was a bit like a continuous tape because he'd go back to the beginning again and go through the same routine. If you were in the Crack with him, John'd say, 'Hello, squire, is that a bad tooth you've got or are you smoking a pipe?' Then you'd forget that and maybe a couple months later you'd hear the same line. It was always funny, but it was more funny the first couple times around."

Paul socialized with John and his new art-school friends during his lunch break or in the Crack. Associating with an older and hipper crowd than the one at the institute was an ego boost for Paul, and most of the art students accepted him because he was a friend of John's. "He was accepted because he was fast on his feet and fast with his wit," says Tony Carricker. "If John said 'This is Paul from next door,' if he was bringing him in, then he was all right. Paul always had more to him than the polished, diplomatic bugger that he appears to be today. Paul could put it around quite a bit, he just did it with more charm, but he still did most things that John did. McCartney was no pushover as a personality. Paul had wit and he was funny."

Although John seemed tough and outgoing, his need to be loved and accepted was often unfulfilled. He wanted to be popular among the other art students and went out of his way to be noticed, but he felt awkward around those who had genuine artistic talent. John had been frustrated since his first week in school until the day his composition instructor found his sketchbook. "I was in the studio one afternoon," remembers Arthur Ballard. "I picked up this sketchbook and thumbed through it and suddenly I'm falling around laughing. It was filled with stories and satirical drawings of me and the other staff members. They were really funny and I thought, This is marvelous! I asked one of the students, 'Who on earth does this belong to?' and he said, 'Oh, that belongs to John Lennon.' I was amazed! I was able to say to him, 'Look, you've got a lot of talent. Don't bother with composition, carry on with this kind of work. This is superb!' "

The stories (influenced by Lewis Carroll) and the line drawings (influenced by English artist Ronald Searle) in Lennon's sketchbook reflected the style of his later books, *In His Own Write* and *A Spaniard in the Works,* and Ballard's appreciation of them gave John an enormous boost. He respected Arthur Ballard and gained confidence in his artistic abilities from Ballard's praise and encouragement. "There was an awful lot of talent there," says Ballard. "Immediate expression, simple line drawings—something very well understood. That's what surprised me, because when he was trying to do what the other students were doing, John was obviously not very interested. They showed me a brand-new John Lennon. They showed me that the boy could think!"

Around Christmas 1957, John met a Scottish-born art student named Stuart Sutcliffe, who, until his death in 1962, had an important intellectual and artistic influence on Lennon. Stuart had entered the art school in 1956 and acquired a reputation as an artistic prodigy. His fellow students envied and admired him, and his teachers predicted a promising future. Sutcliffe's artwork was far superior to the paintings produced at the college in the past.

Stuart had style, flair, a compassion for mankind, and the curiosity of a child visiting the zoo for the first time. Like many geniuses, he was a contradiction in terms: peaceful, yet quick tempered; loving the world but hating its stupidity; shy, yet extroverted when he chose to be. At seventeen he was tremendously energetic, always doing things twice as fast as everyone else and never giving up no matter what he did.

"Stuart was one of those few intensely creative people that you meet," says Bill Harry, the founder of the *Mersey Beat* newspaper who was then a student at the school. "While ordinary people go to art school because they like to draw, certain people go there because they're really dedicated. You know that they intend to do something with their lives, because they mean it—they're not playing games like most art students. Now and again you spot these people and see the intensity they've got, because it's something more than talent. Well, Stuart had it more than anybody I knew at the school."

Sutcliffe's thoughts and passions ran deep. Hungry for knowledge, he seemed to draw more from the experiences of life than from his classes. Once he took a job emptying trash cans so he could talk to people and gain insight into their lives and thoughts. "Stuart was trying to find people who weren't sleepwalking and who weren't going through life talking about nothing things," says Bill Harry. "I think he was eager and thirsty to talk to people who had something to say, new ideas, fresh points of view and different outlooks on life."

Sutcliffe's personality struck a responsive chord in John Lennon. Though their mutual interest in rock 'n' roll attracted them initially, as they grew closer each came to admire the other for his own special talents. Stu basked in the glow of John's extravagant nature and envied his ability to play the guitar and his knowledge of rock 'n' roll. John, for his part, had never encountered anyone like Stuart; he was awed by his new friend's intelligence, his skill with a paintbrush, and his creative brilliance.

Regarded as the school's leader in new fashion trends, Sutcliffe adopted tight-fitting jeans and a James Dean image. Lennon, inspired, became a brooding character stalking around the college in a tweed jacket, stovepipe trousers, and sneakers, his hair combed high and greased back in a DA. Stuart's appearance didn't ruffle the instructors, who knew he was a gifted art student, but John's intimidating aura singled him out as a troublemaker. "The Teddy-boy look had a very bad flavor as far as the Establishment was concerned," says Arthur Ballard. "By wearing clothes of this kind, it just wasn't being different, it was taking up a cause. The staff at the art school were mostly conservative types and they were so prejudiced about things that were different. I suggested to John that he should play it down a little, that he was only attracting attention when it wasn't necessary and putting up the backs of these bastards he was going to need. He should attract attention by his work."

Once Lennon began imitating Sutcliffe, McCartney started imitating Lennon.

By early 1958 John and Stuart were close friends. Paul had met Stuart while visiting John at the art school, and did not like the fact that John's attention was being diverted from him. Paul was jealous of Stu's artistic talents, his James Dean image, and of Lennon's admiration for him. Without knowing it, Sutcliffe became Paul's rival.

McCartney succeeded in recapturing John's attention by telling him that he was composing songs—another interest attributable to his father. Paul remembers sitting at the foot of the family piano when he was ten years old, listening to his father play a song he had composed called "Walking in the Park with Eloise." The first song McCartney recalls writing was "I Lost My Little Girl," which had a harmony he got from his father.

Paul's songs were simple and built around three chords— C, G, and G7—but they were enough to alert Lennon to McCartney's musical progress. Once Paul revealed his new-found creativity, John, not to be outdone, also began composing.

Their new mutual interest in creating original material fortified their friendship. After school they would go to Paul's place and work out their own songs together, often imitating Buddy Holly. From the beginning of their songwriting partnership, Lennon and McCartney established a simple approach to composing original tunes. One would start something and the other would pick up on it, or one would have a song virtually finished except for a bit the other would provide.

The songs that John and Paul wrote were not of much artistic significance with their elementary lyrics, inane rhymes, and melodies that echoed the hits of the day. But the pair gained years of experience and practice over their contemporaries in the 1960s by developing a songwriting method and style early in their careers. And they made a deal that whatever songs either of them wrote they would put both their names on it. A few of the songs they wrote then, such as "I Call Your Name" and "One after 909," were later rearranged musically and lyrically and recorded by the Beatles. The Quarrymen played many of these early compositions, including a version of "Love Me Do" with different words, but the group never performed them in public. "We would play their songs, and it was good to play them," says Eric Griffiths, "but for a group at that time, if you didn't play the popular songs, nobody wanted to hear you."

During the spring and early summer of 1958, John's mother figured prominently in his life. In the years that had passed since John was sent to live with Mimi, Julia had given birth to two daughters (fathered by John Dykins), but she watched with delight the way her son was growing up and how his personality had developed. Julia contributed to John's delinquency by encouraging his rebellious behavior, reinforcing the notion that everything he did was all right. John, of course, found her approval a great deal more pleasant than Aunt Mimi's nagging lectures and endless advice. Mimi sought to limit Julia's influence by keeping John away from his mother—indeed, for some time John did not know that she lived just a fifteen-minute walk from Menlove Avenue. Once he discovered this, however, and recognized the conflict between his mother and his aunt, he cunningly played Julia against Mimi to get what he wanted. Chris Walley remembers that "John would go up to his auntie and say, 'I need a new pair of shoes, auntie, what about it?' and she'd say, 'Can't have any this week, John, I haven't got the money.' John'd say, 'Well, I'm going over to me mother's because she said she'd get them for me.' So he'd go over to his mother's and get the shoes, shirt, and whatever else he wanted, then he'd come back to Mimi."

At an early age, John used his confusing relationship with Mimi to get away with doing whatever he wanted. When living with her became unbearable to him, he would run away to Julia's house for several days until an argument with his mother or with John Dykins forced him to leave. His family situation distressed him and he rarely talked about it with his friends. "John was very cagey about his family," says Rod

Murray. "He never let on whether his mother or father were alive or dead. While he appeared to be a very open person, full of exuberance and willing to do anything, John had this blank spot. He didn't like talking about his family. You'd think that a guy who'd laugh at just about anything, including people with one leg, wouldn't care."

As John reached his midteens, however, his need to be closer to his mother grew stronger. At seventeen and a half, he was the perfect image of Julia: independent, anarchistic, witty, and musical. They were developing a deeper relationship than ever before, and John came to regard her as a young aunt or an older sister. One afternoon, John and John Dykins awaited Julia's return from a visit with Mimi. They were both concerned that she was late. Sometime during the late afternoon on July 18, 1958, a policeman appeared at John Dykins's house in Allerton, announcing that Julia had been killed by an automobile driven by an off-duty policeman.

The effect of her death on John was horrifying. He recalled it as "the single worst event" in his life. None of his friends, including Paul, could feel his special anguish and despair. Paul had known his mother for most of his life; John had just begun to know his. Paul had a father to comfort him after his mother's death; John did not. His grief was intensified by the suddenness of her death, so soon after they had grown close. Now he felt a stabbing loneliness, and he was more bitter than ever.

John went to the Liverpool Art School to see Arthur Ballard, who remembers finding him outside his studio the following day. "Tears were trickling down his face," says Ballard. "He came up to me and I asked, 'What's the matter?' and he said, 'My mother's just been killed in an accident.' I felt terribly sorry for him. I got Geoff Mohammed and said, 'John's outside and he's terribly upset. Take him for a coffee.' The rest of the art group heard about this; there was a good deal of affection toward him."

Chris Walley recalls that John "went into a shell after Julia died, because I think deep down—he never really told us— John felt an awful lot for his mother. He hadn't shown it before, and I think it's often a fact of life that people show their affection after they've lost a loved one rather than when they're alive. I think this was the case with John. He was seen dressed in black for several weeks after her death."

John vented some of his anguish through sick and cruel humor, laughing at the misfortunes of others. His callousness and disrespect knew no limits, and his friends were always fearful of the bitter words that rolled off his tongue. He cared little for what he said to people and enjoyed inflicting verbal abuse on others. Tony Carricker recalls: "We were walking in the City Centre one day and there was a guy with no legs going around in a wheelchair, and John said in a loud voice, 'Some people will do anything to stay out of the army!' Once, a girl was sitting at a table with us at school and she was hanging about and wouldn't leave, so John started getting really obscene and more and more obscene, and it was getting personal. I was feeling sorry for her and thought, You silly bitch, why don't you get up and go, because it's only going to get worse. Eventually she stuck it out for as long as she could and left.

"He had a very clear mind for humor—the Lenny Bruce bits where you see the clarity of a situation straightaway and make a joke about it. If it happens to be cruel toward somebody, then tough tit. He was straight to the point, no messing about."

John turned his artistic talents to sketching monsters, disfigured babies, and antireligious cartoons. When Pope Pius XII died on Lennon's eighteenth birthday, he made a cartoon of the deceased pontiff rattling the gates of Saint Peter with the caption "But I'm the Pope, I tell you!" There were times when his humor bordered on the macabre. Once he gathered his friends together for a séance. "All the lights were turned down and we were supposed to put our fingers on a glass tumbler," says Chris Walley. "Well, the tumbler was supposed to move in a certain way—and it did! Whether this was one of John's practical jokes where he made the tumbler move or some outside force, I'll never know. John didn't let on whether or not it was him."

3

One day in early 1958 Paul McCartney brought a friend named George Harrison to the art school and introduced him to John Lennon. Harrison was a year behind McCartney at the Liverpool Institute and had the reputation of being an exceptional guitarist. Paul felt that George should be one of the Quarrymen, but Lennon was reluctant to invite him to join the group, feeling he was just a kid following him around.

During his career as a Beatle, George Harrison was considered a nonentity. He had neither Lennon's brashness nor McCartney's charm, but his image as the "quiet Beatle" was an important ingredient in the overall character of the group. Harrison, more than the others, disliked and later came to loathe the hysteria that surrounded the Beatles in the 1960s, modestly proclaiming that he never wanted to be famous. During a concert performance, George could be seen playing his guitar three steps behind Lennon and McCartney, content to let them bask in the limelight while he provided the occasional backup vocal and sang lead on one or two songs. His quiet demeanor was explained as a habit he'd had since his teens of removing himself from a situation to observe and listen to what was happening around him, then deciding what was enlightening or absurd.

George was the youngest child of Harold and Louise Harrison, born on February 25, 1943, at 12 Arnold Grove in Wavertree, Liverpool. Harold was a steward in the merchant navy when he married Louise in 1928. When George was two years old, Harold left the sea and worked as a bus conductor, then as a bus driver in Liverpool. During the years that her husband was at sea, Louise remained at home caring for her children: Louise, Harold, Peter, and George.

Harold was a loving but stern father. Louise, the more lenient, had a cheerful, optimistic outlook on life and simply wanted her children to be happy. The responsibility of supporting a family of six on a bus driver's salary, supplemented by government welfare checks, forced the Harrisons to live a somewhat humble existence, but George remembers his childhood as happy and undisturbed, except for his annual illness, usually tonsillitis.

Louise Harrison remembers her son as a little boy who was always full of fun and well liked by the neighbors; a strong-willed, independent, and outgoing youth. Before George began school, at Dovedale Primary in 1949, the Harrisons moved from Wavertree to a council estate at 25 Upton Green in Speke, where nearly all of his childhood memories begin, and where he always played with his brother Peter. George enjoyed sports such as soccer, cricket, and swimming, and when his parents saved enough money to buy him a bicycle, he spent many hours traveling all over Liverpool.

George passed his eleven-plus examinations at Dovedale Primary and was accepted into the Liverpool Institute in 1954. During his first year at the school, he earned passing grades and was considered a good student. In his second year, however, he became bored and fed up with school. He grew resentful of the authority of his teachers and hated the way they force-fed students according to narrow-minded traditional rules that discouraged independent thinking. As he drifted farther from the mainstream of the student body each term, his teachers singled him out as a troublemaker in need of reform. Hardly a day passed when George was not scolded, thrown out of the classroom, or sent to the headmaster's office for his impudence. Harrison quietly rebelled against the staunch authority he loathed by dressing like a Teddy boy, which made him stand out among the more obedient schoolboys. His hair was the longest and he wore wild-colored clothes with skin-tight pants and blue suede shoes.

The skiffle craze had all but died out when George, at age thirteen, asked his mother to buy him a guitar from a school-mate who had lost interest in the fad. He expressed a desire to play the instrument after his brother Peter acquired one. George's interest in the guitar was different from John's and Paul's—he was intrigued by it technically, curious about how it worked and how it was mastered. In the beginning his progress was discouragingly slow, and there were many frustrating moments when he felt he would never learn how to play. At such times he would store the guitar in his closet for several weeks until he was compelled to try again. Once, his curiosity led him to disassemble the instrument. Unable to put it back together, he returned the guitar to the closet, where it remained for a month until Peter repaired it.

During this learning period, Louise Harrison was a constant source of inspiration to her son, encouraging him to persevere whenever he wanted to quit. She would sit with George for several hours a night, patiently listening to him play and watching his fingers as they awkwardly fumbled up and down the guitar neck. He continued to practice until the noises he produced became comprehensible songs. His excitement at finally playing the melody of his first song inspired him. In his enthusiasm he formed a skiffle group called the Rebels featuring Peter and two schoolmates. The group auditioned for a show at the Speke British Legion Hall and lost, but they were hired at the last minute when the main act failed to appear. The Rebels knew only two songs and played them repeatedly throughout the night. Harrison recalls that the group performed a few times after that appearance before they disbanded.

When rock 'n' roll descended on England, George was fascinated by the sounds produced by American guitarists such

as Chuck Berry, Carl Perkins, Elmore James, and Elvis Presley's lead guitarist, Scotty Moore. "Heartbreak Hotel" was the
song that did it for George. He tried copying the guitar riffs
from rock 'n' roll and blues records he obtained from a cousin
in the merchant navy, or by listening to Radio Luxembourg.
Realizing that his cheap guitar was inadequate to produce the
same effects, he persuaded his eldest brother, Harold, to sign a
purchase-form guaranty for a better instrument—a £120 Club
Thirty electric guitar from Hessey's Music Store in the City
Centre.

Paul McCartney's appearance in George's life in late 1956
had the same effect on George's guitar playing that it had on
John Lennon's. They met on the hour-long bus trip to the
institute and struck up a conversation that turned to the subject of the guitar. Since Paul and George did not live far from
each other, they began playing their guitars together after
school. Paul's skill inspired George to practice diligently day
and night, stopping only when his fingers were too sore to
continue. "George liked the technical side of music," says Bill
Harry, "not so much the vocalizing. He was one of these guitar
nuts—a guy who would be sitting around learning, doing all
the intricacies. He used to play these numbers with interesting
guitar work."

Around the time that Paul joined the Quarrymen, George
began playing in a group called the Les Stewart Quartet. The
two friends did not see much of each other after school, but
they still met every day on the bus ride into the City Centre
and during their lunch hour. Early in 1958 Paul began bringing Harrison with him to the art school or to the Crack to see
John, but George's youthful presence among the other art students initially made Lennon uncomfortable.

During the spring and summer of 1958, George occasionally performed with the Quarrymen when Eric Griffiths was
unable to play. After each of these engagements, Paul made a
point of asking John what he thought about his friend's ability,
then casually mentioned that it was a shame that someone of
Harrison's talent had to perform in a group other than the
Quarrymen. Lennon was always looking for ways to improve
the band, but though he knew that George's skill on the guitar
exceeded his own and McCartney's, he was reluctant to ask

him to join because of the age difference between himself and Harrison, who was then only fifteen.

In August 1958 the Les Stewart Quartet broke up. On the day they were to perform in a newly opened club called the Casbah in West Derby, Liverpool, Les Stewart had an argument with Ken Brown, one of the members of the quartet, and refused to play. George told the club owner, Mona Best, about John and Paul, and they joined George and Ken Brown for the engagements. Paul was neat, but John was a bit of a beatnik. They sang "Long Tall Sally."

The boys received 15 shillings (about $2) each that day, and John finally asked George to join the Quarrymen. Eric Griffiths, who was forced out of the group by Harrison, feels that by introducing George to the group, Paul was trying to reduce John's influence. If so, the plan backfired, because Harrison, much to McCartney's discontent, was bowled over by Lennon's personality.

From September 1958 to April 1959, the Quarrymen played regularly at the Casbah. Colin Hanton had left the group by then, but Ken Brown remained, making the Quarrymen a quartet of guitars. Tony Carricker frequently saw them play at the Casbah and remembers: "I was very impressed with Paul's voice, and George was a good guitarist—he could do the solos note for note. John was not as impressive as Paul as a singer or as a guitarist. John *was* very impressive as a personality—overwhelming. As musicians and singers, Paul had the best voice, George played the best guitar, and John played rhythm."

The boys were playing tunes by Buddy Holly, Chuck Berry, and Bo Diddley, as well as Gene Vincent's version of "Ain't She Sweet." "George had his Club Thirty guitar and Brown had a semiacoustic guitar and a little amp," says Tony. "Brown'd sing 'Apple Blossom Time' very gently and very nice, and John or George would plug into his amp halfway through and wreck him at every opportunity. Brown thought he was getting a group; he didn't know he was getting three rock 'n' roll maniacs who just plugged him out of the amp, cut him off, and turned him down. They were pretty hard on Ken Brown."

In September 1958, when John, Paul, and George returned

to school to begin a new term, their preoccupation with music left little room for their studies. Paul, in his fifth year at the institute, made only halfhearted attempts to pass. At age sixteen, he was uncertain about his future but still thinking about becoming an English literature teacher. George had begun his fourth year at the institute and was making no effort to pass. Since entering high school, he'd become progressively wilder in behavior and appearance. His teachers eventually gave up trying to reform him and allowed him to sleep at his desk in the back of the room if he did not disrupt their classes.

John, in his second year at the art school, had little interest in his classes except as an alternative to finding a job. In the early summer of 1958, he'd had a taste of the workingman's life when he worked at a building site with Tony Carricker for a weekly wage of £10, which he used to buy an electric guitar. "John hated every minute of it," remembers Tony. "My father and I used to pick him up at a railway station, and John used to tell me, 'Oh, God! *Oooh.* I pray every morning that the train will break down and I won't have to go to work!' My father was the foreman on the site and he eventually made John a teaboy because he was useless. We had a big kettle to heat water for the men's brew, and John lit a fire under it and forgot about it and went drifting off, dreaming somewhere, and burned the bloody ass off the kettle. There was no brew for the fellas' tea and they went berserk!"

After six weeks at the building site, John's loathing for the life of the working class prompted him to tell Tony one day, "Look, I'm not working. I don't give a tap what I do, I'm not working at all. I'll play me guitar in pubs for the rest of my life, but I'm not working!" Lennon preferred the art school's easy life-style. "He never knew what he wanted to be," says Tony, "but he knew what he didn't want to be. We were doing absolutely nothing, just enjoying ourselves, running round town, getting drunk quite a lot and cutting classes. Doing exactly what we felt like doing, which any eighteen-year-old does because he knows he's never going to get another chance to do it."

Lennon brought his guitar to school every day and would play it in the classroom, sitting atop a desk, before the teacher arrived. Says Tony, "John'd be strumming away on the guitar, and as Arthur Ballard walked in, John'd say, 'Here's another little ballard for you,' and he'd start strumming something else. He was that fast on his feet. John was genuinely funny. He made you *laugh*, and said things that you wouldn't say."

John's teachers, however, were not amused. "John was a bugger for getting into trouble," says Rod Murray. "He would play funny tricks. In those days the big minimal paintings were popular, with a totally orange canvas with a big green blodge in one corner and a line drawn down the side. One of the students in the fourth year was doing something like this, and all the staff members were saying, 'What wonderful paintings! He's really made a breakthrough!' What John did was he whizzed home, painted a lot of paintings that looked like these, took them to school, and stood them around in the same studio with this guy's work. The next time the staff came around, they looked at these paintings as well and said, 'Oh, yes! Absolutely amazing!' and turned them around and found 'Lennon' written on the back. It was really embarrassing for them."

In the months following their Casbah debut, John, Paul, and George became important parts of each other's lives. The songwriting rivalry between McCartney and Lennon intensified as Paul tried to maintain the edge, a challenge to which John responded. George, cocky and confident, was too engrossed in his guitar to be concerned about songwriting, but a nonmusical rivalry existed between him and McCartney, both of them seeking John's attention. George was a disciple of Lennon's then—a young teenager seeking the approval of an older teenager. In his eyes John was the epitome of a rocker: cool, hip, and rebellious to the core. Eager to win John's acceptance, George often sided with him against Paul.

"It wasn't a mystical communion between personalities," says Bill Harry. "They were unlikely collaborators when you think what John was like at the time compared to George, who hardly spoke and was just a guitar freak. They were tied to each other by the music. When they played, they created a fusion that they were all part of." Tony Carricker adds: "You've got the combination that they all play guitars, they're all a bit unique in personality, and they're all quite funny and

a bit unconventional. Paul and George were certainly unconventional. They were fifteen- or sixteen-year-old boys and
they'd come into the art school where the big boys were—
where the older women were—and were not intimidated in
the least. George was a young kid, but he had a bit of a bite to
him and a bit of nerve. The lack of intimidation is probably
what drew them together, because they laughed at everything."

George was accepted by John's college friends, though his
youth and naïveté made him a target for their practical jokes.
"George was one of the funniest ones," recalls Rod Murray.
"We used to tell him sad stories because he had one of those
faces that echoed whatever it was you were telling him. One of
us was always the ploy storyteller. We'd be in the Crack with
George and someone would come in and say, 'My God!
There's been a terrible accident up the road!' and George
would go into shock. 'It was an old lady and her dog got run
over,' and he would go 'Aww.' 'But I think it's going to be all
right,' and his face would brighten up. George would be
watching whoever was telling the story, and everyone would
be watching George."

Through their friendship with Lennon's crowd, Paul and
George encountered interesting personalities and different
ways of life at an impressionable age, which made them more
culturally aware than other boys their age at school. They felt
proud to be accepted by the older, arty set.

John dated many girls from the art school and generally
made their lives miserable, even getting violent and hitting
them. According to Tony Carricker, Lennon was never lacking
for women. "John was sexually precocious and he was getting
more than many boys in those days because they had inhibitions and John had none of them. If girls found him attractive,
it was because he was a bit of a bastard and a lot of young
women then dearly loved to cry. So if they were looking to cry,
John'd make them cry."

An art student from Hoylake named Cynthia Powell sat
behind John in lettering class. An introverted girl and a hard
worker, she was annoyed by his habit of borrowing supplies
from her without returning them. A year passed before
Cynthia realized that she liked him, but she was too shy and

intimidated by Lennon's brashness to talk to him. In December 1958 they met socially at a party held in the flat of Austin Davis, a teacher at the art school. "I went in with John," remembers Tony Carricker. "He told me beforehand he reckoned he quite fancied her. 'What do you fancy her for?' I asked. I went in with him and he went out with her. After that, it was John and Cyn."

Their relationship bewildered all of their friends—the two were so different from each other. George told John that he liked Cynthia—except for her large teeth. Others commented that Cynthia did not look anything like Brigitte Bardot, who was Lennon's dream girl then, and they gave Cynthia an all-around hard time.

John did not make the relationship easy for Cynthia. The blind rage he was experiencing made him insensitive to her feelings and he verbally and physically abused her, criticized her upper-middle-class background, and was constantly borrowing money from her to buy cigarettes or beer. By his own admission, he was a male chauvinist, and Cynthia was quiet enough to let him get away with it. "Cynthia was a very level-headed girl," says Chris Walley, "and a very nice girl, but not the type that would appeal to John on a long-term basis. She was a girl who was trampled on by John, but you feel that if it was a woman who was going to be rebellious, it wouldn't have lasted. It needed to be someone that let him do whatever he wanted without being interfered with."

Under the influence of their relationship, Cynthia changed from a conservative-looking woman into Brigitte Bardot's likeness, bleaching her brown hair blond and adopting casual clothing. She allowed John to vent his frustrations on her and continued to love him no matter how hard he trampled.

By the spring of 1959, John, Paul, and George were all that was left of the Quarrymen. An argument over money after a performance at the Casbah brought Ken Brown's stay in the group to an end. After his departure, the boys added a piano player named Duff Lowe to their lineup and the group appeared under various names hastily thought up for a performance. One such name was the J. Page Four: *J* for John, *Pa* for Paul, and *ge* for George.

There was a vagrantlike quality to their lives then. John, Paul, and George spent many uneventful days together wandering the streets of Liverpool or playing their guitars. Acting as anti-Establishment layabouts helped strengthen the bond between them. In those days of personal poverty and uncertainty over what tomorrow would bring, the boys felt closer each day, sharing everything from the clothing on their backs to the little money they had between them. Their satirical wit became sharper as each tried to outdo the other in the cocky comedic style of Liverpool.

As a performing band, however, they made little progress. Duff Lowe left them after two performances, and after that the bookings were scarce. They entered and lost numerous talent shows and contests, and in mid-1959 the group finally broke up. But they kept playing together in each other's homes. They listened to everything from contemporary music to rhythm 'n' blues performers like James Brown, Ray Charles, Sam Cooke, Larry Williams, and Link Wray, who influenced Lennon's own rhythm style. John, Paul, and George firmly established their musical preferences then. John and George liked the more rocking and experimental sounds, while Paul preferred the mainstream pop music.

John and Paul tried to succeed as a duo called the Nerk Twins, a name that Paul and his brother used when they sang for relatives. Lennon and McCartney appeared at parties and played tunes that they could sing in harmony, but the Nerk Twins made little headway and stopped performing after a few dates.

Meanwhile, the boys' parents and guardians wrung their hands in frustration over the musicians' lack of interest in school and the direction their lives were taking. George failed his examinations at the institute and in the summer of 1959 obtained his parents' consent to quit school. Harrison applied for a job as a window dresser at Blacklers, a department store in the City Centre, but was made an apprentice electrician instead. During the time that John and Paul were performing as the Nerk Twins, George tried to join a group called Rory Storme and the Hurricanes, but was turned down because of his age.

Much to Jim McCartney's relief, his son was receiving fair

grades at school and had passed his exams the year before, leading his father to believe that he would enter a teachers' college after graduating from the institute in 1960. But Jim eventually realized that Paul's interest in rock 'n' roll was more than a hobby and would interfere with his education. As a single parent, he had a difficult time keeping Paul in line and frequently clashed with him over his Teddy-boy appearance. He forbid Paul to wear tight-fitting trousers which Paul got around by taking his trousers to a tailor every week and having just a fraction taken off each time.

After Julia's death, John's life with Mimi became one continuous row. She was thoroughly convinced that he was becoming a bum. "John once told me," recalls Tony Carricker, "that he used to follow Mimi up the stairs, dead quiet, and yell 'Boo!' at the top of his voice or clap his hands loudly, trying to give her a heart attack." Finally one day he told Mimi he was leaving. "Everyone else at school lives in flats," he said. "I feel like a baby living here at home."

John, Stuart Sutcliffe, and Rod Murray moved into a flat at Gambier Terrace on Hope Street, across from the Anglican cathedral, which became a dirty hangout without furniture except for beds.

One month later, John stopped by Menlove Avenue to visit Mimi for the first time since moving away. She noticed that he looked thinner and invited him to stay for dinner, but his pride made him refuse. A few days later he returned and devoured steak and mushrooms.

On October 29, 1959, John, Paul, and George regrouped under the name Johnny and the Moondogs to audition for an amateur talent contest called the "Carroll Levis TV Discoveries Show" at the Empire Theatre in Liverpool. The boys passed their audition and were invited to perform in the final show at the Manchester Odeon in early November. They were elated by the news—this was their chance to break into the big time.

The Moondogs arrived in Manchester by train and performed two Buddy Holly songs. John, without his guitar, sang the lead vocals while Paul and George, standing several paces behind him, provided the instrumentation and the harmony. They received a mild round of applause, but because the contest was running late and they feared they'd miss the last train back to Liverpool, they weren't able to stay for the second half of the show, which would determine the winner. To compensate, John managed to steal an acoustic guitar from one of the contestants on their way out.

Around the time of the Moondogs' performance in Manchester, Stuart Sutcliffe became a minor hero at the art school. One of his works, which he called *Summer Painting*, was selected to appear in the John Moore's Art Exhibition at the Walker Art Gallery in Liverpool. The show opened on November 19, 1959, and gave Merseyside a chance to see the best artwork being created in the country. Stuart did not win a prize for his work, but the Moore family, feeling sorry for him, bought the painting for £60.

Sutcliffe's sudden wealth tied in with John's plans. After the talent show, he'd begun thinking about forming a proper group. They desperately needed a bass guitar and a set of drums to complete the lineup, but both instruments were expensive and it was difficult to find musicians who were not already in a band. John mentioned this to Stuart and Rod Murray, and told them that whoever could get an instrument was in. Sutcliffe was eager to join a rock 'n' roll band; he'd often told Lennon how much he envied and admired him for being able to play the guitar. "I went off and began to make a bass guitar," says Rod Murray, "But Stuart went to Hessey's and bought one, so he was in the group. I never did finish that bloody guitar."

Stuart did not know how to play, but he desperately wanted to learn, and the others said they would teach him. Says Bill Harry, "He was almost like a fan. It became an obsession with him—a new direction." John wanted Stuart in the group for more than musical reasons: Stu was his best friend— which was reason enough for Paul's resentment and jealousy. Stu was also the one person Lennon could turn to for the truth—in contrast to Paul, who seemed a bit phony.

John also began thinking about a new name for the group. They all liked the music of Buddy Holly and the Crickets, and

Lennon was especially amused by the bug concept, but he did not want to copy or extend on the Crickets with something like "the Cricketeers." Stuart suggested the name Beetles, which John liked but was unable to leave alone. The American beat poet Jack Kerouac was popular among art students then, and since Lennon enjoyed playing with words, he used the word *beat* to form the name Beatles, meaning both "beat" and insects.

The name met with laughter from several musicians they knew, but the boys liked the name and the clever play on words. All the groups in Liverpool incorporated the lead singers' names into their titles, and it was suggested to the Beatles that they do the same. But there were two lead singers in the band, and if the boys had to have a long title, they wanted one that reflected a group. Eventually they decided to call themselves the Silver Beatles. Naming and renaming the group had little effect on their musical direction, but it did show that they were beginning to take themselves seriously.

4

In the spring of 1960 there were hundreds of rock 'n' roll bands throughout Liverpool, and the Silver Beatles, without a drummer or an air of professionalism, did not figure prominently on the scene. The top groups were Rory Storme and the Hurricanes, Cass and the Casanovas, Kingsize Taylor and the Dominoes, and Howie Casey and the Seniors. While these groups were earning up to £10 a night at "jive halls," the Silver Beatles rarely got a booking. When they did, it was for parties or dances at the art school, for which they received only a handful of shillings. "They were an amateurish group at the time," says Bill Harry. "When they were getting their first gigs, they'd work at a small place that would fit maybe twenty or thirty people. They were regarded as the art-school band because of John and Stuart. The Silver Beatles were looked upon with affection and booked on art-school gigs, but the top-of-the-bill bands were traditional jazz bands. The students liked the group, but they weren't anything sensational."

Their daily life was a monotonous routine of wandering around Liverpool, hanging around the art school, drifting over to the Kardomah Café, or a place called the Coffee Pot on Renshaw Street. "They were constantly broke," says Bill Harry. "For instance, there'd be three or four of them sitting around a table, wondering whether they've got an extra penny to buy some toast with jam on it. This was the time when they used to try and exist for a day, go out with a girl and maybe have only five shillings on them. So they existed and hung around the coffee shops or spent time rehearsing."

They became frequent visitors at a coffee shop on Slater Street called the Jacaranda, a small club located in the Bohemian section of the city—Liverpool 8. The Jac, as it became known to its patrons, was the social haven for an assortment of weird personalities, ranging from poets to pimps. It was operated by a man named Alan Williams, whom the boys came to know while decorating floats for the Arts Ball fete in 1959. Initially, Williams wanted nothing to do with them; compared to the other musicians who frequented the club, the Silver Beatles were a scruffy lot. But in time he grew to accept their presence as part of the Jac's decor.

When the Silver Beatles met Alan Williams, he was not connected with the rock 'n' roll scene in Liverpool. The closest he had come to being involved was through a West Indian steel band that played calypso music in the Jac's basement at night, and through his acquaintance with the beat musicians who patronized the club. John, Paul, George, and Stuart felt privileged to be in the company of these local celebrities, who treated them indifferently and laughed at them behind their backs. Through these musicians, Williams learned of the thriving beat scene on Merseyside and discovered that promoters were earning a lot of money by staging dances. Aroused by this, he decided to try his hand at it, and co-promoted a successful show starring Gene Vincent at the Liverpool Boxing Stadium in May 1960. His partner was pop enterpreneur Larry Parnes, whom the British entertainment world had dubbed "Mr. Starmaker." The Silver Beatles were impressed, and decided that Williams was the man who could get things organized for them.

When they approached him, however, he didn't exactly jump at the chance. Williams recalls that John Lennon came over to him one evening at the Jac and said, " 'Hey there, Al, why don't you do something for us?' He looked awfully scruffy. A right bloody layabout. 'Do what?' I responded, fully remembering the evening when the Beatles had been breaking their necks to listen in to the conversation between Parnes and me. I didn't think at that time they were intent on becoming a full-time professional group. As far as I knew, music was only their hobby for making a bit of pocket money.

" 'You know, don't fuck about,' said John. 'You and Parnes were talking the other night about using groups. How about us?' Lennon started talking about the instruments they played and how they were developing. I knew they didn't have a drummer.

" 'Just a minute,' I said. 'Who's your drummer? You gotta have a fucking drummer!"

" 'Yeah,' said John, 'we haven't got one. Right. No fucking drummer.' So just to push him a bit more, I went on: 'How do you expect to have any decent sound without a fucking drummer? You better get one before you come talking to me about doing things for you.'

" 'We can get by in a pinch,' said John. 'It's not really necessary, is it? A drummer?'

"I couldn't believe my ears. 'You can't come here talking about having a group without a drummer, John. It just won't work. You haven't a proper band, a real sound.'

" 'Oh, Christ,' said John. 'I don't know any fucking drummers.'

"I told John I would see what I could do about finding a drummer."

In the days that followed, Williams allowed the group to practice in the Jac's basement in the afternoons. At each session he heard a chorus of reminders from the boys to "get things going." Through Brian Cass, the leader of Cass and the Casanovas, they found Tommy Moore.

"I was playing drums with various groups in Liverpool then," recalls Moore. "I wasn't with anyone in particular; I was just playing to enjoy meself. Then somebody said to me that a group was looking for a drummer, a group called the Silver Beatles. Well, that name was just *vaguely* known in Liverpool then."

Tommy had met the group once before at the Temple Restaurant in Dale Street, a gathering place for musicians to meet and jam together in a room above the restaurant. "When they arrived at the Temple," recalls Moore, "they were known as the Quarrymen. As far as I was concerned, they were playing novelty music."

Tommy Moore joined the Silver Beatles in the spring of 1960; and after a week of rehearsals in the Jac, Alan Williams began to book the group with the understanding that he would receive ten percent of its earnings. Williams found work for the Silver Beatles, but he was not their manager as he has claimed. "In the time that I was with them," says Tommy, "he looked after us. I wouldn't say that he was a manager. He was only interested in the money or whatever he could get out of it. He never attended any of the rehearsals or gigs. As far as I know, he just made the bookings through other people. We just used his van and were paid in buttons at the end of the night. I don't know too much about it, because there was too much going on behind my back. Alan wasn't involved with it that much. He had his club to run, so I don't see how he could get involved."

The Silver Beatles' first professional booking was on May 20, 1960, at the Grosvenors Ballroom in Seacombe, Wallasey. For the next month, the group played steadily around Liverpool, mostly in Seacombe or at Neston Hall in Wallasey. These were rough places and fights often broke out between rival Teddy-boy gangs and bouncers while the groups were performing. "John loved the fights," says Tommy Moore, "and he used to think it was funny watching someone get kicked in the head. He'd say, 'Ooh, did you see that?' He gloated at anything like that."

When the Silver Beatles were not booked elsewhere, they alternated sets with the steel band in the Jacaranda. "I lost a lot of sweat in the Jac," says Tommy. "We used to play from midnight to about four in the morning for cups of coffee and a jam buttie [sandwich]. I don't remember getting paid. The only time we got paid was when we played out, and Alan was more interested in keeping us in the Jac because we were bringing in the people." The group had gained a minimal following of students and friends from the art school and the Jac became a hangout for them. Their equipment was primitive and girls would take turns holding up microphones.

The Silver Beatles' repertoire consisted of songs by Jerry Lee Lewis, Little Richard, Fats Domino, Gene Vincent, and the Everly Brothers. "It was just a matter of rattling songs off, one after the other, just to make the night go by," says Tommy Moore. "We played one Everly Brothers tune in particular, 'Cathy's Clown' . . . I remember that the drum part was difficult for me at the time. We did a couple of good blues numbers, too. All that mattered to us was that it rocked." Moore, a jazz enthusiast, often persuaded the others to play a couple of jazz tunes, but "there was no way they could have played jazz and made a living of it," he says. "They just couldn't get it."

Lennon and McCartney continued to write songs together, but their tunes were never heard by the public because they didn't have the confidence to include them in the group's repertoire, and in fact seemed embarrassed when anyone asked about them.

Tommy Moore was with the Silver Beatles during an important phase of their development—when they were playing their first professional jobs—and retains vivid impressions of the four. "I didn't like John Lennon at all," he says. "I saw him in those days as a down-and-out—a bit of a tramp. He was so hardheaded, you couldn't insult him, no matter what you said. He was a bit of a beatnik and wore a dirty old jumper, denim jacket, sandals, long hair combed back over his collar, and glasses. Paul was a real homely lad, but a nice fella. I didn't have too much to do with George. He was the electrician of the group and used to do all the spot work on the equipment. And Stuart was a bad bass player, but he tried his best. The others never gave him any encouragement. They were always kidding him."

John, Paul, and George were wild but harmless delinquents, and the concensus was that they would never amount to anything. In comparison to the other Liverpool groups, the Silver Beatles were little more than a garage band. Chainsmoking, drinking, and always connected to their guitars, they went home only to sleep or change clothes. Their irreverence kept them from being truly professional. "I used to do me own bit on the drums," says Tommy, "a solo to keep the crowd happy and on the floor while the others were off and had a bit of a break behind the stage. So I'd be playing for some time and I'd turn around every so often to see where they were and when they were coming out, and all I'd see is John Lennon pulling faces at me from behind the curtain."

The boys *were* trying to learn, though, and as they played more, their skill increased. Still, their unconventional and unprofessional attitude irritated Tommy Moore. "I was getting a bit fed up with things," he says. "No one was telling me how much we were supposed to get paid for a gig or what job was down the line. Everything was so secretive. So I said to John one day outside the Jac, as we were getting our equipment into the van, 'You know what, John? I'm getting a bit cheesed off with all this business here.' John said, like a typical Scouser, 'Why? You're getting paid, aren't you?' I said, 'Well, yes, but what are we getting paid? Buttons!' He said, 'What else do you want, then?' I said, 'There's nothing happening, nothing is materializing. In the near future, I'm bailing out and going back to me old job in the factory.' He said to me, very seriously, 'I'd sooner die first, mate, than go to work.'"

The boys learned that Larry Parnes was returning to Liverpool in June to hold auditions at the Wyvern Social Club for a backup group to tour with one of his singing stars, Billy Fury. The tour represented the big time to the Silver Beatles: £100 for the group; billing behind Fury; performances in major cities; and the chance of being managed by Larry Parnes. Realizing that they would be competing against the best Liverpool bands, the boys practiced incessently in the Jac.

But on the day of the audition, Tommy Moore couldn't make it. The group would have lost its chance to perform, but Johnny Hutchinson, the drummer from Cass and the Casanovas, agreed to sit in with them at the last moment. They played several instrumental numbers that impressed Fury, who told Parnes that he wanted the Silver Beatles. But Parnes had detected a problem: Despite the attempts of John, Paul, and George to cover up for him, Stuart's ineptness on the bass guitar was apparent. They were asked to play once more, this time without Sutcliffe. A silence fell over the club for a minute, and then John said firmly, "No!" Alan Williams, who saw his ten-percent commission vanishing before his eyes, tried to coax them to play—even Stuart tried to persuade them—but

Lennon and a reluctant Paul and George stood by their decision. Parnes, amused and puzzled, still thought they were good enough to send on a tour of Scotland as the supporting group for another singer he managed, Johnny Gentle. Parnes refused to pay Stuart because of his inability, but John, Paul, and George agreed to share their earnings with him.

Excited about traveling to Scotland, Paul, George, and Stuart adopted stage names for the tour: Paul became Paul Ramon; George changed his name to Carl Harrison (after Carl Perkins); and Stuart became Stu de Stijil. John, however, did not change his name, as he never liked any better than his own, although once an MC introduced him as Long John and the Silvermen.

The tour began inauspiciously for the group, as Tommy Moore recalls: "When we went up to Scotland, we didn't have any money at all. It was Alan's idea that the money would be sent to us in advance from Larry Parnes in London. All I was interested in was getting on with the tour; I wasn't interested in who was doing the business. It was our understanding that Alan was looking after the financial part of it and that the money would be sent to us from London to hold us over." They were each supposed to receive £15 a week, and before the start of the tour Larry Parnes got a telephone call from a frantic John Lennon asking "Where's the bloody money?" It didn't arrive, and the Silver Beatles left for Scotland in June 1960 with virtually no cash.

When Johnny Gentle first met them, he was shocked by their appearance. "I wondered what on earth Parnes had sent me," he remembers. "They were the roughest-looking bunch I had seen in my life, hopelessly fitted out with no stage gear. Paul and Stu had black shirts. I lent John a shirt of mine and went out and bought one for George, but we were so broke that we couldn't afford to buy one for the drummer, so he wore white." Lennon told the pop singer, "This is our big break. We've been waiting for this!" Johnny Gentle replied, "Jesus Christ!"

The boys traveled throughout Scotland in a minibus and were generally well received. Throughout the first week, however, John, Paul, and George constantly teased Stuart while they performed. The teasing was always instigated by Lennon.

"Stuart wasn't the type of lad to argue over anything," says Tommy. "They used to mock him, stick him because of his ways. They'd get on him about his playing, shout at him on-stage. He had something none of us had: looks. It was often said by the many girls we knew in Liverpool that he would have made another James Dean. Believe me, he was the image of him—a real good-looking lad, Stuart was. I don't know what it was with them, but if anybody looked better than they did, they'd give him a rough time. Lennon would try and give me a rough time, so I'd give him one back and threaten him. The way they were carrying on in general, I thought, What the bloody hell is going on here? Once I get back to Liverpool, this is it!"

One night during a performance, John unplugged Stuart's bass guitar from its amplifier while his back was turned. As Stuart struggled to play the proper notes, the others watched in silent hysteria, particularly Paul, who enjoyed seeing "James Dean" make a fool of himself. At the end of the show, Sutcliffe asked them how he did. Lennon said he didn't know, and that next time Stu should be sure his guitar lead was plugged into the amp. Confused by John's comment, Stu looked at his amp and saw that the jack was lying on the stage. Paul and George exploded with laughter; Sutcliffe blushed in embarrassment.

This practical joke nearly cost the Silver Beatles their job. After the concert, several girls complained to the tour promoter, Duncan McKinnon, about how bad the group sounded. McKinnon, who had heard similar comments the nights before, wanted to send the Silver Beatles back to Liverpool. "We all sat down together in a bar in Inverness and went over each number until the boys got the right sound," says Johnny Gentle. "They were terribly depressed. I felt sorry for them and persuaded McKinnon to let them finish the second week. One night, after we'd finished a show, a girl came up and asked for their autographs. John was so thrilled, he couldn't stop talking about it and asked me if I thought they should chuck up everything and go full-time."

After the first week, financial problems washed away whatever enthusiasm the boys still had for the tour. "On the way up there, it was fairly exciting," says Tommy. "The idea of just traveling was exciting. After the first few dates, things got a bit sticky and I started getting funny feelings about the tour, particularly about Alan. I told the others in a hotel, 'I don't like the looks of this at all.'"

Financial hardship forced the boys to take drastic measures. Tommy recalls: "We literally had to scrounge for food. In the hotel we were staying at, I felt like a tramp. We kept getting telephone calls saying that the money was on its way, but it never came." They smuggled food from the restaurants they ate at—saltines, bits of cheese wrapped in paper, slices of bread and dinner rolls—back to their hotel rooms and divided their haul. Once John was so hungry that he ordered a huge meal and walked out of the restaurant without paying. "We walked in front of him and he sort of used us as a shield," says Tommy.

To add to their problems, toward the end of the tour the group was involved in an automobile accident with an elderly couple near Banff. "Johnny Gentle could never go on stage unless he had a few drinks," says Tommy. "He was just starting out on his first tour, and whenever we were with him, he was always under the influence. One night Johnny had a few drinks and after the show he suddenly got it into his head that he would drive the minibus. Well, he got behind the wheel and took a wrong turn and—*bang!* All I remember was waking up in a hospital."

John, Paul, George, Stuart, and Johnny Gentle escaped injury, but all the equipment fell on top of Tommy Moore, who was sitting in the rear of the minibus. While Tommy lay in a hospital bed under sedation, Duncan McKinnon had a talk with him. "They were in a sticky position," Moore remembers. "I was in the hospital, things weren't going well on the tour, and they couldn't find another drummer. Even if they did, there wasn't enough time to rehearse. So against doctors orders, I left the hospital."

Tommy arrived at the theater drowsy from the effects of the drugs and with stitches in his upper lip, two teeth missing, and a bandage around his head. John exploded with laughter upon seeing him, and mocked and needled him throughout their performance, making faces, trying to stretch the stitches in Tommy's lip by making him laugh. Occasionally John would turn around while performing, look at Moore, and burst out laughing. "Lennon must have thought, This is it; this time I'm gonna have a go at him," says Tommy.

The tour ended in Dundee in late June 1960. "We said goodbye to each other at the railway station," says Johnny Gentle, "and as my train pulled out, they were still saying, 'Ask Larry Parnes if he wants us again!'" According to Tommy Moore, the tour was a disaster; all five of them returned to Liverpool penniless, and the behavior displayed by Lennon, McCartney, and Harrison finally forced him to quit the group.

The Silver Beatles had left Scotland believing that they were now a professional group, but upon their return to Liverpool they found themselves performing once again in small clubs for cups of coffee and jam butties. They also played a series of bizarre dates, one time backing a beat poet named Royston Ellis, who introduced John, Paul, and George to their first drug—Benzedrine, from the inside of a Benzedrine inhaler. Everybody talked all night.

Another time, Alan Williams booked the Silver Beatles to perform behind an exotic dancer named Janice in the New Cabaret Artists Club, a strip club in Liverpool's Chinatown district. Although the boys didn't know her repertoire, they did well enough, all the while enjoying the show.

For nearly a year John, Paul, and George had pursued the elusive "big break" that would catapult them to instant stardom. But the most obvious opportunities, such as talent shows and the Scottish tour, rewarded them with only frustration, and none of the three took disappointment too well. In the summer of 1960, Alan Williams offered them a chance to perform in Hamburg, West Germany. This was hardly the chance of a lifetime, they felt; no one associated Hamburg with rock 'n' roll, or with the starmaking machinery that would make them famous. But it was an opportunity to travel abroad—and in retrospect, Hamburg *was* their big break: Hamburg made the Beatles.

Although Alan Williams was responsible for booking Liverpool groups into Hamburg, those close to the Beatles and to the beat scene at that time say that he stumbled onto the German club scene. "Brian Cass used to sleep in the basement of the Jacaranda," says Bill Harry, "and would make telephone calls all over England looking for work for the Casanovas. One evening Cass placed a call to a nightclub owner named Bruno Koschmider in Hamburg. So Allan was in the Jac one morning and the telephone rang and someone said, 'Alan, there's a man calling from Germany!' Allan answered the telephone—he didn't know what it was about—and it was Bruno Koschmider returning Cass's call, asking about booking groups. Alan figured out what it was about and said he could do it and arranged to meet Koschmider in London."

Bruno Koschmider, who had a reputation for ruthlessness, operated two nightclubs in Hamburg: the Kaiserkeller and Indra. When his star attraction left, Bruno flew to England to search for new talent. He wanted groups who could entertain his customers with loud, fast, rousing rock 'n' roll—the sort of groups Alan Williams said he managed. Williams and Koschmider met at the Two I's Club in London, and from that meeting the Hamburg-Liverpool link was established: Alan would book Merseyside's top groups into Bruno's clubs.

The Silver Beatles were the furthest thought from his mind, however. The first Liverpool band he booked at the Kaiserkeller was Howie Casey and the Seniors. Cass and the Casanovas were originally scheduled to perform at the Indra Club, but they canceled at the last moment. Williams asked Rory Storme if the Hurricanes would go, but Rory turned him down because of a previous commitment in Wales. Alan then approached Gerry Marsden, of Gerry and the Pacemakers, and he, too, said no because the Pacemakers were dubious about the Hamburg circuit. With only days remaining before the starting date at the Indra, and fearing that his deal with Bruno might fall through, Williams resorted to the Silver Beatles.

John, Paul, George, and Stuart were eager to go, but they could not perform without a drummer, and if they didn't find one in a hurry, Williams would have to get another group. They remembered that the owner of the Casbah Club, Mona Best, had a son, Peter, who played the drums. Pete Best, age nineteen, was strikingly different from John, Paul, and George. He was a conservative rock 'n' roller, another James Dean type—good-looking enough to stir jealousy in Lennon, McCartney, and Harrison, yet quiet enough to make him tolerable. They auditioned him and he was in, going to Hamburg with them two days later.

Their families did not share their enthusiasm for the trip. Going to Hamburg meant that John, Paul, and Stuart would have to quit school. John was failing at the art school and was supposed to complete work for his degree, but did not attempt to pass. (While the Silver Beatles were in Germany, a few of John's friends turned in a portfolio of artwork bearing his name, but their efforts, too, received failing marks.) Stuart hastily produced several paintings and passed, but this stirred the wrath of Arthur Ballard, which he directed at Alan Williams for interrupting the career of a brilliant art student. For Paul, working in Germany was an excuse to quit school. His letter to the headmaster at the institute read: "Dear Sir, I've got a great job in Germany and I'm earning £15." Paul then had Alan Williams persuade his father to let him go.

The boys cockily ignored their families' advice to stop wasting time and get serious about finding a trade. The lure of travel abroad was too strong to resist. With their equipment packed on top of a minibus, Alan Williams drove them to New Haven, where they boarded a ferry to the Hook of Holland. The minibus was stored in the hold, and upon their arrival in Holland, Williams drove the group to Hamburg. Their entry visas classified them as "students."

Hamburg was a teeming city—the German equivalent of Liverpool—when the Silver Beatles arrived there in August 1960. Both cities were major seaports, geographically parallel to each other, with reputations as tough towns. But Hamburg's notoriety exceeded Liverpool's. All the seedy elements of Europe had found a home in the St. Pauli district (Hamburg 4), where the Indra and Kaiserkeller clubs were located. The area, dotted with whorehouses and strip clubs, was inhabited by gangsters, prostitutes, pimps, drug addicts, and assorted other shady characters. Anything illicit was available in the St. Pauli.

The depravity of the area centered on the nightclubs that lined a mile-long avenue called the Reeperbahn. Here club owners employed an army of dockworkers ostensibly as waiters but in reality as bouncers to maintain order. They carried a variety of weapons—handguns, switchblades, truncheons, and knuckledusters—and did not tolerate trouble from anyone. Arguments over checks were settled with threats or with clubs on the head. When fights erupted, a phalanx of "waiters" charged in, separated the combatants, and beat the hell out of them, the band onstage lending momentum to the brawl with a sound track of hard-driving rock 'n' roll. St. Pauli was a volatile and intimidating area, but charged with an electricity that gave Hamburg 4 its fascinating character.

In this Barbary Coast atmosphere, five musicians from Liverpool—the oldest twenty (Stuart) and the youngest seventeen (George)—would live and perform for four months. Their new home was an eye-opening experience for each of them. "It was the very fact that they were in a foreign city with alien sounds and smells," says Bill Harry. "Hardly any of them had been out of England in their lives. They thought only the rich could travel abroad, and the mere fact that they could go to another country and play music was completely mind-blowing! They were bombarded with new sensations all the time."

But expectations of a glamorous life in Hamburg were abruptly shattered the moment they arrived. Koschmider, from the outset, showed little concern for their well-being and remained indifferent throughout their stay. He housed them near a rest room in the rear of the Bambi Theater, where the smell of excrement permeated the air. It was damp and they slept two to a room.

However disgusted they were with their accommodations, the boys were too tired from the journey to complain to Bruno.

The next day they were taken to the Indra Club for their first night's work—and from all accounts, they were not well received. Koschmider failed to give the Silver Beatles any billing out front, nor did he inform the public that he had recently converted the Indra from a strip joint to a nightclub featuring live music. The clientele, expecting to see nude women, was not happy when a rock 'n' roll band appeared instead.

Another shock was learning they had to perform eight hours a night, six days a week, starting about five in the evening. After a night's work, the boys returned to the Bambi for some sleep, only to be awakened early in the afternoon by the noise of the film being screened in the theater.

Despite all this, their abilities improved dramatically.

When they began performing at the Indra, they were nothing more than background music—drums, four guitars, and two battered amplifiers—receiving little attention from the audience. They soon found this monotonous, and Bruno began insisting on a boisterous show, so John started toying with the derelict crowd, teasing them, having a go at them as he did with everyone else. Paul and George joined in, both because Lennon was doing it and because they were being plied with liquor. Lennon would leap about like Gene Vincent, the numbers would last twenty minutes just to stretch them out, and if an amplifier went Paul would just start pounding out chords on the piano. They got cocky—and they started getting good.

The boys thought they were the ones having fun, ridiculing their audience, but the Germans responded with laughter—they liked the strange, mocking, foreign rock 'n' rollers onstage. Bruno Koschmider, pleased, kept urging the boys to *mak shau, mak shau* (make show). When the audience clapped or pounded tables, virtually all the group's inhibitions were wiped away. During their first season in Hamburg, they learned the art of entertaining and developed a style, stage presence, and as a result of having to play eight hours a night, a compelling, hard-driving sound.

Performing eight hours a night also forced the group to expand their repertoire from twenty-five numbers to fifty. They began relearning the rock 'n' roll tunes they had played in their skiffle days, and they practiced when they weren't playing. Maintaining this pace forced John, Paul, and George to share the vocal responsibilities, which ultimately strengthened the harmony of their singing. Now, whether they played Chuck Berry or Jerry Lee Lewis, they played it differently than anyone else. They also filled out their repertoire by playing the original tunes of Lennon and McCartney, who had penned nearly eighty songs by then.

At times the Silver Beatles stretched the limits of the audience's tolerance. One night they goose-stepped onto the stage yelling "Heil Hitler!" But it was John's antics that most stirred the audience. He once appeared onstage wearing nothing but a pair of swimming trunks; another night with a toilet seat circling his neck. He'd shout obscenities at the crowd, calling them "Fuckin' krauts," "Nazi's"—anything to provoke a response.

It was bold of the group to mock the intoxicated crowd with obscene gestures and insulting references to Nazism. Though the West German government had passed a law prohibiting the display of the old regime, the audience enjoyed the show and pushed the boys even farther. The group's name, pronounced with a German accent, "Die Silber Pedels," meant "the Silver Pricks," which only enhanced their image with club patrons.

Hamburg was a halcyon period in the boys' lives. They were young, living in a somewhat exotic place with temptations confronting them at every turn, and able to do practically anything they wanted without fear of reprisal—"good dirty fun" in Paul's words.

The area often exploded into violence. Brawling was commonplace in the clubs, which fascinated the boys because it reminded them of cowboy movies. Once, while they were performing, a man was shot in the head because he insulted a gangster's girlfriend. And the district was inhabited by homosexuals, transvestites, pimps, and prostitutes.

The raucous performances at the Indra lasted several weeks, until finally the club was closed by the police. The Silver Beatles then joined Howie Casey and the Seniors at the Kaiserkeller Club, where each night both groups continued to push themselves to the point of exhaustion. Preludin, Cylert, and Didrex and other uppers helped them maintain the frenzied pace.

By the end of three months, the group had dropped the "Silver" from their name and grown confident enough to loudly express their resentment at Bruno Koschmider's indifference. One night, tired of stomping on a rickety stage supported by empty champagne crates, they decided they wanted a new platform built so they stomped through it during one of their epic hour-and-a-half renditions of "What I'd Say."

The Liverpool groups became famous in the St. Pauli district for their music, their antics, and their personalities. The huge audiences they attracted to the Kaiserkeller gave the Beatles their first taste of success, and they wrote letters to Bill Harry expressing their amazement at their newfound energy and sense of direction. "I think they saw new horizons," says Bill Harry. "They suddenly found that there was something different from playing for the rest of their lives in Liverpool. I don't think they thought of big success before that time. But to me, they were *so* excited. They weren't swollen heads; it was *enthusiasm.* They were just brimming over with excitement and more confident in themselves and completely excited that their whole lives were opening up for them."

Little mattered to the Beatles but their music and their stage show, and later they would feel it was the peak, for people came to see them for who they were, not because they were famous. In the time they had to themselves, the boys spent their money as quickly as they earned it or sought comfort in the arms of Reeperbahn prostitutes. In Germany they received an education that was ignored in the wealth of Fab Four publicity written about them in the mid-1960s.

By November 1960 the Beatles had enhanced their stage presence by adopting a black-leather image, in striking contrast to the scruffy appearance they projected in Liverpool and Scotland, and very different also from the Teddy-boy look they'd sported when they first arrived in Hamburg—mauve sports coats, black dress shirts, drainpipe trousers, and crocodile shoes. During their time off from performing, they had noticed a clothing shop in the St. Pauli area that sold black leather apparel—a look that Lennon, in particular, liked because one of his rock idols, Gene Vincent, wore leather. When each of the Beatles had saved enough money, they bought black leather jackets and trousers, black T-shirts, and black cowboy boots embroidered with silver. This look suited the character of Hamburg 4 and the rockers who frequented the Kaiserkeller, now including students from the Hamburg Art School, similar to the art-school crowd in Liverpool.

Klaus Voorman, a student at the school, was one of the first to discover the Beatles. "I went to see the group and found them quite fascinating," he says. "They were so different— somewhat strange-looking, but fantastic onstage. I was in awe of them and too shy to introduce myself. I came back the next night with a record jacket I had designed. When they were on break, I walked up to John and showed him the jacket." According to Klaus, Lennon did not want to be bothered—he didn't like Germans. "He told me," says Klaus, " 'I'm not the artist. Talk to Stuart—he's the artist.' "

The following night Voorman brought his girlfriend, Astrid

Kirchnerr, and afterward the couple talked to their friends about the group and persuaded them to come to the club. Soon a group of art students became regular patrons of the Kaiser-keller and began socializing with the five musicians.

The Beatles' contract with Bruno Koschmider was due to expire in December. Feeling nothing but contempt for Bruno, they decided to search for new opportunities. During their time off, they frequently visited Tony Sheridan at the Top Ten Club, which was a bigger and better venue than the Kaiserkel-ler. When Bruno's henchmen reported to him that the Beatles were spending too much time there, Bruno suspected that his star attraction was planning to jump clubs and he told them to stay away from the Top Ten, but they ignored his warning.

The last straw, as far as Bruno was concerned, came when the Beatles auditioned for club owner Peter Eckhorn one afternoon. Within forty-eight hours, their stay in Germany came to an end. When the Beatles performed later that evening at the Kaiserkeller, the police raided the club and dragged George Harrison off the stage. The authorities later learned that George was underage and ineligible for a work permit. He was detained at a St. Pauli police station and deported the following day.

John, Paul, Stuart, and Pete decided to remain in Hamburg and play at the Top Ten. They set fire to a contraceptive on the club wall as a final goodbye. But as they were leaving the police threw them in jail on Koschmider's complaint that they had set fire to his club.

Pete and Paul were ordered to leave the country; John and Stuart, without a group, made their way back to England. In early December 1960, the Beatles returned to Liverpool with their tails between their legs. Their enthusiasm for performing vanished following their defeat by Koschmider. Although John, Paul, and George had experienced their share of bad breaks before, this time failure was harder to accept—they had come so far. They had also spent all their money. All were despondent that Christmas.

More disappointments awaited them on their return. No one had heard about their success in Germany and promoters were not standing in line to hire them. No one even knew who the Beatles were then. Moreover, Alan Williams, who had promised the group steady work upon their return from Germany, lost his club in a fire. These setbacks almost broke up the Beatles.

The Hamburg experience, however, had forged an ever-strengthening bond between them. They had been together twenty-four hours a day, eating together, sleeping, clowning and occasionally coming to blows. As strangers in a foreign land, they had come to rely on one another for support. John, Paul, and George especially felt responsible for the bulk of the musical labors. After they returned to Liverpool, the realization that they had built their world around the group re-kindled their resolve. If they had not traveled to Hamburg as mates and returned to Liverpool as brothers, the Beatles story might have ended there. But their families' determination to put them to work in the nine-to-five world triggered a resentment they nurtured in each other and strengthened their determination not to fall into the pit of conformity.

There were few options open to the boys. Paul and George had left the institute, and John could not return to the art school. The Beatles decided to resume playing as a group because, it seemed a shame to let the Hamburg experience go to waste. Alan Williams secured two mid-December dates for them at the Grosvenors Ballroom, and Mona Best booked them into the Casbah for one night.

Their most significant booking, however, was arranged by Bob Wooler, an emcee at the Litherland Town Hall. He persuaded a jive-hall promoter named Brian Kelly to include the Beatles on the bill of a Boxing Day promotion at the Litherland on December 27, 1960. Kelly placed posters outside the Litherland proclaiming in large fluorescent letters, THE BEATLES, DIRECT FROM HAMBURG! Since the Beatles were not known in Liverpool, the posters led people to believe that Kelly had hired a German band. "The posters caused a certain amount of curiosity," says Brian Kelly, "and I remember the first reaction to their name: 'Beatles—you've spelt it wrong, mister.' 'Beatles? Where'd you drag them from?' 'Beatles? Who are they?' " But on the day the Beatles were to perform, he had to turn away 200 kids. "This is where December 27, 1960, comes in, which is certainly a historic date," says Wooler, "because this was the beginning of Beatlemania. That name came about because of the British press in 1963, but it really happened at the Litherland Town Hall on that particular date."

That night Bob Wooler placed the Beatles as an insert act in the middle of the show. "There was this expectant crowd," he says. "Something very special was going to happen for them. The curtains were closed; we primed each other as to exactly what we were going to do. In my vocal buildup to the audience, I attempted to instill in them that this was a special act and not your run-of-the-mill group that they'd been used to week in and week out—that this was an act with a dynamic difference! I announced, 'Here they are, direct from Hamburg, the sensational Beatles!' As the curtains swept open, Paul launched into 'Long Tall Sally.' "

The audience was spellbound by their performance, and even the Beatles did not understand what had happened when teenage girls began to scream. "There was that indefinable difference," says Wooler. "I had a stage-eye view of the audience and they were just captivated. In fact, they gravitated to the footlights. There was a tall, high stage at the Litherland and you literally had to look up, and from the stage you'd see a sea of faces. I went off to the side of the stage and into the audience to have an audience-eye view, and it was quite stunning."

Brian Kelly recalls: "At that particular moment, I was by the cashier and there was certainly a change in the atmosphere—so much so that we closed the doors and all the bouncers and I went into the ballroom to see what the hell was wrong! But something did occur and we didn't like it; it wasn't a familiar feeling. We went in and saw a group onstage performing and the audience was right up at the front of the stage, all squeezed in watching in adoration, not dancing! I had seen this type of reaction before, but it wasn't as effective. I never saw the whole hall stop and watch."

Bill Harry, who was in the audience that night, recalls: "The Beatles wore black leather jackets and trousers, and . . . all this black leather and the fact that kids thought they were a group from Germany who spoke very good English added to the impact."

The Beatles' overwhelming performance at the Litherland placed Bob Wooler in an awkward position with the other groups on the bill. "Oh, I was really in for it that night from the other groups," he says, "because the Beatles were booked in the best spot of the evening. The groups were saying to me at the end of the night, 'Who the fuck *are* they? What's the idea of bringing them on, then? Kelly didn't tell us about this!' And I had to say, 'Now, now, it's a *special* night. A special Christmas attraction.' They said, 'Well, who brought them, Santa Claus?'"

John, Paul, and George have each pointed to this date as the moment when they first came to believe that the Beatles would succeed in Liverpool. It was the first time the hometown crowd stood and cheered.

PART TWO

WHAT'S FROM LIVERPOOL?

Circa 1961 to February 1964

5

The Beatles' success at the Litherland Town Hall led to a series of bookings at two other venues run by Brian Kelly: the Ainstree Institute and Latham Hall. The audiences at both clubs quadrupled, but instead of dancing, kids stood in front of the stage staring at the group in awe and adoration, screaming their approval at the end of each song. Recognizing the group's box-office potential, promoters approached the Beatles each day with offers to play at their venues, and the boys found themselves in the unique position of having their pick of the best halls, dates, and fees. With the increasing number of bookings being offered, the responsibility for handling the group's business affairs was delegated to Pete Best. A friend of Pete's named Neil Aspinall, who owned a minibus, was hired as their road manager.

Hamburg had taught the boys how to deal with unruly crowds, and in fact England's Teddy boys seemed like mischievous grammar-school brats compared to the Reeperbahn bouncers who played soccer with a drunk's face while the Beatles indifferently rocked onstage. Still, they were fearful of the violence that erupted between rival Teddy-boy gangs wherever they performed in Merseyside and often got caught up in it, with amps getting smashed and a general riot as they played "Hully Gully."

The Beatles realized the scope of their local popularity when they performed at the Litherland Town Hall on Valentine's Day. After the group played "Wooden Heart," a girl was selected from the audience to receive from the band a specially made wooden heart, which Paul was supposed to present to her. When she came up on the stage, more girls followed and McCartney suddenly found himself surrounded by a hundred adoring fans.

The Beatles weren't the only group that improved while in Germany; Rory Storme and the Hurricanes, and Howie Casey and the Seniors also returned to Liverpool with a dynamic, hard-driving sound. But although Hamburg instilled a new vitality in all the groups that performed there, the Beatles emerged as the premier band in Merseyside. "They wrote original material and the other groups didn't," says Bill Harry. "That was a big edge. They also came back with an image in black leather, and the other groups came back looking the same. They had this image, the original material, and their looks—they were a better-looking band than any other group."

Through the efforts of Bob Wooler, the Beatles began appearing at the Cavern Club at 8 Mathew Street in the City Centre. From March 1961 to August 1963, they gave more than 292 performances there. Liz Hughes, now co-owner of the Beatles Museum on Mathew Street, was one of their early fans and she remembers: "Mathew Street back then was a very dark, sort of dreary little road with seven-story warehouses all the way down either side. Very little light—only natural light got through. The Cavern door was literally a hole in the wall. It was an arch doorway painted at the top in red and white and blue with 'The Cavern' scrawled up the side. The stairs had crumbled to nothing at one side, so you walked down sideways on these stone steps. When you got to the bottom, you were in a cellar, stone walls, no decor to speak of at all. If you touched the walls, your hands came away wet because with all the bodies down there, the walls used to sweat!"

At night the Cavern swelled with 200 teenagers who listened to beat music for three hours. The heat from their bodies drove the temperature in the club to over ninety degrees and created mists of steam that seeped through the doorway into Mathew Street, blending with the smell of rotten fruit that lay on the brick pavement. When girls fainted from the heat, the only way to remove them from the club was to pass them over the heads of the crowd. The musicians standing beneath the Cavern's arched ceiling had almost no headroom. As they performed, condensation streamed from the stone walls and onto their amplifiers, shorting them out. Instead of storming off stage in a huff, the Beatles laughed and led their fans in singing sea chanteys until their equipment was working again.

It was at the Cavern Club that the Beatles established themselves as folk heroes. There was John Lennon—a lean street punk, fostering a tough-guy image, perniciously witty, cocky and brash, swearing at the crowd whenever someone interrupted him while he tuned his guitar. Paul McCartney, whom Bob Wooler introduced as "the Noel Coward of rock 'n' roll"—charming and sincere, the spokesman for the group. George Harrison—quiet and unassuming, looking serious as he played lead guitar, nicknamed the "great stone face." Stuart Sutcliffe—standing with his back to the audience, wearing sunglasses to conceal his eyes from the fans as he earnestly played the bass. And Pete Best—keeping to himself, content to remain in the background while observing the antics of the others, yet ironically the most popular of the group.

"The atmosphere was absolutely unbelievable," says Liz Hughes. "This was the start, if you'd like, of hysteria, the first time it had ever been known in Britain. No one had manipulated them or fashioned them in any way. They were so different from the run-of-the-mill groups around with suede-collar jackets. Whatever these lads happened to get up in that morning, they played in that day. People would be shouting, 'Play this!' or 'Play that!' and they'd answer you back. They'd shout, 'Oh, shut up!' or they'd say, 'Oh, er, yeah, in a minute.' They were always very free."

The Beatles had combined their unique personalities and a musical repertoire into a stage presence remarkable to the eye and ear. They were rowdy, raw, and boisterous. Their eating and drinking onstage and their mockery of anything or anyone only added to their appeal. "There was a certain arrogance about them," says Bob Wooler, "but at the same time, there was a disarming quality. One moment they would be superior and the next moment they'd realize that they had been and try to atone for it. It was this contrasting combination of attitudes that made them so fascinating. When they were together, all thinking and on a combined attack, they were absolutely devastating. They could demolish a person. John, Paul, and George would combine and, *my God*, it was so difficult, because they'd bounce remarks off one another and onto the victim."

Though individualists, these three possessed great strength as a unit and their shows were fascinating to watch because they abided by no rules. This was an extension of John Lennon's energy. Though Paul and George were two distinct personalities, John's influence on them was unmistakable. Their attraction to him developed into a strengthening of personal style and wit, an evolution of defense against his brashness.

In April, two months after George Harrison's eighteenth birthday, the Beatles returned to Hamburg to perform at the Top Ten Club, splitting among them £150 a week. They were joined by Tony Sheridan, the singer/guitarist from England who had immigrated to Germany to establish a career as a nightclub performer. They all shared an attic room, complete with bare boards and freezing drafts.

John's girlfriend, Cynthia Powell, who had found their four-month separation too much to bear the last time the group played in Germany, traveled to Hamburg to be with him during her two-week Easter holiday from college. Cyn stayed at Astrid Kirchnerr's apartment in Eims Butteler Strasse, but occasionally John persuaded her to spend the night with him in the Beatles' attic room above the club. Cyn recalls that she must have loved John a great deal to sleep with him in those dank and crowded quarters.

Two weeks after the Beatles arrived in Hamburg, Stuart wrote to Alan Williams and informed him that they were not going to pay him his ten-percent commission. The decision, made by Lennon, was based on the fact that they themselves had made the arrangements to play at the Top Ten, hence Alan was not entitled to an agent's fee. Having been exposed to the hard business tactics of Bruno Koschmider, and having achieved success in Liverpool and Hamburg, the boys were not about to be led by a would-be impresario who lacked the expertise to guide them beyond strip clubs and coffee bars, and whose scope was such that Liverpool fame was the biggest anyone could attain. A point they overlooked, however, was that it was Williams who had enabled them to obtain entry visas and return to Hamburg. He had written to the German consulate in Liverpool explaining the circumstances that had led to their deportation and, ironically, expressing the belief that they were "fine lads" who had been exploited by an unscrupulous entrepreneur.

The Beatles had been in Hamburg for nearly a month when Stuart announced that he was leaving the group. Stu had never developed into a good bass player and had continued to play only the simplest bass lines. This had led to many rows with Paul, who was eager to play the bass and felt that Stuart was holding the group back. Paul's constant needling had once provoked Stu into picking him up and throwing him against a set of drums, which quieted McCartney for a while.

Stuart's decision to leave the Beatles, however, was not prompted by his clashes with Paul but by his desire to devote more time to painting—and also by the fact that he and Astrid had fallen in love. Their attraction was intellectual as well as physical. Astrid was different from the shallow types he normally encountered. Advanced, aware, in tune with Stuart, she encouraged his artistic absorption and convinced him that he was wasting his time with the Beatles. "Stuart reached the stage where he had to decide between his art or the guitar, and he decided to stay with his art," says Bill Harry. "I think when he picked up the guitar, Stuart thought he could do both, and eventually realized that he couldn't." Sutcliffe's decision was hastened when a visiting sculptor, impressed with the musician's artwork, invited him to join his master class at the Hamburg Art School. Upon Stuart's departure, Paul took over the bass guitar. The Beatles moved one step closer to musical unity; Stuart went on to produce his finest work.

* * *

One evening in early May, Bert Kaempfert, a producer for Polydor Records in Germany who gained international fame in 1960 with the recording "Wonderland by Night," visited the Top Ten Club and was impressed by Tony Sheridan and the Beatles. Over drinks Kaempfert asked them if they would make a record for him. His studio was a dilapidated radio station used by the British army after World War II and later remodeled into a recording facility. Kaempfert didn't know what the boys should play, so he just told them to do what they thought best.

Tony Sheridan and the Beatles spent an entire morning in the recording studio. From that session came "My Bonnie," "The Saints," and "Why?" on which the Beatles backed Sheridan, and "Ain't She Sweet," sung by John Lennon. The group also recorded their first original tune, "Cry for a Shadow," an instrumental written by John and George. After the session, Kaempfert signed Tony Sheridan to a recording contract with Polydor Records, which released "My Bonnie" and "The Saints" in Germany on a single in June 1961. Polydor's marketing department thought the name "Beatles" was repulsive and listed the group on the record label as the Beat Brothers. Though he was impressed by the Beatles, Kaempfert did not secure a record deal for them because they were Liverpool-based. Instead, he signed the group to Bert Kaempfert Productions on May 12, 1961. The agreement made Kaempfert the Beatles' first manager.

In June 1961 the Beatles, now a well-seasoned quartet, returned to Liverpool. The marathon sessions at the Top Ten had whipped the band further into shape—particularly Paul, who was learning to play the bass guitar—and had given John, Paul, and George an opportunity to work on their harmonies, something the Beatles had rarely done before.

During the early 1960s, the strongest musical influence in England emanated from London-based bands—primarily the Shadows, whose style and image were copied by nearly every aspiring group in the country. Singers modeled themselves after the pure pop styles of Cliff Richard or Adam Faith, whose conservative public image pleased the British establishment: They were clean-cut and performed in tailored suits.

The beat scene in Liverpool, however, had acquired a life outside the mainstream of the British music industry. The bands were rough and raw-looking, clad in old jeans, sweaters, and leather jackets. Although there were a few groups that preferred the tailored look—Rory Storme and the Hurricanes, for example—nearly every Merseyside band had a style and image of its own. "It wasn't an exact copy of American rock 'n' roll," says Bill Harry. "The kids played it in their own way and had their own instrumental lineups. With American rock 'n' roll at the time, there was a lot of saxophone work in it. The American rock bands had quite big lineups. In Liverpool the average lineup was about four kids with just guitars and drums. Groups like the Beatles, the Searchers, and Gerry and the Pacemakers developed their own style of three-part harmony with lead, bass, and rhythm guitars, and a drummer. That was a very common lineup. They seemed to adapt the American music in their own style, but this was a hard-driving beat that the Liverpool groups used to do."

The "Mersey sound" (so named by journalists in 1963) was a fusion of American rhythm 'n' blues and an unsophisticated style of playing that made Liverpool groups easily distinguishable from other British bands. They sang with a Liverpudlian accent, accompanied by an overpowering guitar sound. "The difference between the music of Liverpool and that of the rest of the country was that we didn't use echo chambers," says Bob Wooler. "So Liverpool groups had a raw sound while the rest of the country had a twangy sound."

Another difference between Liverpool bands and London bands was the types of music they performed. The British music industry then was following the direction of the American by releasing easy-listening pop songs, while Liverpool groups were performing gutsy rock 'n' roll and obscure rhythm 'n' blues tunes. As a seaport, however, Liverpool had a significant advantage over other English cities: Liverpudlian seamen in the merchant navy, who sailed to New York and traveled America's eastern seaboard, returned home with a supply of rhythm 'n' blues records that were not available to the British record-buying public until the mid-1960s. There was a wealth of this material available to musicians who had a friend or relative in the merchant navy. Many beat groups acquired a vast repertoire of these obscure rhythm 'n' blues tunes through Bob Wooller, who played his rare and extensive collection of American rock 'n' roll discs at the jive halls in Merseyside. Wooler was a confidant of the Beatles, who often sought his advice about business and music, and the group had access to his collection.

Liverpool teenagers in 1961 did not analyze the music or what was happening in Merseyside—they just enjoyed themselves. Cellar clubs like the Iron Door, the Zodiac, the Mardi Gras, the Blackcat, and the Peppermint Lounge sprouted throughout the area in competition with the Cavern Club. Since the vibrancy of the beat scene did not interest the local press, who wrote only about the national pop stars, Bill Harry launched the *Mersey Beat* newspaper in the summer of 1961. For nearly a year, Harry gathered information about the beat scene: the groups, venues, and promoters. "I believed then that nobody knew the extent of the scene," he says. "I found that it was far bigger than anyone ever realized. All the groups thought there were just a handful of bands, and when I came out with a list of well over three hundred bands, everybody's minds were blown! They just couldn't believe it! I thought at the time, Surely there's never been so much music in one city before. It was almost the equivalent to what was happening in New Orleans at the turn of the century with hundreds of groups in one city; tens of thousands of teenagers going out three or four nights a week to see the bands. It was completely unique."

Bill Harry named *Mersey Beat* after the river Mersey, the beat that a policeman or a reporter covers, and the beat of the music. The first issue, dated July 6, 1961, featured a story about Gene Vincent, and eventually the paper became a vital source of information about the Liverpool groups, especially the Beatles. In each *Mersey Beat* issue, Harry promoted the Beatles by including an article about their progress in Liverpool and Hamburg. No other Merseyside group had such coverage.

John Lennon and Paul McCartney were regular contributors to the paper. (Much of John's poetry, later published in his book *In His Own Write*, debuted in *Mersey Beat*.) In the first issue, Lennon wrote a tongue-in-cheek history of the group, called the "Dubious Origins of the Beatles," in which he explained the derivation of the group's name.

By now the Beatles played regularly at the Cavern Club, and their following had grown immensely. Bob Wooler recalls: "Whenever they played, they had this corps of supporters. Just a devout loyalty. There are countless examples of kids camping outside the Cavern because they wanted to be in the front row of seats. This was proof of their dedication." In the afternoon, shop assistants who worked in the City Centre would queue in Mathew Street to see and hear the Beatles perform during lunchtime sessions. At night the girls who sat in the first two rows of seats patiently removed curlers from their hair and applied makeup during the performances of the other groups, making themselves attractive for the moment when the Beatles walked on stage and began their show.

Despite the scope of their success, the Beatles were frustrated with the day-to-day routine of performing in the same venues. They were confident that the group had the talent to succeed in the big time, but they were desperately waiting for something to happen for them. Although John, Paul, George, and Pete were earning more money each week than the average workingman in Liverpool, they did not want to spend the rest of their lives performing in cellar clubs and jive halls as some of the other beat groups seemed destined to do. John Lennon was prepared to do *anything* to get out of Liverpool. Paul tried to generate interest in the group by writing letters to journalists, hoping they would find the Beatles newsworthy and write about them, but his letters were ignored.

To escape the monotony of their life-style, Paul and John abruptly canceled a string of bookings and went to France for a week in late September. It was during this brief vacation that the two began sporting the French-styled haircut (hair combed over the forehead) popular among the art students in Hamburg—the five-point haircut created by Vidal Sassoon in 1959. When John and Paul returned to Liverpool, George, too, adopted the style, but Pete Best did not. The Beatles were the only group in Merseyside to sport this image. Liverpool's groups stood apart from London's, and now the Beatles stood apart from everyone else.

6

In autumn 1961 Stuart Sutcliffe, who was living in Hamburg, sent John Lennon a copy of the single "My Bonnie" b/w "The Saints." The disc then came into the possession of Bob Wooller, who hosted a half-hour record session in the Cavern Club. "I met George Harrison on a bus one day," says Wooler, "and George said that Stuart Sutcliffe had sent them this record. I said, 'Let me play it!' It wasn't really a Beatles record, because they were doing a backing chore for Tony Sheridan. But the mere fact that they could listen and say, 'Oh, that's me!' or 'Oh, I did that bit!'—that was really something. They were, of course, excited because hardly anyone in Liverpool had made a record before."

Wooler played the record repeatedly during his Cavern disc session. "Naturally, I plugged 'My Bonnie' and 'The Saints.' I said, 'The Beatles are on record! If you want this record, go and ask for it at the record shops.' Of course, it wasn't available, but this was to stimulate interest and, hopefully, bring supplies into the country."

One fan who responded to Wooler's plug was a teenager named Raymond Jones. On October 29, 1961, he walked into the North End Music Store (NEMS), a furniture and record shop on Whitechapel Street, and told proprietor Brian Epstein he wanted a copy.

Epstein was proud of NEMS's ability to fulfill any customer's request, but when it came to the German recording, he came up empty. Several more inquiries for the record that same day threw Epstein into a panic. Peter Brown, a NEMS employee, recalls: "We had a fabulous stock system—a very intricate stock system. Our boast was that we could guarantee that if we didn't have a record in stock, we could get it within twenty-four hours. In those days the record industry was much smaller than it is now, so we were able to stock pretty much the entire catalog of the major American labels. When somebody asked Brian for a Beatles record and he couldn't find it, he went crazy!"

Epstein was the image of the English businessman: well dressed, refined, even aristocratic. He was also a complex man: Within him lurked a frustrated homosexual, an inner man struggling to discover some means of self-expression. Born on September 19, 1934, Brian was raised in a wealthy environment by parents who provided him with an excellent education and taught him to appreciate art, beauty—the finer things in life. However, they expected their son to carry on the management of the family business—the North End Music Stores—and this gnawed at him, for he wished to succeed on his own without the cushion of an established family enterprise. He often pursued flights of fancy that his parents believed were silly and distracted him from his real work—and indeed his projects and ideas were all costly, in time and money, and always ended the same way. Whenever Brian saw the chance to solo in a new project, he went at it with gusto, putting forth every effort for a short time, then quickly dropping the idea when he lost interest.

For example, after spending a year in the Royal Army Signal Corps as a clerk, Brian, who enjoyed the theater throughout his life, entered the Royal Academy of Dramatic Art in London. Though a number of his classmates—such as Susannah York, Peter O'Toole, and Albert Finney—achieved acclaim, Epstein did not complete the course. Desiring never-theless to have something to do with the entertainment world, even after the Beatles became the success he'd hoped they would, he poured his personal fortune into a series of unsuc-cessful theatrical productions.

In 1951, when he was twenty-two, Brian formally rejoined the family business, finding that NEMS had incorporated a record department within the store. Clive Epstein, Brian's younger brother, recalls: "The record department interested Brian. When he saw what our plans were, he decided to come back into the business, devoting his time and efforts to the record department, which became extremely successful under his guidance." Brian displayed an ability to attend to all mat-ters of business and detail, however trivial. He established a system with pieces of string and paper clips that alerted him when their stock of any record was low.

By autumn 1961, however, Brian felt that he had con-quered every aspect of record retailing, and he was again bored. It was during this period of restlessness that Raymond Jones requested a copy of "My Bonnie." Epstein learned from one of his assistants that the Beatles were playing at the Cavern Club, just a hundred yards from NEMS's Whitechapel address, and made arrangements to visit the club to find out more about this mystery record and the Beatles. On November 9, Brian arrived at the Cavern to see the group play during a lunchtime session.

Epstein later said that he regretted his decision to visit the Cavern the moment he descended the stone steps of the club; the murkiness and the smell of perspiration nauseated him. But once he saw and heard the Beatles, his misgivings van-ished. He had never seen anything like them and was drawn by their magnetism.

Bob Wooler acknowledged Epstein's presence over the house microphone after the Beatles completed their first set. The boys knew Brian Epstein—"They were regular loiterers at NEMS," says Peter Brown, a former NEMS employee and friend of all four of the Beatles, "either talking to the shopgirls or using up the sound booth without purchasing records, much to Brian's distaste." When Brian walked over to the stage, he was greeted by a bewildered George Harrison. "What brings Mr. Epstein here?" George asked, shaking hands. Brian explained that his shop had been getting requests for their record. They played the record for him, which he liked but thought was unexceptional, and he stayed for the second half, liking the Beatles more and more.

Brian could not compare the liveliness of the Cavern Club nor the excitement he felt over the Beatles to anything he had known before. As he watched the Beatles, a new idea, unlike his previous ones, formulated in his head: He wanted a piece of the action. When John, Paul, George, and Pete completed their second set, Brian approached them again. A meeting with him might prove beneficial to their careers, he told them, and proposed that they meet "just for a chat" at his Whitechapel office. The boys were a bit suspicious of his intentions, but they agreed and a date was set. "I think the music industry and everything that went with it was something Brian stumbled across," says Clive Epstein. "I don't think he was actually looking for that type of activity. He more or less thought, Here's an area I've never considered before; maybe it's something I could dabble with. He had a reasonable income from the family business, and of course a little more income was always great. Although Brian never invisioned it turning out like it did, I think the idea of an extra activity, which at the same time supplemented his income, interested him."

Brian Epstein was one of many local agents who had approached the Beatles with management propositions, but the Beatles refused to associate themselves with someone they considered a loser. They knew they were the best group in Liverpool, and they wanted a manager who understood their hunger to become stars. They had established themselves as the conduit of new trends in Merseyside. They did not flaunt their hipness; it simply showed—onstage or wherever one encountered them. Brian Epstein was challenged by this, for despite the group's rough exterior, their intelligence was evident and their worldliness rare for men their age.

Epstein's desire to meet with them naturally intrigued the group. "They didn't know what to think of Brian," says Bob Wooler. "I had been their adviser ever since that first Litherland booking and they often took me into their confidence.

They said to me, 'What do you think, then?' and I said, 'Well, nothing lost by going along and hearing what he has to say, is there?' They asked me to come along and have a look at this fellow and tell them what I thought afterwards."

On December 3, 1961, the Beatles, minus Paul, arrived with Bob Wooler at Epstein's office at the appointed time. Paul was taking a bath. When he arrived an hour later, the meeting began. Epstein, who hadn't been expecting to see a stranger at the meeting, "was looking very quizzically at me," says Wooler, "and eventually John realized that the intros hadn't been completed, and he introduced me as 'Oh, this is me dad.' It was an interesting meeting, though. Brian didn't know quite how to handle the situation. It was a very halting and unforth- coming performance from all. I accepted one or two glances from the boys, but they were interested in what he had to say. They would hear a person out, be polite, and if they took the mickey out of that person afterwards, well, that was their way. They were great at parodying people; taking off on people in an unkind manner. But Brian did say that he was interested in the possibility of seeing what he could do for them."

Another meeting was suggested for the following week. This gave Brian time to inquire further about the Beatles. He heard that Alan Williams had been involved with them at one time and asked his opinion. "My advice to you," said Wil- liams, "is to have nothing to do with them. They'll let you down." John, Paul, George, and Pete also had time to think about Brian Epstein. Despite their mocking, the fact remained that he owned a large record store, had a lot of influence, and appeared businesslike. Brian was certainly a contrast to the working-class types who managed other Liverpool groups. Why he wanted to bother with them was a mystery to the group. "Brian came from a money family," says Bill Harry, "and a majority of the people in Liverpool didn't have money, and here was a guy who had it all, moving into another envi- ronment. In some ways, people suggested that he really en- joyed this environment because it seemed a bit seedy, coming from his upper-class background and going into a sweaty little cellar club with guys in black leather. It was a bit like slum- ming, you know."

Brian Epstein was drawn to the Beatles not only for musical reasons but because he saw something in them that Alan Williams and Bert Kaempfert had failed to see: their raw sex appeal. Epstein also knew enough about what sounded good to recognize their recording potential, and the Beatles' main concern then was securing a record contract. "The Beatles were aware that the peak was a record," says Bob Wooler. "They weren't thinking in terms of being bigger than Elvis, they were thinking in terms of 'We want a record!'" And the Beatles believed that Brian Epstein was the man who could make this possible.

A week later, on December 10, 1961, the group arrived at NEMS for their second meeting with Epstein and they struck their deal immediately. Epstein did not have a contract for the group to sign, yet the Beatles accepted his offer with the knowledge that his only experience in the music world was retailing records.

Although there was a vast difference between Epstein's background and that of the Beatles, he had one thing in common with them: He was hungry for recognition. Epstein would not be content to point to a clip-and-string inventory system as his major accomplishment. He felt that he had creative contributions to make to the entertainment world, and the Beatles were the perfect vehicle for his aspirations. They were exuberant, flashy, and wild, which excited him. He was fascinated by the idea of living vicariously through these boys.

Brian next had to convince his parents that his involvement with the Beatles was unlike his previous ventures and wouldn't conflict with his responsibilities in the family business.

7

Brian Epstein's subsequent visits to the Cavern Club strengthened his determination to secure a record contract for the Beatles. He was sure that through his involvement with record retailing he could arrange an audition with a record company. Initially he tried to persuade the local press to write about the Beatles and their popularity to show artists-and-repertoire executives that there was hometown interest in the quartet. He wrote to *Liverpool Echo* columnist Tony Barrow, who was known to his readers as "the Disker." To Epstein's surprise, Barrow's reply came from Decca Records in London, where Barrow also worked as a publicist. "Brian was asking if I would write about the Beatles," says Tony, "and I had to write back to him and say that mine was strictly a record-review column, and until they had a record out, I really couldn't write about them."

Of all the record companies in England then, Epstein's best connections were with Decca, so in mid-December 1961 he traveled to London to meet with Tony Barrow. "After he'd gone," Barrow recalls, "I rang through to the marketing department because I knew that Epstein was a record retailer. So I said to marketing, 'Because he's a record shopman, he may very well think that his band has got to have a Decca audition.' They said, 'Epstein—is that the name of the shop?' I said, 'No, the shop's called NEMS.' They said, 'Oh, NEMS! The North End Music Stores. Yes, they're very big customers. His group *will* have to have a Decca audition,' which of course they then did get."

Chances are that Decca would have agreed to a recording test even if the Beatles had been tone-deaf. NEMS was an important client to the sales department, who gathered that if they did not appease the record magnate from the north, Decca could lose the account. Dick Rowe, the head of the artists-and-repertoire department, sent one of his men, Mike Smith, to hear the Beatles at the Cavern Club. "When Mike came back," recalls Rowe, "I said, 'Well, what are they like?' I wasn't excited, but I was very interested because there was a lot of underground talk about them. Mike said, 'Oh, they're great!' I said, 'Well, you better bring them down and give them an audition.' "

Although Brian gave the Beatles the impression that he was a man of influence, he was definitely an amateur in the music industry. When he heard the news that Decca had arranged a recording test for the group, he was overwhelmed—by disbelief. He telephoned the boys and asked that they meet him at a café in Liverpool. There, the five of them—four scruffy-looking musicians and a well-dressed businessman—sat around a table and talked about the beat scene for a while. Then Epstein, beaming, told the group they had an audition with Decca.

John, Paul, George, and Pete were stunned by the news. They had asked Epstein to manage them only two weeks ago, and already he had secured a recording test for them with a major record company. Any initial skepticism about Brian vanished; they were confident that he was the right man.

Brian and the Beatles celebrated throughout the night and into the early hours of the morning, "getting drunk with power," as Epstein recalled. That night the cultural gap between them grew narrower and their relationship became less businesslike.

On New Year's Eve 1961, they all departed for London. Brian traveled by train and checked into the posh Park Lane Hotel in Mayfair. The Beatles braved the wrath of winter and drove 200 miles in a van, along with Neil Aspinall and their equipment. They were booked into cheaper accommodations at the Royal Hotel in Russell Square. During their first night in London, the boys roamed the snow-covered streets and talked about what was ahead of them the next day. The city, cold and impervious to these four provincial boys, made them nervous and uncomfortable. Excitement over the Decca audition gave way to fear and panic. The recording test was crucial to the realization of a dream, and the Beatles were suddenly very aware of the many barriers that existed between them and a recording contract. Decca was London, and the Beatles were Liverpool, which was, in the eyes of the south, "hicksville." Their awareness of London's prejudice cowed them before they walked into the Decca recording studios. On the morning of the audition, Brian Epstein encountered four nervous and apprehensive musicians.

Shortly before noon on January 1, 1962, they arrived at Decca's West Hampstead studios. Brian, knowing that leather jackets and jeans would make a bad impression, had persuaded the boys to dress neatly for the audition. They sat in the lobby of the studio, chain-smoking with anxiety that intensified when Mike Smith failed to appear at the appointed time, annoying them and making them feel shabbily treated. When Mike Smith arrived an hour later, the audition began.

As they were preparing themselves in the studio, Smith told them to put away their battered amplifiers and use the equipment left over from a previous session. Paul was distracted by a red light glowing in the studio and asked if it could be turned off, but Smith refused, explaining that the light prevented people from walking in during the session. Their unfamiliarity with the studio created even more tension. "At that original session, I'm sure it was a situation where these four bewildered souls get put into a studio and a microphone gets put up in front of them," says Mike Smith. "I

Cynthia and John, circa 1959. (Courtesy the authors)

Tony Carricker *(left)* and John outside the Crack Pub, circa 1959. (Courtesy the authors)

Quarry Bank High School, John Lennon *(left)* and Pete Shut-
ton *(right)*. (Courtesy the authors)

Paul (*second from left*) and John (*second from right*) performing with the Quarrymen, fall 1958. (Courtesy Dezo Hoffman/Rex/RDR)

Brian Epstein at the Cavern Club.
(Courtesy Camera Press)

George and Ringo outside the Cavern. (Courtesy Dezo Hoffman/Rex/RDR)

The Beatles in Key West, 1964. (Courtesy Bob Bonis)

John relaxing in Key West. (Courtesy Bob Bonis)

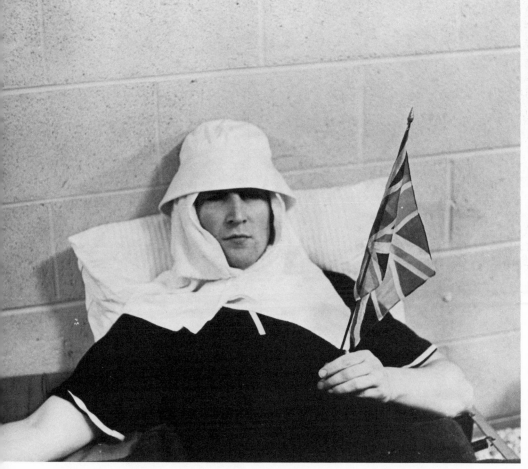

Paul plays bass backstage before a concert at RFK Stadium in Philadelphia.
(Courtesy Bob Bonis)

George concentrates as he tunes a guitar backstage before the concert at RFK Stadium in Philadelphia. (Courtesy Bob Bonis)

George and John confer backstage before the concert at RFK Stadium in Philadelphia. (Courtesy Bob Bonis)

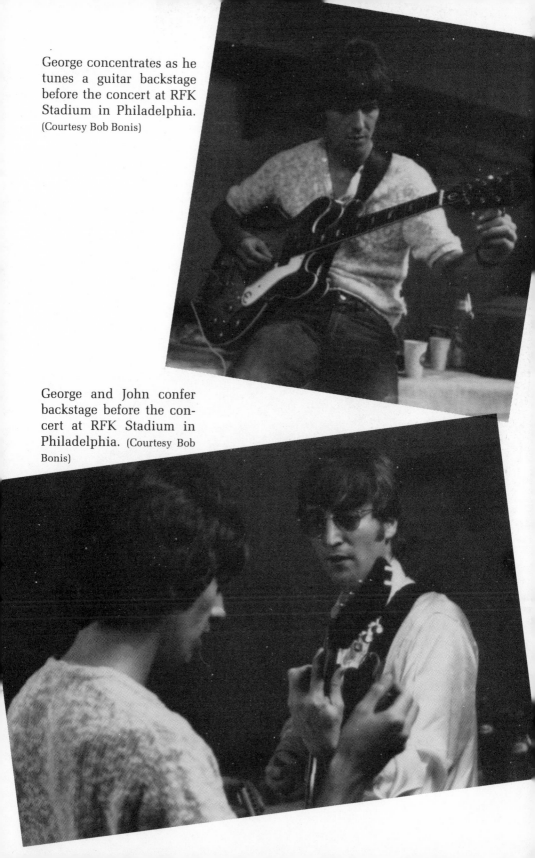

George at Abbey Road Studios, September 1962. (Courtesy Dezo Hoffman/ Rex/RDR)

Ringo at Abbey Road Studios, September 1962. (Courtesy Dezo Hoffman/Rex/RDR)

John and Paul recording "Love Me Do" at Abbey Road, September 1962. (Courtesy Dezo Hoffman/Rex/RDR)

Rehearsing a Lennon-McCartney composition for producer George Martin. (Courtesy Rex/RDR)

Fall 1962. (Courtesy Dezo Hoffman/Rex/RDR)

Rehearsing for "The Ed Sullivan Show." (Courtesy Wide World Photos)

The "boys" as they were presented to a Beatle-crazed world. (Courtesy Dezo Hoffman/Rex/RDR)

wasn't aware of their nervousness. I would think that they were probably playing their part as well as I was playing mine. I was trying to be, I suspect, the cool, sophisticated record-company executive, and here was a group *lucky* enough to come into the great Decca studios and be able to have an opportunity to perform. I mean, it was a *big deal* in those days to have a record contract."

The group spent three hours in the studio recording eleven songs. Paul sang "Red Sails in the Sunset," "Till There Was You," and "To Know Her Is to Love Her"; George sang "Memphis" and "The Sheik of Araby"; and John sang "Please, Mr. Postman," "Money," and "Three Cool Cats." They also recorded three Lennon/McCartney tunes: "Like Dreamers Do," "The Love of the Loved," and "Hello, Little Girl." The Beatles, however, did not perform well for Decca. Their cockiness and strength crumbled in the studio, and once the boys were overpowered, there was no magic left to their sound. Their nerves were taut throughout the session, the beat and tempo lagged, and their voices cracked from the tension. "When I saw the Beatles onstage, I was *knocked out*, I was *entranced*, I thought they were *fantastic*," says Mike Smith. "It was only when they came into the studio that I discovered they weren't very good. The thing that stuck in my mind was how bad McCartney was that day."

When the test ended at three o'clock, the boys quietly put away their instruments and were told that Decca would be in touch. The drive back to Liverpool seemed longer than the trip down. The air of excitement and anticipation that had accompanied them to the capital was replaced by pessimism. They were haunted by their mistakes, but knew they had to wait patiently to hear what Decca thought of their audition.

Upon their return to Liverpool the Beatles began performing under a heavier booking schedule. Their spirits lifted when a popularity poll in *Mersey Beat* voted them Liverpool's top beat group of 1961. (John, Paul, George, and Pete had bought extra copies of the paper and voted for the Beatles under assumed names.) Brian Epstein saw the publicity advantages in the title "Top Beat Group" and made sure that Decca was aware of this success, hoping that it would shape their thinking about the test. Brian was as impatient as the Beatles to hear from Decca.

On January 24, 1962, Epstein signed the Beatles to a management contract. The agreement was innocent in its simplicity and guaranteed him twenty-five percent of their earnings. The signing took place in the Casbah Club, witnessed by Alistair Taylor, who was a NEMS employee and a friend of Brian's. Taylor endorsed each of the boys' signatures, but not Epstein's; he refused to sign the contract, explaining that he did not have complete faith in his ability as a manager and did not want the group tied to him should he prove incapable of giving them the best representation.

Though the Beatles signed the document, they felt that Epstein's commission should have been kept to twenty percent. Brian said that the additional five percent was needed for business and promotional expenses. Remembering that several promoters in Merseyside had taken advantage of them before, the Beatles began to wonder again about Epstein's motives and intentions. Unknown to him, Brian was once more in the position of having to prove himself to the group. And unknown to the Beatles, Epstein's refusal to sign the contract protected him from being legally responsible for the group, because the agreement was invalid.

Officially, however, Brian Epstein was now the manager of the Beatles. The group was solely responsible for their music; Epstein was responsible for making them stars—not an easy task. In the coming months, the greatest obstacle Brian Epstein had to overcome was the Beatles themselves, who questioned his actions every step of the way and fought the discipline they believed he was trying to impose upon them.

Following the signing of the management contract, Epstein assumed control of the group's affairs and direction. As captain of the vessel that was the Beatles, he brought order to the group, handling their business with his usual flair for detail and organization. Knowing that the boys had a reputation for arriving late at bookings, Brian determined to correct this unprofessional habit by providing each of them with a typewritten memo on his personal stationery informing them of the time and place of an engagement. Because the group was earning barely £10 a night, he did not take his twenty-five percent commission; but as their earnings increased, so did his. Their first booking under his management was on February 1, 1962, in West Kirby. The following day he arranged an out-of-town date in Manchester.

Meanwhile, Epstein had his hands full with the Beatles. Though they were a close-knit group, their egos were displayed in the subdued but fierce rivalry between John and Paul. Epstein was introduced to this clash of power early. He would occasionally drive John, Paul, and George to their bookings in his Ford Zodiac while Pete rode with Neil Aspinall in the van. Since their dates were usually north of where they lived, it was easier for Brian to pick up John, George, and Paul in that order, and he was not aware that Paul was annoyed about being picked up last until Paul rebelled.

Brian had secured two bookings for the Beatles on the same day, but when he arrived at Paul's house on Forthlin Road with John and George, Paul wasn't ready and deliberately took his time, knowing that it would upset Brian, who prided himself on being punctual. After waiting fifteen minutes in the car, Brian told Paul to take the bus and meet them at the venue. McCartney, furious, refused to play, and the Beatles subsequently missed their first job that night, which angered Brian. He told John and George that if this was the way they were going to behave, he wanted nothing to do with them. Lennon telephoned Paul, persuaded him to take the bus, and the Beatles got to the second booking in time. After the show, McCartney and Epstein argued, and Brian learned that Paul's display of temperament was based on his belief that being picked up last meant he was less important to the group. Thereafter Epstein made sure that John, Paul, and George were treated as equals.

From the moment Brian became their manager, he instilled in the boys a sense of pride that fed their already inflated egos. He regarded the Beatles as more than a local sensation and insisted that promoters treat them with the respect accorded major pop stars. On one occasion, when a promotor paid him £10 in coins, Epstein became furious and said, "If you want the Beatles again, you'd best treat them like professionals!" Realizing that promoters were earning huge profits from the Beatles' shows, he also began to increase their fee per booking.

"Brian really devoted himself to the Beatles," says Bill Harry, "and he was determined to win with them. This is the point: Brian wanted them to be winners and he had to fight all the way and he didn't take any messing. When he made the announcement that he managed to get fifteen pounds for a Beatles gig, all the promoters in Liverpool laughed because that was an unheard-of sum of money then. He kept making these announcements that he'd do a certain thing for the Beatles, and he'd end up doing it."

The Beatles began to take Brian Epstein seriously, too, which prompted him to take a bold step: the refinement of their image. Promoters outside Liverpool refused to book the group because of their menacing black-leather attire. Brian bluntly told the boys that their present image would prevent them from progressing beyond Liverpool jive halls and Hamburg nightclubs, and that they had to make certain compromises if they wished to succeed in a conservative-minded music industry. He felt strongly that if they combined their personal magnetism and energy with an air of innocence, they would gain wider appeal, perform in bigger and better venues, and earn more money.

The gradual transition from menacing to innocent—from leather to suits—took three and a half months. First Brian encouraged them out of their leather jackets, then jeans; then he got them to wear sweaters onstage and, finally, suits.

Their first performance in suits was at the Cavern Club. Bob Wooler recalls: "I was doing the commercials at the Cavern: 'The Beatles will be appearing in their new suits! For the first time on Merseyside, the Beatles appear in suits! And came the night and of course it was jammed-packed. It was a sweatbox and everyone sweated and the Beatles went on stage and *they* sweated and all their suits began to rot as they were wearing them—coming apart at the seams. They said to Brian, 'This is ridiculous!' and he was furious because he hadn't gotten sweatproof suits for them."

Despite their reluctance, Paul, George, and Pete accepted the new look. John, however, fought against changing his image and would leave his tie undone—until Paul would tighten it. Though some of their fans disliked the group's new image, feeling that they had sold out to the Establishment, the Beatles eventually realized that Brian was right.

The intensity of the connection between Epstein and the Beatles was focused on the relationship between John and Brian. Fascinated by Lennon's boldness and underlying intellect, Brian wanted to reach him and win his friendship, but he knew that Lennon trusted few people, particularly aristocratic, bourgeois capitalists, whom John resented because of his own poverty. Lennon was not so insensitive as to be unaware of Brian's sincerity and genuine affection for them all, but he and the others often hurt Brian with their cruel humor. When one or more of the boys walked away from him, Brian expected the chuckles, the laughing whispers about his effeminacy or his conservative background. This cruelty was a staple of the Epstein-Beatles relationship, and no one could hurt Brian more than Lennon.

Though Brian Epstein's homosexuality became publicized after his death in 1967, he had supposedly confided to a friend that his interest in the Beatles was triggered by his attraction to John Lennon, who was then unaware of Brian's feelings toward him. According to Bob Wooler, the group knew that Epstein was a homosexual before they were formally introduced to him in the Cavern Club, but their stay in Hamburg had exposed them to a variety of sexual life-styles, and they were not prejudiced against Epstein. They believed he was the one person in Liverpool who could help them realize their dream of signing a record contract, and it didn't matter whether he was heterosexual or homosexual as long as they got what they wanted.

The dominant bond between John and Brian then was their conviction that the Beatles could become stars—a belief reinforced by the reaction of teenagers wherever the group performed. They had strong personalities, an irreverent wit, and a style uncommon among British pop performers. Though promoters and managers in Liverpool laughed at Brian's claims that the Beatles would one day be bigger than Elvis Presley, it was not the talk of a fool. "This was something that Brian and John believed," says Clive Epstein. "I don't know about the others, but I do know that Brian and John discussed the scope of the Beatles for many hours. He may have done so with the others, but with John in particular Brian discussed the whole formula and image for many hours." Epstein told Lennon that he was not only the leader of the Beatles but their strength as well. If the group was going to have any chance of succeeding outside Liverpool, said Brian, it would be up to John because Paul and George looked up to him.

The launching of the Beatles in England, however, was not as easy as Brian and John had imagined. Three months had passed since their audition for Decca, and the company had yet to report a decision. Mike Smith had tested another group, Brian Poole and the Tremelos, on the same day the Beatles auditioned. "Mike brought the tapes from both tests to me," says Dick Rowe, "and the Beatles weren't very good. They sounded completely different from a record Brian Epstein left me earlier that featured guitarist Tony Sheridan. I thought, What's this guy up to?—because I saw no connection between what they'd done at their audition and on the record he'd left me."

The final decision was made by Mike Smith. Dick Rowe recalls: "I thought, Mike has seen both groups, so he's got one up on me. So I said to Mike, 'It's up to you—which one do you want?' So he thought, the Beatles are up in Liverpool; it means that I've got a long train ride every time I want to say good morning to them, whereas the other group lives nearby. Mike thought he could work with Brian Poole and the Tremelos all the time."

Rowe says that the Tremelos' audition wasn't too impressive either, but he didn't fight Smith's choice because he didn't like Brian Epstein. "I don't like people who—I guess because he was wealthy—don't wait to be asked to come into an office," he says. "He'd open the door and walk in. I'm really not that kind of person, but he was so much like that that I really didn't take to him. So when Mike said he wanted Brian Poole and the Tremelos, the decision didn't mean that much to me. If the Beatles had done a great audition, I would have said, 'Mike, you're out of your mind! This group's fabulous!' My eyes and ears were open, and I was very conscious that they were copying American records. So I put it all together and said, 'Go on and sign the Tremelos.'"

In March 1962, after numerous telephone calls to the artists-and-repertoire department, Brian was invited to meet with Dick Rowe. Over coffee, Rowe immediately came to the point: "Not to mince words, Mr. Epstein, we don't like your boys' sound. Groups of guitars are on the way out."

Brian, stunned, continued to try to sell the record executive on the glowing future of the Beatles. "You must be out of your mind! These boys are going to explode! I'm completely confident that one day they'll be bigger than Elvis Presley!"

Dick Rowe, however, was of a different opinion, and was blunt with him. "The boys won't go, Mr. Epstein. We know these things. You have a good record business in Liverpool. Stick to that!"

Decca offered Brian the services of Tony Meehan, a former member of the Shadows and then an artists-and-repertoire man, to produce a demo recording for the Beatles at a cost of £100, but Brian refused. Epstein, heartsick, made his way back to Liverpool with the bad news. On his arrival at Lime Street Station, he telephoned Paul and asked him to contact the others to meet at Joe's Cafe in the City Centre "for a little talk." They drank endless cups of coffee and talked about the future of the group and the beat scene, until George asked about Decca. Stunned by the answer Brian gave them, they all talked about how rotten the record companies were and how the A-and-R men didn't know anything.

Epstein approached the HMV, Columbia, Pye, and Phillips record labels. He told the A-and-R chiefs how popular the Beatles were in Liverpool, more popular than the established stars of the day, but they all turned him down. All they wanted was another Shadows.

On April 11 the Beatles returned to Hamburg for a seven-week booking at the newly opened Star Club in the St. Pauli district. Hamburg was a refreshing change for the group, particularly in the light of the ups and downs of pursuing a record deal. John, Paul, and Pete flew to Hamburg (George arrived later, having missed the flight) and were met by Astrid at the airport. John looked around and asked, "Where's Stu?" Astrid told them that he had died the day before.

It had begun months earlier, she said, with headaches that in time grew so severe that the pain brought Stuart to frantic fits of violence and long stupors. This drove Astrid into sheer panic. They consulted several doctors, all of whom told them that his condition was not serious and attributed the headaches to stress and exhaustion. During the last two months of his life, Stuart had worked hard preparing for his first art exhibition in Paris, organized by his teacher, Eduardo Paolozzi. On April 10, 1962, Stuart collapsed in the apartment he shared with Astrid, and died in her arms on the way to the hospital in an ambulance. An autopsy report said that the cause of death was a cerebral hemorrhage.

Upon hearing the news, John Lennon wept uncontrollably. And later, during the Beatles' first performance at the Star Club, he went wild trying to relieve his grief. "He gave one of the most hilarious shows I'd ever seen," says Klaus Voorman. "It was as though he'd gone mad and showed his lunacy with sheer comedy. It was John's way to trying to cheer us up; his way of letting out the hurt. At one point he raised his leg over the shoulder of a blonde who was close to the stage and looked down at her breasts. We understood what John was doing. He was deeply touched by Stuart's death because he loved him. When Stu died, John displayed the madness and absurd reality of life by acting the clown."

Stuart Sutcliffe was the closest friend that John had had since Julia's death. Many of his thoughts and beliefs about life and art evolved from Sutcliffe's original ideas. John viewed the loss of his friend as the act of some lunatic power directed against him personally.

Brian Epstein, in the meantime, was in England, still trying to secure a record deal for the Beatles. His inability to produce results placed a strain on his relationship with the group. In their frustration, they blamed Epstein for the rejections and started to wonder whether he was the right person to guide them. Yet there were forces working against Brian and the Beatles of which they were then unaware. British record companies were simply not interested in vocal groups, which was the reason why Pye, HMV, Columbia, and Phillips refused to listen to the audition tapes. "In those days groups didn't write their own songs," says Mike Smith. "Groups weren't even allowed in the studio, because you had solo *artistes* and session men and people who wrote arrangements. The producer found a song that he thought was a hit, brought it into the studio with an arranger, and it was recorded. It was really unusual for a group to get into a studio."

There was also the fact that British record companies cared little about performers from outside London, hence anyone who wanted to be discovered had to be London-based. It was here that performers were molded into the style and image that conformed to the needs of the record industry. The power and control of the music business was in the hands of a select few, and these people determined the direction of the pop scene and the musical tastes of teenagers. The accepted style was that of the balladeer, not the radical sounds emanating from the north of England. Brian Epstein was, in essence, trying to sell a product that did not interest anyone in the music business.

Brian's disappointment deepened. His parents were pressuring him to abandon his latest venture and concentrate on the family business. Harry Epstein asked his son whom was he employed by—the four scruffy musicians or him? Brian's lack of expertise as an agent led him into a mild depression, which at times grew to the point of despair. The numerous rejections did not undermine his faith in the Beatles' potential; rather, he blamed himself. He had approached the artists-and-repertoire departments of these record companies in the belief that they would immediately audition the group lest they lose NEMS's business. What Brian did not know was that these A-and-R executives were not as concerned about losing one distributor for their product as were the marketing executives, and that the A-and-R men were not about to be bullied by someone who thought he was a big shot.

In May 1962 Brian decided to give the search for a recording contract one more try, using a different approach. Once in London, Brian stopped at the HMV retail store on Oxford Street to have acetates made from the tapes for a more professional presentation to the A-and-R executives. The reel consisted of the recordings from the Decca audition, a dozen rhythm 'n' blues tunes, and several Lennon/McCartney compositions that the Beatles had recorded in the Cavern Club. At HMV a man named Ken Boast and a dubbing technician named Ted Huntley were impressed by what they heard. While the discs were being cut, Boast offered to help Brian. He arranged for him to meet Syd Coleman, the managing director of Ardmore & Beechwood, the publishing arm of EMI Records.

Coleman, too, found the recordings and the original material interesting and was willing to publish them. Brian repeated his story of rejection for Coleman, who said he knew of a friend who might be able to help—George Martin.

Brian's luck appeared to be changing. In the last two months, he had worked relentlessly for the chance of playing his tapes for a producer. Now he was being handed that opportunity.

George Martin was a learned, polished, soft-spoken man who since 1955 had directed and provided repertoire for the Parlophone label, then the smallest of the three EMI labels in England. Martin was known throughout the organization for the eccentric and offbeat recordings he produced, including a number of comedy records by Peter Sellers and Spike Milligan. Outwardly a confident and successful executive, Martin was in fact at the time desperately waiting for something new and different to fall into his lap. He envied his colleagues' success at HMV and Columbia while he repeatedly came up empty. By the time Brian Epstein walked into his office, George Martin was concerned about losing his job and would have listened to anything, which is why he agreed to meet the Liverpudlian.

Brian arrived at EMI's Manchester Square offices for his appointment on May 9. Martin listened to Brian's sales pitch and the recordings. He thought the tape generally unimpressive, but was intrigued by a "peculiar" quality to them.

Martin later said that the peculiarity he heard on the recording was the group's potential and the fact that they boasted three vocalists who all sang in an engaging style, particularly Paul McCartney, whom the producer thought had the most commercial voice. Martin also liked the lead guitar work of George Harrison. He told Brian to bring the boys to London for a test.

Epstein was filled with relief. It wasn't a contract, but it was clearly a chance, and it rekindled his motivation. He sent a telegram to the Beatles in Hamburg: CONGRATULATIONS BOYS. EMI REQUESTS RECORDING SESSION. PLEASE REHEARSE NEW MATERIAL. John, Paul, George, and Pete were excited and sent a postcard to the Reeperbahn to Brian, saying, "Please wire £10,000 advance royalties!—Paul." "When are we going to be millionaires?—John." "Please order new guitars.—George."

On June 6, 1962, the group arrived at EMI's number three

studio on Abbey Road, St. John's Wood, London, for their recording test with Parlophone. The Beatles immediately liked George Martin when they learned of his work with Peter Sellers, whom they had admired since their schoolboy days. Martin liked them, too, liking their irreverent humor. The Beatles spent three hours in the studio playing a variety of rock 'n' roll standards, as well as a few of John's and Paul's songs: "Love Me Do," "P.S. I Love You," "Hello, Little Girl," and "Ask Me Why." Martin sat poker-faced throughout the session on a high wooden stool. He was not bowled over by their performance, but he heard the group's potential. When the test ended, he told the boys and Brian that he would need time to think it over before he made a decision. The Beatles had heard this before and forlornly returned to Liverpool.

In the month that followed the audition, George Martin played the acetates from the session incessantly, trying to make up his mind about the Beatles and wondering who he should make the leader and finally deciding to leave them as they were.

Before making a decision, Martin wanted to see the Beatles perform in the Cavern. So he traveled to Liverpool, and was astonished by the environment of the club and the reaction of teenagers. He liked their brashness and independence, and when he returned to London in early July informed Brian Epstein that Parlophone was prepared to offer the Beatles a recording contract.

But there was one problem: Martin told Brian that Pete Best's drumming was not what he had in mind for the group. In fact, he went so far as to say that Pete was "a terrible drummer." Epstein had heard similar comments in recent months from John, Paul, and George, who said that neither Best's image nor his beat fit in with the group. While they combed their hair downward, for example, Pete's was greased back. He was simply "too conventional to be a Beatle," they said. For some time they'd wanted a drummer named Ringo Starr in the group.

During his career as a Beatle, Ringo Starr was regarded as the proverbial boy next door, an image that has stayed with him to this day. In the early 1960s, however, the press unjustly labeled him the "downtrodden dummy" of the group. These images were used to describe the way the public perceived Ringo's behavior and his reaction to fame.

Ringo Starr (christened Richard Starkey) was the only child of Richard and Elsie Starkey. He was born on July 7, 1940, at 9 Madryn Street in one of the many people-packed tenements in Dingle, Liverpool. All the problems of greater Liverpool were concentrated in the Dingle. Education levels were low and crime levels high. Those who lived here were stamped with a working-class label that kept a better life and a better job out of reach. Food rationing brought on by the war changed their lives from bad to worse, and the Luftwaffe bombs added paranoia to grief.

Richard and Elsie Starkey were hardworking parents who struggled to survive under these conditions, though three years after the birth of their child, irreconcilable differences forced them to divorce. Elsie retained custody of Ritchie (as Ringo was called then) and moved from Madryn Street to a smaller and less expensive flat at 10 Admiral Grove. She found a job as a barmaid in a pub called the Empress where her jolly sense of humor and forceful nature helped her deal with the rowdy dockers who frequented the pub.

As a youth, Ritchie and his neighborhood friends played in Sefton Park or by the Dingle Jetty. Though Elsie earned only enough to support herself and her son, Ringo recalls that he never lived in squalor; his mother provided him with a comfortable and loving home. Elsie's job, however, kept her away from home afternoons and evenings. He was cared for by a neighbor, but often expressed his loneliness to his mother, telling her he wished he had brothers and sisters.

Throughout his childhood and adolescence, Ritchie suffered several prolonged illnesses that interrupted his education at crucial moments. His grandfather gave him the nickname Lazarus because of his ability to recover from bouts of ill health, including an appendicitis attack at the age of six that confined him to a hospital bed for one year, three months of which he spent in a coma. When he returned to St. Silas Junior School, Ritchie was a year behind his classmates and could barely read or write. A neighborhood girl tutored him, but as

Ringo recalls, "I don't think I ever made up the schooling I missed." He slowly plodded his way through St. Silas until he failed his eleven-plus examinations and had to enroll in Dingle Vale Secondary Modern School in 1951. By then, education no longer interested him. Though he did not rebel like John or George, he spent most of his time playing truant in Sefton Park, pinching pennies from the younger students or using the lunch money his mother gave him each day to buy fish and chips and a ticket to the movies.

In 1953 Elsie married a man named Harry Graves, who was the first real father figure in Ringo's life. He was a gentle man with a quiet disposition, and he encouraged his stepson's interest in music and the drums.

From an early age, Ringo had a passion for the drums and he never cared for any other instruments. He used to bang on empty cans and boxes with pieces of firewood. His grandfather, who played the banjo and mandolin, tried to interest him in one of these instruments, but Ritchie did not express a desire to learn. The first time he recalls playing a real drum was at age thirteen, when pleurisy confined him to a children's hospital for two years. While he was recuperating, he participated in a ward band with the other children, playing the drums.

Ritchie was fifteen when he left the hospital. He was too old to return to Dingle Vale, but his lack of education did not leave him illiterate or stupid. He decided to find a trade or a job, and worked for a brief time abroad a ferryboat that traveled between Liverpool and Wales, then as a steward for British Railways, and then as an apprentice fitter in a Dingle factory. During this time the skiffle craze was the force throughout the land, and like the other Beatles, Ritchie fell under its influence.

The first drum that Ringo owned cost £10—"a one-skin bass drum I used to bang on that drove everybody nuts." Not wanting to discourage him, Elsie and Harry allowed him to practice in a room at the back of the house, though the din could still be heard throughout the neighborhood. Ringo believes his interest in music kept him from becoming a juvenile delinquent.

In 1956 Ritchie acquired a complete drum kit and although

he wasn't any good he joined the Eddie Clayton Skiffle Group, a band made up of friends from the factory where he worked. Though he liked the music of Carl Perkins, Johnny Cash, Little Richard, and Elvis Presley, Ringo was not influenced by any one drummer in particular and learned to play through practice on stage.

After leaving Eddie Clayton, Ritchie played in several other groups before joining the Raving Texans in 1959. The group later became Rory Storme and the Hurricanes—the most successful beat group in Liverpool before the Beatles won the *Mersey Beat* popularity poll in 1961. They received prestigious bookings in Liverpool, at the Butlins Holiday Camp in Wales, and at air-force bases in France. During the group's first season in Wales, Ritchie adopted the stage name Ringo Starr, inspired by all his rings.

Ringo got to know John, Paul, and George while the Beatles and the Hurricanes played at the Kaiserkeller in Hamburg. Eventually John, Paul, and George started talking to him between sets, and throughout 1961 and early 1962 he occasionally played the drums for them when Pete Best was ill.

The situation with Pete Best came to a head in August 1962 when John Lennon told Brian Epstein they weren't happy with Pete Best's drumming and they wanted Ringo instead.

Though George Martin's opinion of Pete's drumming gave the others an airtight excuse, there was a personality conflict between them and Best.

John, Paul, and George treated Pete indifferently. He was alienated from them. They always made sure that he rode in the equipment van with Neil Aspinall, and he was the last to hear the results of the Decca audition, long after the others had heard, when John inadvertently mentioned it in conversation. "Pete was always regarded as 'the other one' and he wasn't considered part of the 'gang,'" says Peter Brown. "He didn't fit in with their mold or zaniness." Bill Harry adds that John, Paul, and George were used to having different drummers and had always thought of Pete as temporary.

Pete Best was an introvert whose somber and mournful expression excited the girls who followed the Beatles. Though John denied that Pete's good looks made them jealous, it was Best the girls mobbed after a Beatles performance, not the others. There were reports in *Mersey Beat* of girls sleeping in his garden in Haymans Green, waiting for a glimpse of him. Epstein knew of Pete's popularity and was reluctant to replace him with Ringo, whose drumming and appearance were unimpressive. Epstein could not understand why Starr was so important to the group.

Ringo, meanwhile, was growing frustrated with the Hurricanes. Though he was earning a better wage than the average workingman in Liverpool, the Hurricanes were going nowhere. In late 1961 he seriously considered immigrating to Texas, but the red tape involved with immigration forced him to give up his dream of becoming a cowboy. In the summer of 1962, after Rory Storme and the Hurricanes finished their commitment at the Star Club, Ringo stayed behind and played drums for Tony Sheridan's group, the Star Band. He had rejoined the Hurricanes in Wales for a season at Butlins when the offer to join the Beatles was made. Ringo accepted immediately but gave the Hurricanes his services till Saturday.

John spoke to Ringo on the telephone and said, "You're in, Ringo, but the beard will have to go. You can keep your sidies, though."

According to journalist George Harrison from the *Liverpool Echo*, who became a close friend of the Beatles during the 1960s, Ringo had long had a secret yearning to be in the group. "On one occasion," says Harrison, "Ringo told me, 'I'd have given anything to join the Beatles. I even worked out a plan to invite them to a party and get them all drunk and tell them afterwards that they promised to take me in.'"

John, Paul, and George thought it unwise to discuss the matter directly with Pete; the right thing to do was have Brian Epstein tell him that he was out of the group. Brian, terribly upset by this, did not know how he would break the news to Best. On August 18, 1962, Epstein called him to his office in Whitechapel Street and told him that the Beatles would be bringing in Ringo Starr as their new drummer. Pete was shocked by the bomb that was dropped on him—and by the way it was done.

Their treatment of Pete Best was a clear example of the Beatles' brutal insensitivity. John was the most guilty, but he at least was candid about it, unlike Paul and George. Their statements that Pete "didn't fit in" and was "too conventional to be a Beatle" were simply rationalizations; the overwhelming mass of fans found Best's conventionality a great balance to the rowdiness of the other three, and in fact Ringo Starr was no less conventional, but he was less of a threat, more likely to stay in the background, content to remain unnoticed. Since 1960 Pete Best had contributed much to the Beatles' success in Liverpool and Hamburg, sharing countless experiences with them. Now that they were about to sign a recording contract, he was told that he was no longer important.

The news of Pete's departure from the group was headlined in the August 23 issue of *Mersey Beat:* BEATLES CHANGE DRUMMERS! A rather stiff statement released by Brian Epstein informed the Mersey fans of the change in personnel. Overnight, Brian Epstein became the most hated man on the beat scene. One night someone vandalized his Ford Zodiac while it was parked outside the Cavern Club. "I think Brian was in fear of his life," says Bill Harry. "The fans turned *vicious.* Brian and the boys were scared because Pete was the most popular of the band, and the fans didn't like the way the situation was handled. People thought it was unsavory. They weren't used to things being covered up. In Liverpool then, there was all this friendliness between groups; they used to help each other out, and there was this sort of honor among them. Pete was virtually sacked behind his back."

Neil Aspinall was forced to choose between the group and his friend. He had lived with Pete's family for several years and had been Mona Best's lover. Initially, Neil decided to quit when he heard that Pete was sacked, but Brian and the others persuaded him to stay with the Beatles as their road manager.

Ringo's first appearance as a Beatle was on August 20 in Ellesmere Port. On their return to the Cavern Club, however, they were met with a big demonstration. Fans marched up and down Mathew Street chanting, "Peter forever, Ringo never!" Brian Epstein hired a bouncer from the club to protect the boys, but as they made their way into the Cavern, one punch connected with Harrison, who had argued strongly for Pete's replacement, and gave him a black eye. During their performance, fans shouted "We want Pete!" after each song. In the days that followed, riots and fights broke out between partisans of the two drummers wherever the Beatles performed.

*   *   *

On the same day that *Mersey Beat* reported Pete's sacking, John and Cynthia were married. Though they had known each other for five years and had lived together off and on for four months in a room Cynthia rented near the art school, they had still considered themselves too young for marriage. In mid-August, however, Cynthia learned that she was one month pregnant with John's child. John broke the news to Aunt Mimi, who told him that she was disgusted and would not attend the ceremony. The wedding was held at the Hope Street Registry Office and attended by Paul, George, Cynthia's brother, and Brian Epstein, who was the best man. Brian's wedding present to the newlyweds was a furnished apartment he rented, though seldom used, on Faulkner Street near the art school. Epstein now had the task of keeping the marriage a secret from the group's fans.

On September 4, 1962, the Beatles left Liverpool for London. Two days later they signed a recording contract with Parlophone Records. The contract was a standard one, guaranteeing them one cent per single record sold and six cents per album—a royalty to be shared between the group and Brian Epstein. The contract was for one year, during which time it was guaranteed they would record two singles.

The boys were about to begin a new phase of their careers—that of recording artists. But while they were excited about signing a contract, they were aware that they now had to prove themselves worthy of all the praise paid them by their fans through *Mersey Beat*.

On September 11, 1962, the Beatles walked into the Abbey Road Studios to record their first single. When they arrived, the boys found that George Martin, not wanting to take a chance on Ringo's untried ability, had brought in a drummer named Andy White to play with them. Ringo was bitter at this unpleasant surprise. Ringo was to have come along only to familiarize himself with the studio.

John, Paul, and George tried to persuade Martin to use Ringo, but Starr's experience with Rory Storme and the Hurricanes was of no consequence to the producer, who remained adamant. Despite their protests, they knew they were in no position to dictate to George Martin. Ringo realized he was being auditioned and began to wonder if he was a bona fide member of the group. Clearly, the other three had yet to accept him as a close mate. He did not know, for instance, that John Lennon was married and found out by accident later.

The Beatles spent the early afternoon rehearsing six tunes before the recording session began. George Martin perched himself atop a high wooden stool in front of them and listened as they played. Ringo sat ten feet behind them playing his drums and ignoring Andy White, who was nearby familiarizing himself with their songs. Prior to the session, Martin had spent time searching for songs for the Beatles to record, but had not found any that were suitable. After two hours, he selected two Lennon/McCartney compositions—"Love Me Do" and "P.S. I Love You"—though it was unprecedented then for an upstart British group like the Beatles to record original tunes for their first record.

From the start, George martin encouraged the boys to acquaint themselves with the aesthetics of recording. Twin-track recording was the best that could be accomplished in the studio then. On one track the Beatles recorded the guitars and drums; the vocals and additional instruments were added on the second. After each take, Martin brought them into the control booth to listen to the playback and explained what they had done.

The Beatles' nervousness was evident throughout the session. "Love Me Do" was recorded seventeen times before George Martin was satisfied that he had a good take. A "terrifying" experience, according to Paul—he can still hear the nervousness in his voice whenever he hears the song. Martin did give Ringo a chance to play, alternating with Andy White on the drums and tambourine during "Love Me Do" and on the maracas for "P.S. I Love You." Nevertheless, Ringo found the experience humiliating and discouraging.

In the days that followed, EMI's publicity department prepared a press kit for the Beatles that contained a photograph and background material on the group for distribution to the music press. In their first interview with a national music publication, the Record Mirror, they talked with journalist Peter Jones for an hour, but their wit and charm failed to impress the reporter, who concluded that the Beatles were "a nothing group in terms of national interest."

8

With a single due to be released, Brian Epstein drafted a new management contract for the Beatles to sign. Whereas the document he'd refused to endorse nine months earlier did not bind him to the group, the new contract, dated October 1, 1962, tied the Beatles to NEMS Enterprises Ltd., a management firm that Brian had established in June. The term of the contract was five years, with the provision that "either party to this Agreement may terminate this Agreement by giving three months notice in writing to the other party by registered post or by his or their last known address to expire on the anniversary of each year of the Agreement." The contract guaranteed NEMS twenty-five percent of the group's income and control over most aspects of their professional work. The agreement was signed by Brian Epstein and the Beatles, and by Jim McCartney and Harold Harrison, since Paul and George were still under the age of contractual consent.

On October 5, 1962, Parlophone released the Beatles' first

single, "Love Me Do" b/w "P.S. I Love You." George Martin had intended to issue "P.S. I Love You" as the A-side because it was the more commercial of the two tracks, but he changed his mind when he learned that singer Peggy Lee had made a record with the same title, which he felt would be confusing to the record-buying public. The boys were excited about having a disc out and exuberant when they heard "Love Me Do" on the radio for the first time. George Harrison says he went "all shivery" when he heard the record played on Radio Luxembourg.

Still, the single failed to set the music industry ablaze, and in fact only one music journalist from the national press took the trouble to review it, saying even though it dragged midway it was "not a bad song."

Tony Barrow reviewed the single locally in the *Liverpool Echo*, and the group's following eagerly bought the record upon its release. But many were disappointed with the selection of the songs, preferring instead the R-and-B tunes.

EMI all but ignored the single. Brian Epstein telephoned George Martin daily and complained, but Martin could not bring himself to tell Epstein that EMI had no faith in the Beatles and their record. Upon hearing the name of the group, an EMI executive had asked Martin if this was one of his comedy recordings. Others laughed at his claims that they would be hearing more from the Beatles in the future. Putting their songs on plastic was a merchandising venture calculated to produce a small return on a minimal investment—less than £2,000. It was almost impossible for EMI to lose money on the deal, considering the minuscule royalty paid to the group as well as the Beatles' large following in the north.

Brian Epstein once again consulted with Tony Barrow, who recalls: "Brian came to me and said, 'Is there anything else that ought to be done for this record?' I said, 'The one extra thing I can think of is, quite apart from whatever the EMI press office does, you might well have an independent PR man working on the record who could mail out stuff himself— photographs and background material—to the record columnists.' Epstein asked, 'Could you do that?' and I said, 'Come on now. How can I sit at a desk at Decca and write about an EMI act?' "

Brian's offer, though, interested Barrow, who ultimately agreed to coordinate the press for the Beatles on a part-time basis while continuing to work for Decca and the *Echo*. Tony avoided a conflict of interest by arranging to have London publicist Andrew Oldham, who later became manager of the Rolling Stones, act as the Beatles' official press officer. "I took Oldham to lunch to talk over the whole situation," recalls Tony, "and over lunch, Andrew and I came to the agreement that I would use his phone number and office address, and that I would tell him what to send out."

Still Liverpool-based, the Beatles were booked solidly in Merseyside in late 1962. Brian Epstein promoted a majority of these dates to gain show-business experience and notoriety on the beat scene. The Beatles appeared as one of the supporting acts for Little Richard at the Tower Ballroom in New Brighton and at the Empire Theatre in Liverpool. These were exciting moments for the group, particularly for Paul, who had admired Little Richard for years. It was also the largest crowd they had ever played for. The Beatles impressed Little Richard, who said, "Man, those Beatles are fabulous. If I hadn't seen them, I'd never dreamed they were white."

Toward the end of October, "Love Me Do" made its appearance on the national record charts, entering at forty-eight in the *Melody Maker* and virtually nibbling its way up the charts until it peaked at twenty-four in *Disc Weekly*. The boys monitored its progress in all the music papers, getting more and more excited as the song crept up. The moderate success of "Love Me Do" was attributed to the strength of the group's following in Liverpool. Later it was rumored that Brian Epstein had bought a chart position for the Beatles by ordering large quantities of the record to be sold in NEMS—an accusation he denied.

George Martin believed he had a hit group on his hands, but he was uncertain about the songs they should record, feeling their songs just weren't strong enough. Martin contacted a music publisher named Dick James, a retired singer whom he had produced in the 1950s. "I played him a song written by Mitch Murray called 'How Do You Do It?' and he liked it," says James. "George said he was recording a group from Liverpool called the Beatles. 'Beatles?' I said. Then he spelled it—clever name. . . . I said, 'Liverpool! What's from Liverpool?' I used to play vaudeville in Liverpool and it was a good place to leave on a Saturday night."

Martin took the song and showed it to the Beatles at a November 26 recording session. They were less than enthusiastic and proceeded to sabotage the recording. John and Paul then showed him a song they had written called "Please Please Me," which Martin had heard at the last session and hadn't been impressed with. Paul told him that they had improved the arrangement, as the group then demonstrated. Martin did like the tune better this time, and after rearranging the introduction and ending and lifting the tempo, the Beatles recorded it. At the end of the session, Martin told them they just made their first number one record.

For an up-and-coming group in the early Sixties, the idea of artistic freedom did not exist—the producer's word was law. But the relationship between George Martin and the Beatles was unique. He gave them an unusual degree of artistic freedom by allowing them to choose their own material and to participate in the mixing sessions. He was, in essence, the one who showed them how to realize their musical ideas. George Martin knew he was dealing with four determined and temperamental musicians, and that a productive association could not be based on autocratic rule or suppressed creativity. He gave them a chance to produce a song of their own because he wanted them to prove themselves as songwriters. If John and Paul had been unable to compose a better tune, the group would have had no other choice but to release "How Do You Do It?" as the follow-up single to "Love Me Do."

Brian Epstein, meanwhile, wanted the Beatles to have wider exposure through a theater tour of England. In December 1962 he signed a contract with promoter Arthur Howes for the exclusive presentation of the Beatles in England. "I received a telephone call at home one Sunday morning from Brian Epstein," Howes says. "Brian said, 'I have a group here in Liverpool called the Beatles.' I said, 'What do you want me to do, Brian, send you up some spray?' Of course, Brian was so taken with his group that he saw no humor in what I said. But I was always prepared to give a new group a try on my shows. I had a big show going then in a place called the Peterborough Embassy. I told Brian I could put the Beatles on the show, but I could only pay for their petrol to come and do the show to see what they were like."

Arthur Howes booked the Beatles for a ten-minute spot in a December 10 concert headlined by Frank Ifield, but the audience's response to the group was poor. "It really wasn't their type of show with Frank Ifield," says Howes. "Everybody was sitting on their hands, not showing any sort of reaction, because this was a new sound to hit England. It was fantastic in Liverpool, but it hadn't reached the rest of the country. I had great confidence in them, but the manager of the Embassy Theatre couldn't understand it all. He couldn't understand the sound, or *noise*, as he called it. I said to him, 'Well, as far as I'm concerned, they may mean nothing now—they're bottom-of-the-bill—but at this time next year, they'll be top-of-the-bill, and in two year's time they'll be superstars.'"

In mid-December 1962, the Beatles returned to Hamburg for their fifth and last time. They were booked into the Star Club for two weeks during which time they shed their new image and happily reverted to the rowdy antics of their old Hamburg days. Without Brian around, the boys acted as they pleased, even going so far as to wear monkey suits and scare away another club's patrons—and winding up in the police station yet again.

Epstein had remained in London to make sure that "Please Please Me" would be plugged strongly. He decided not to assign the publishing rights to Ardmore & Beechwood, because they'd done so little to promote "Love Me Do." George Martin told him that he needed a publisher who was hungry; someone who would work day and night pushing it. He arranged for Epstein to meet Dick James at his office in Charing Cross Road.

"Brian brought along an acetate of 'Please Please Me,'" says James, "and I put it on the turntable and I hit the ceiling. I said, 'This is fantastic! It has a very unusual construction—the falsetto effect, the novelty of the way it's written, the performance—smash, number one!'

"Brian just sat there with his mouth open because no one had said this to him before. His battle so far had been all uphill, and the fact that he was listening to someone who was really enthused excited him. I said, 'What's been arranged for television?' and he said, 'Nothing. Apart from George Martin, you're the first person to hear it.' So I picked up the telephone and called Phillip Jones at ABC Television. He had a pop program called 'Thank Your Lucky Stars' that went out on Saturday afternoon. I said, 'Phil, have you got time to listen to an acetate I've got here?' and he said fine, and Brian is just sitting there with his mouth open. He'd never seen anything like this before. Play a record over the telephone? You only see it in a Hollywood movie!

"I played it to Phil and he said, 'Yeah, it's very good—great. When's it coming out?' I asked Brian when the record was being released, and he said January eleventh. Phil said, 'Right, you're in the program recording the Sunday before its release.' So I said to Brian, 'Is that okay?' and he just nodded with his mouth open. I said to Phil, 'Send the contracts to Brian Epstein, NEMS, Liverpool. Brian will do the business; I'm just fixing the plugs.' Suddenly I'm fixing the plugs and I haven't even got the song. So I said to Brian, 'Are you going to give me the song?' Brian said, 'You've got it.' 'Thank Your Lucky Stars' was a very big pop plug. I said to Brian, 'When can the boys be available for interviews or come down to do live performances for the BBC?' He said, 'You fix them, they'll be there.'"

During their final visit to Hamburg, three of the Beatles' sets were recorded one night by Ted Taylor, the leader of Kingsize Taylor and the Dominoes. The tape, which was released on an album in 1977, captured the Beatles on the eve of national fame. John can be heard teasing a barmaid named Bettina and insulting the audience: "I don't know if you can understand me or not, but piss off! You got that? Christmas or no Christmas!" Taylor offered to sell the tape to Brian Epstein in the spring of 1963. In a letter dated May 9, 1963, Epstein told Taylor: "As there does not appear to be any commercial value to the recordings, I can only offer you £20 for your time and effort in producing the tape recording." Taylor declined the offer and placed the tape in a desk drawer in a Liverpool recording office, where it remained untouched and forgotten for over a decade.

The Beatles won the *Mersey Beat* popularity poll once again in 1962, but at the outset of 1963 few outside Liverpool had even heard of them. A national popularity poll conducted by the *New Musical Express* toward the end of 1962 gave the quartet fewer then 4,000 votes, presumably all from Liverpool. The big question was whether they had staying power and whether they could make it outside Liverpool.

The pace the Beatles maintained that January was arduous. After fulfilling their commitments in Hamburg, they flew directly to Scotland on New Year's Day and began a five-day tour. Apart from a series of one-night stands in the north of England, there were numerous appearances on light-entertainment radio shows, such as "Talent Spot" and "Saturday Club." Once "Please Please Me" began ascending the charts, Arthur Howes booked the Beatles on their first national tour of England as the opening act for singer Helen Shapiro.

The tour began on February 2, 1963, and in the first shows the audiences seemed bewildered. Kids were dumbfounded by what they saw and heard, while theater managers complained to Howes that the Beatles were overamplified. The group was using specially built coffin-shaped amplifiers made by Adrian Barbar of the Big Three (formerly Cass and the Casanovas) that gave more volume and depth to their sound.

After their first paid performance in Peterborough, the Beatles returned to London to record their first album. EMI, still skeptical about the group's potential even though the single "Please Please Me" was developing into a hit, did not want to invest too much time or money in the session, so the album had to be recorded in one day. George Martin had considered recording it in the Cavern Club, but the acoustics were unfavorable. So they mapped out a session of the tunes the boys played most often and therefore were most familiar with. They recorded twelve tracks, starting at ten in the morning and ending at eleven at night.

The session appeared to be over and the boys were relaxing in the control room, drinking tea and talking, when Martin said he needed one more song. Thoroughly exhausted from the session, the boys returned to the studio and decided to record "Twist and Shout." The recording heard today captured John Lennon in the process of losing his voice and is stronger for the rawness.

In late February the Beatles rejoined the Helen Shapiro tour and found that their audience reception had improved. Now that "Please Please Me" had entered the Top Ten, kids were better acquainted with the group and seemed more interested in seeing them than the star of the tour, which led to a strained relationship between the boys and Helen Shapiro. On March 2, the day before the tour ended, "Please Please Me" topped the *Melody Maker* singles charts. John, Paul, George, and Ringo were ecstatic about having their first number one disc. So of course were Brian Epstein, George Martin, and Dick James, now convinced they had a hit group. "Please Please Me" was the first of twelve consecutive Beatles singles to top the charts in Britain.

With an album due to be released, Brian Epstein committed the Beatles to a twenty-one-city tour just six days after the Shapiro tour ended. This time they were booked as the opening act for Chris Montez and Tommy Roe. Again, however, it soon became obvious to the tour promoter that the audiences were coming not to see the headliners but to see the Beatles. Arrangements were made for the group to close each night as the stars of the tour.

The ovations increased during the last eight dates of the tour after Parlophone Records released the Beatles' first album, *Please Please Me*, on March 22, 1963. The LP reflected the Beatles' stage show at the time of the Helen Shapiro tour and captured the excitement reminiscent of the early days of rock 'n' roll. *Please Please Me* topped the album charts three weeks after its release and remained there for an unprecedented six months.

The national press nevertheless continued to give the group short shrift. The *Liverpool Echo*, which had applauded their success with the "Please Please Me" single, later asked whether the Beatles were going to be "one-hit wonders." Journalists from the national press, who had seen the Beatles, regarded the group's image as a gimmick. The quartet also had to contend with the tag "from Liverpool." Brian Epstein was told, "You'll never make it from the provinces. Move down to London and you'll really get moving."

Despite the problems that Tony Barrow encountered with the press, he never fabricated stories about the Beatles to attract publicity. "You could not have possibly put a PR image to the Beatles," he says. "There was nothing any of us could have come up with that was better than the original. The natural image was there and it would have been pointless to put anything on top of that." The points that Barrow stressed in his releases were the correct spelling of the group's name, the music of Lennon and McCartney, and the fact that the Beatles were unlike any other pop stars around then. The releases overlooked the fact that John Lennon was married, though rumors flourished in Liverpool that he was. In those days it was important to keep that sort of information from the fans.

Brian Epstein knew there were two forces working against the Beatles: a record organization that displayed little confidence in them and a disinterested national press that regarded the group as a novelty act. Epstein also realized that it was not going to be easy establishing this "extraordinary new group," because every aspect of the Beatles was contrary to what was acceptable in British pop. Their image and the fact that they were a vocal group who provided their own instrumentation and most of their repertoire were considered revolutionary. The London-controlled music industry was not accustomed to *outsiders* implementing change or influencing the musical tastes of teenagers, and they believed that the record-buying public would not accept a provincial vocal group with a weird name, long hair, and an overamplified sound. The lack of promotional support from EMI led Epstein to believe that the only way to establish the Beatles in England was through consistent concert, television, and radio appearances.

Disc jockeys, however, recognized the excitement that the Beatles were bringing to the pop scene and pushed their next single, "From Me to You" b/w "Thank You, Girl," released on April 11. John and Paul had composed "From Me to You" on a bus trip from Shrewsbury to York while the Beatles were touring with Helen Shapiro. The title was inspired by the letters column in the *New Musical Express* called "From Us to You." "Thank You, Girl" was originally to be the A side, but "From Me to You" was so strong it was the lead song. "From Me to You" topped the British singles charts one month after its release and remained there for seven weeks.

Music journalists began to acknowledge the star potential of the Beatles after their April 21 appearance in the *New Musical Express* "Poll Winners Concert" at Wembley Stadium. The concert was a significant date for the group and was interpreted as a sign of having arrived in the British music industry.

In early spring 1963, the Beatles were still living in Liverpool, though the group's concert schedule allowed them to spend only a few days with their families between bookings. Paul, George, and Ringo stayed in the homes in which they were raised; John and his wife had moved from their Faulkner Street apartment to Mimi's home on Menlove Avenue. The baby that Cynthia had been expecting was born on April 8, 1963, at Sefton Hospital in Liverpool. At the time, the Beatles were performing out-of-town concert dates, and though John telephoned Mimi each night after every show for progress reports, he did not see his wife and newborn son until a week later. Cynthia waited for her husband's return to name the baby, who was christened John Charles Julian Lennon.

Before John left the hospital, he told his wife that Brian Epstein had invited him to travel to Spain for a few days, and asked if she objected. Cynthia recalls that she was stunned by the question, but suppressed her true feelings and said no. During their three-day holiday, Brian admitted to John that he was a homosexual and had feelings for him. Their trip started rumors on the Liverpool beat scene that Lennon and Epstein were having a love affair. John ignored the stories that were circulating in Liverpool about him and Brian until Paul's twenty-first birthday party, when Bob Wooler implied that they were lovers. Lennon lost control of himself, knocked Wooler to the ground, and kicked him in the face. Wooler later filed assault charges against John, but decided to drop them after Brian Epstein paid him £100.

Following the group's concert appearance at Wembley Stadium, they flew to Teneriffe in the Canary Islands for a twelve-day vacation that almost cost Paul McCartney his life. One day he swam too far from the shore and the ocean current began pulling him into deep water. He was saved by a native of the island who reached him in time and dragged him to safety.

Upon their return from the Canaries, the Beatles traveled to London for a May 9 concert appearance at the Royal Albert Hall. After the show, Paul met a seventeen-year-old actress named Jane Asher, who had been commissioned to write a story about the group for a BBC program called the "Radio Times." McCartney immediately fell for her. When she finished her interview with the boys, Paul asked her for a date, and so began their five-year relationship.

The success of the *Please Please Me* album and "From Me to You" overlapped the group's third national tour, which they headlined with American singer Roy Orbison. The tour began on May 18 in Slough and covered twenty-one cities. In some cities the Beatles were pelted with jelly babies, a candy George Harrison had mentioned that they liked, and on June 7, 1963, they heard faint screams during a performance in Glasgow, Scotland—the first indication that hysteria was beginning to brew.

Throughout mid-1963 the Beatles performed steadily on a string of one-night stands. They played a charity date at the Grafton Ballroom in Liverpool for the National Society for the Prevention of Cruelty to Children and gave a series of concerts in Merseyside. On July 21, hundreds of teenagers converged on the Queen's Theatre in Blackpool and prevented the group from entering through the stage entrance, forcing them to go up some scaffolding to the roof of the theatre.

Everyone working for the Beatles behind the scenes began to feel the growing pains of success. Brian Epstein, who had moved his management firm from NEMS's Whitechapel address to offices by the Royal Liver Building, had to hire additional secretaries and office assistants to help him run the daily affairs of the company. Road manager Neil Aspinall's job—driving the equipment van to the venues; setting up the drums, guitars, and amplifiers for a performance; then loading the equipment back into the van after a show—had become too much work for one person. He was grateful when Epstein hired Malcolm Evans, a former bouncer at the Cavern Club, to assist him as the group's second road manager.

In London, Tony Barrow, who had left Decca in May and joined NEMS full-time, coordinated the press-and-publicity division from Monmouth Street. The London staff realized that the Beatles had arrived by the growing number of inquiries made by fans. "At the beginning," recalls Jo Bergman, Barrow's personal assistant, "there was Tony chain-smoking in one office and typing with one finger. Then the stacks of mail began to arrive and we had to organize the fan club. We took upstairs offices, and there was this pornographic bookstore downstairs. So there was this real bizarre setup where you had these perverted men downstairs and Beatles fans trickling upstairs."

George Martin was working around the clock in the Abbey Road recording studios. He was producing three groups managed by Brian Epstein—the Beatles, Gerry and the Pacemakers, and Billy J. Kramer and the Dakotas—as well as other acts on Parlophone, and administering the label's day-to-day affairs. In 1963, the number one position on the British pop world's singles charts was dominated by groups managed by Brian Epstein and produced by George Martin. By the end of the year, this association accounted for eight number one records.

Dick James, who was securing television and radio plugs for NEMS-managed groups, had formed a music-publishing company called Northern Songs to publish the compositions of Lennon and McCartney. "It was always agreed with John Lennon and Paul McCartney and Brian Epstein that I would have an individual song assignment for 'Please Please Me' and 'Ask Me Why,' " says James. "From then on, all the songs that they wrote I had on trust until the company was formed and until Paul was twenty-one. I didn't even have a contract with them until August—I had a gentleman's agreement. Most of the industry knew that I didn't have a piece of paper signed, and they were romanced by all the industry. But Brian, John, and Paul said, 'We have a deal with Dick James.' "

On August 3, 1963, the Beatles returned to Liverpool and gave their 292nd—and last—Cavern Club performance. Since New Year's Day, the group had averaged at least one appearance on Merseyside each month, but many of their hometown fans complained nevertheless that the Beatles had deserted them. Letters poured into *Mersey Beat* saying, "They're not our Beatles anymore," to which John Lennon later replied that the letter writers were not the true fans. John, Paul, George, and Ringo were told that their Liverpool fans were not buying Beatles records because they wanted the group to fail and thus be forced to return to Merseyside.

Though teenagers were hearing Beatles records on the radio and seeing them perform in concert, the group's consistent personal appearances on pop radio shows, such as the BBC's "Saturday Club," contributed greatly to their popularity. Teenagers were delighted to hear these four energetic, witty, humorous, and irreverent pop stars say the most outrageous things, unlike the pop stars of the past, who hid behind their image and carefully phrased their answers so as not to offend anyone. These qualities endeared the Beatles to teenagers and won more fans for the group.

The record that opened the door to national fame for the Beatles was "She Loves You" b/w "I'll Get You," released on August 23, 1963. It was recorded on July 1 at the Abbey Road Studios.

In early October, Brian Epstein consolidated NEMS's Liverpool and London offices by moving his business to the capital. Once the Beatles began making an impression on the music scene, Epstein had found it inconvenient traveling to and from London to conduct business. He and the Beatles were harshly criticized by the *Liverpool Echo* for having "deserted the city that made them," but the Beatles no longer felt they belonged to Liverpool; the luxuries and excitement of the studio, hotels, and the road were far more alluring to them than their life-style in Merseyside. They did not sever their ties with Liverpool, however, and when Beatlemania descended on England, being Liverpudlians became an additional press benefit to their image.

Epstein had hired a journalist from the *London Daily Express*, Brian Sommerville, to work specifically as press officer for the Beatles while Tony Barrow supervised the press-and-publicity division of NEMS. (Andrew Oldham left NEMS in June to become the manager of the Rolling Stones.) After the group's October 13 performance on the television program "Sunday Night at the London Palladium," the British press would never again ignore the Beatles. While the group rehearsed for the show in the afternoon, thousands of teenagers gathered outside the theater on Argyll Street. At one point, fifty fans broke through a network of doors and surrounded the Beatles onstage. The press and television camera crews were present to cover the chaos in the street.

"Sunday Night at the London Palladium" was then the most popular and widely viewed television program in England, and the Beatles were booked as the main attraction. They sang five songs that evening: "I Want to Hold Your Hand," "This Boy," "All My Loving," "Money," and "Twist and Shout." Their departure from the Palladium was difficult; the streets were packed with teenagers. For the first time, the Beatles feared for their safety.

After the show, Brian Epstein, the Beatles, and their families celebrated at the Grosvenor Hotel in London. Tony Barrow, writing in the *Echo*, said, "Four immensely happy, if slightly weary, Beatles were trying to make themselves believe that they had really topped the television bill at the most famous variety theater in the world. Bunches of proud Beatle parents were present to assure the boys that it all happened. Television and radio newscasters confirmed the whole thing from a hi-fi combination set in the corner of the room. The host—group manager Brian Epstein—sat behind a busy telephone, sipping Scotch and replying to the ceaseless press inquiries."

The following day, several London dailies published photographs and articles on their front pages about the show and the hysteria on Argyll Street. The *Daily Mirror* coined the term *Beatlemania* to describe the phenomenon. "That's the time where you can point to and say, from then on, the press were running after the Beatles rather than the press officer running after the press," says Brian Sommerville. "The Beatles hit the right day when there wasn't very much happening. Sunday night has always been a good time to interest the national press in doing something on show business. Not much else is happening in politics, and there isn't going to be any big news on Monday left over from Sunday, short of a train or air disaster. The press was looking for a story."

Overnight, the Beatles became the most widely discussed topic in the country. For Britons, the group's arrival on the national scene was a pleasant diversion from the day-to-day problems that plagued England. On the strength of their success at the Palladium, the Beatles were invited to appear in the biggest show-business event of the year—the Royal Command Performance. The group was performing at the Floral in Southport when the announcement was made. Brian Epstein was not with them then and the boys had to face a horde of journalists alone. This was their first experience with reporters from Britain's national press, who are known to be the toughest in the world. They wanted to tear the Beatles apart and deliberately asked questions that cast the group in a negative light. For example: "Do you think the Beatles from Liverpool should desert their fans by appearing before the boiled shirts and jewels of the privileged of London? Do you really think that you should presume to play for the queen?"

To this Paul replied, "Why shouldn't we? She's our queen too, you know."

Ringo said simply, "I want to bang my drums for the Queen Mother. Is there anything wrong with that?"

According to Jo Bergman, the general operation at NEMS became "even more bizarre." No one in the office could pick up the telephone to call out, because someone would be ringing in. The Monmouth Street office was inundated with requests for interviews and photo sessions. One journalist told Brian Epstein, "By Christmastime, it will be impossible to look at the front page of any newspaper in England without seeing a reference to the Beatles." Epstein was suddenly alarmed by the dangers of overexposure by the media. "After the London Palladium show," says Brian Sommerville, "if the press would have had their way, the Beatles would have made no more records, done no more live shows, and made no more radio and television appearances. It would have been press, press, press, which is ridiculous—that would have killed the whole thing. The Beatles' function then was to make records and live appearances. The amount of photo sessions being demanded and the number of interviews being requested was so enormous that there wouldn't have been any time to do it. As a result, relations with the press became very difficult because people were saying to me, 'You're selecting interviews to be done for all sorts of sinister reasons and rejecting me because I'm not in with you or giving you some payola.' "

John, Paul, George, and Ringo each adjusted to fame, though it took many brief encounters with the public to convince them that they were celebrities. "The day after the Palladium show," says Jo Bergman, "Brian asked me if I would pick up John and take him to his lawyer because John was going to sign a lease for an apartment. I picked up John in a taxicab and the driver gave him that kind of look and said, 'Oh, I saw you on the telly last night,' and said that he liked it. I thought that was interesting, that a taxi driver at that point would have recognized him. Then John decided that he needed some milk or something for breakfast, so he ran into a store and was astonished that people in the store recognized him. It was like suddenly stopping and thinking, Hey, wait a minute. What is this? Kids are one thing, but grown-ups?"

Lennon was determined not to allow his newfound fame to restrict his life-style or affect his existence. The Beatles enjoyed photo sessions, but they were not enthusiastic about interviews. In the beginning of his relationship with the group, Brian Sommerville had a difficult time persuading them to meet with the press. "Given the right approach," he says, "I don't think any one of the four would be impossible. If there was something of any urgency that I wanted them to do, there would be some resistance from George Harrison, a certain lethargy from John Lennon, some playing up from Paul McCartney, and an uncomplaining willingness from Ringo Starr. But take away the urgency of a situation and I could get any one of them to do more or less anything, as long as I chose my time."

Fame did not greatly change their personalities or work habits, but it did change their standard of living. Brian Epstein did not dole out money carelessly to the boys, because the process of receiving money from their current success was slow, but they were able to buy things on credit. "It was the acquisition of things that I thought was interesting to watch because they were a bit childlike," says Brian Sommerville. "Every day was Christmas for acquiring new presents. We went down to the BBC for some broadcast, and when we arrived, we discovered that we had a two-hour wait. George said, 'I want some shirts,' and we went to this posh store in Piccadilly called Simpson's. We drove around the back and I went in to make the arrangements with the store manager. I told him, 'I have the Beatles out in the car. Have you a room where they could select some shirts?'

"Well, this bloke didn't believe me. While I was arguing with this man, I happened to glance at the revolving door, and the boys were coming in; they got fed up waiting for me. The shop's assistants couldn't believe it, and there was pandemonium in Simpson's for a little while. The manager suddenly realized that this wasn't a joke and immediately commandeered a lift, got us all into it, and whisked us up to his office. The various departmental heads visited them and brought their wares carried by their assistants. The boys were saying, 'I'll have a dozen shirts.' 'I'd like to see some jewelry.' They spent a hell of a lot of money, but they didn't pay any money. The bill was sent to NEMS. It was like watching four kids enjoying themselves, knowing that daddy was going to pay."

During their youth, John, Paul, George, and Ringo had considered a one-pound note a lot of money, and to see their income per concert jump from £150 to £1,500 within a short time was mind-boggling. Whatever their income, though, the Beatles had always spent their money as quickly as they earned it, and they continued to do so now, particularly Lennon. This love of spending was the incentive for the group's desire to be successful. "Their ambitions were limited at first because they never dreamed that they would get to the heights that they achieved," says Bill Harry. "I think the main thing in their minds was having an enjoyable time playing and earning enough money to scrape by on. When they asked Ringo Starr, in the television documentary 'The Mersey Sound,' what his ambition was, he said it was to earn enough money to be able to open his own hairdressing salon. That was his ultimate ambition in life! Their ambitions were small in those days. It was only after success started to happen that people in Liverpool realized that the sky was the limit."

On October 24, the Beatles embarked on a short tour of Sweden, accompanied by a contingent of reporters and photographers. During concert performances in Stockholm, Borås, and Eskilstuna, Swedish teenagers displayed all the symptoms of Beatlemania. Upon their return to London, the boys were greeted at the airport by 12,000 screaming teenagers standing in the rain. The reception astonished the Beatles. Paul asked a reporter, "Has all this been going on while we've been gone?" Amid the hysteria and confusion, the departure of the queen and then prime minister Sir Alec Douglas-Home was delayed and the reigning Miss World passed through the terminal ignored by the media, and an American television entrepreneur named Ed Sullivan, waiting to board a return flight to New York, also witnessed the chaos and made a note of the group.

The Beatles received even greater proof of the extent of their popularity when the dates for their next national tour, billed as *The Beatles Show*, were announced. It would be their most extensive British tour, with performances in thirty-three cities, and fans began queuing all over England a month in advance to purchase tickets. The *London Times*, in its first story on the group, said that forty policemen were needed to control thousands of teenagers buying tickets in Newcastle. Similar stories appeared in other newspapers, one saying that teenagers standing in line to purchase tickets in freezing weather looked "more like a death watch than a prelude to a joyous Beatle event." In the city of Hull, 8,000 kids waited for three days to buy 5,000 tickets. When all the seats had been sold, a riot broke out among those turned away. The need for police supervision was questioned in the House of Commons by a member of Parliament: "Shouldn't we withdraw the police and see what happens?" George Harrison responded to that question in the press, saying, "If they do, the injuries would be their fault. We don't want people to get hurt."

Before the Beatles played their first date, they knew that this concert tour would be unlike the previous four. On the one hand, they were thrilled to know that they had inspired this fervor; but on the other hand, the group did not know what to expect. One of the questions they asked themselves then was "If fans are rioting to buy tickets, how will they behave during the shows?" None of the Beatles understood what had happened to the group, because fame, as Brian Epstein recalls, "had suddenly exploded around them."

The tour began on November 1, 1963, and progressed as far as Leeds before being briefly interrupted by the Beatles' return to London on November 4 to perform in the Royal Command Performance. When they arrived at the Prince of Wales Theatre in the afternoon to rehearse for the show, they were greeted by hundreds of teenagers who had been waiting for them since eight in the morning. "Fingers protecting their eyes, they burst into the Prince of Wales Theatre, inches ahead of 200 screaming fans," reported the *Echo*. Inside their dressing room, reporters all had the same question: "Are you nervous?" To which John Lennon replied, "There won't be many in the audience—about a thousand—and we've certainly played before many more than that, but it's the people who are in the audience, that makes us nervous."

By showtime the scene outside the Prince of Wales Theatre in Piccadilly Circus was more chaotic than the demonstration outside the Palladium. The Queen Mother and Princess Margaret were forced to break tradition by using the side entrance instead of participating in the ceremonial arrival at the front door. The Beatles gave a twelve-minute performance, singing "From Me to You," "She Loves You," "Till There Was You," and "Twist and Shout."

They were scared stiff. Paul broke the ice by saying, 'I'm going to sing a number from *The Music Man*, which has already been recorded by our favorite American group—Sophie Tucker.' Before their final number, "Twist and Shout," John gave the highbrow audience a slight slap in the face by stepping up to the microphone and saying, "On this next number, I want you all to join in. Would those in the cheaper seats clap their hands?" He looked up toward the gallery of private boxes: "The rest of you, just rattle your jewelry." The jab at the upper class amused the audience and became the most notable Beatle quote of the year. John's comment, though, was not ad-libbed, as *Echo* columnist George Harrison recalls: "They said to each other days before that they shouldn't use the normal corny routine. John said, 'Why don't I tell them to rattle their fuckin' jewelry?'"

The following day every British newspaper printed a report of the show, including a comment from the Queen Mother, who gave a group a royal stamp of approval, saying that they were "young, fresh and vital." A *Daily Mirror* review of the performance explained why the press liked the Beatles:

> How refreshing to see these rambunctious young Beatles take a middle-aged Royal Command Performance by the scruff of their necks and have them beetling like teenagers. It's plain to see why these four energetic, cheeky lads from Liverpool go down big. They're young, new. They're high-spirited, cheerful. What a change from the self-pitying moaners crooning their lovelorn tunes from the tortured shallows of lukewarm hearts.

The day after the Command Performance, the Beatles resumed their tour. Wherever they traveled, the scene was always the same: a police escort to their hotel, where they were greeted by hundreds of fans and reporters; a police escort to the venue and then back to the hotel for dinner and rest. Early in the morning, the boys departed for the next town. As their car drove out of the city, people lined both sides of the street and waved goodbye. The Beatles enjoyed the reaction of fans at their concerts, but rarely could their music be heard above the jetlike screams of the audience. Each time John or Paul would tell an audience to be quiet, the kids screamed louder.

Though the group had its critics among the ranks of the British press, journalists could not compare the hysterical reactions of teenagers during a Beatles' concert to anything they had seen before. "I've stood at the back of theaters in England and watched an entire audience leave its seats and rush the stage," says Brian Sommerville. "It was as if they did it in time to the music. A cynic could have stood there and said, 'That's been fixed; that's been arranged.' But the reaction was spontaneous. I found these occasions very exciting."

The Beatles were performing in theaters that seated 2,000 to 3,000 fans, while hundreds more, unable to purchase tickets, waited outside, hoping at least to see the Beatles after the concert when their car drove away. The enormous crowd in the street, however, made the group's departure from a theater virtually impossible and often dangerous. On several occasions John, Paul, George, and Ringo had to assume disguises (in Birmingham they dressed as policemen) to elude the crowds. "They seemed to like touring more and more," says Arthur Howes, "but it became difficult as their popularity grew. We had to start getting them in laundry vans and hampers, in and out of hotels and venues. Eventually it became almost like a military operation to get them to a theater." The boys were overwhelmed by the adulation of their fans, but fame had been with them then for only one month, and any inconvenience they experienced from it was tempered by their belief that Beatlemania would likely be temporary.

In any case, it was obvious that Brian Epstein had done a remarkable job. The British press and public viewed the four young pop stars as adorable and innocent—which in many ways they were.

Few outside of Liverpool knew that the group had played in a strip club or about their experiences in Hamburg. Beneath the Fab Four aura that they projected then to the British public and later to the world, the Beatles were the same people they'd been in 1960–61. The only difference was that now they had an image to protect—it was their livelihood. Though in 1962 they'd been unable to visualize how changing from leather to suits would benefit them later, they now knew that the look had contributed greatly to their success, and each was determined to maintain it and reap the financial rewards it brought until Beatlemania disappeared. Bill Harry recalls that when the Beatles changed their image and signed a recording contract, John Lennon asked him to return certain photographs that, if published, would have tainted this Fab Four look.

"Photos from Hamburg had shown them with flick knives, pep pills, looking mean and evil," says Harry. "I'd not published the Hamburg pictures. John Lennon sent me a number of photographs, including shots of him standing on the corner of the Reeperbahn reading a newspaper, dressed only in underpants. This had been at a time when there were stories circulating of him urinating from his flat onto the heads of churchgoers. When Brian took over the group, John requested the photographs back, and his wild behavior began to take a back seat to the polished new image they were given."

Though the Beatles' image was a publicity device, the group's music was their purest outward expression—totally free of the embellishments attached to their image. Throughout the Beatlemania years (1963–66), they never emasculated their music for PR purposes.

On November 22, 1963, Parlophone Records issued the group's second album, *With the Beatles*, which was characterized by the quartet's enthusiasm during the early stages of their fame. Although the LP did not feature any songs released as singles, each of its fourteen tracks found its way onto the singles charts—an unprecedented feat in the British music industry then.

With the Beatles featured six cover songs, seven Lennon/ McCartney compositions (including "All My Loving," which Dick James was unsuccessful in persuading the group to release as a single), and George Harrison's "Don't Bother Me," his first original composition on his first songwriting since collaborating with John on "Cry for a Shadow" in 1961. The title was inspired by Bill Harry's incessant urging that he write a song.

"I saw no reason why George shouldn't stir himself and start writing," says Harry. "At the Blue Angel Club, I tackled him about it night after night: 'Listen, George, have you written any numbers yet?' One night I caught him coming out of the Cabin Club on Wood Street and took him to the *Mersey Beat* office round the corner to talk for a few hours, pursuing the idea that if he could create original material early in the group's career, he should be able to do some writing now. It reached the stage where George almost cringed when he saw me, aware of what I was going to ask him.

"Finally, he did. He told me at Blackpool that he appreciated what I'd done, that he couldn't stand the thought of me badgering him again and again, so he sat down and tried to write—and it worked. 'I sat down to write, thinking that you'd keep bothering me until I did, and the title came into my head, 'Don't Bother Me.' "

With the Beatles, which sold 750,000 copies by the end of November, replaced the group's first album in the number one position on the charts and remained there for six months.

A single was issued at the end of November, "I Want to Hold Your Hand" b/w "This Boy," which had advance orders of nearly 1 million. By December 1, "She Loves You" and "I

Want to Hold Your Hand" had each sold 1 million copies, which stunned the British music industry: Million-selling discs were rare in England, and two by the same artist was a feat no other performer had accomplished before. Upon its release, "I Want to Hold Your Hand" became an immediate number one record.

As the year came to a close, the British press filled its pages with praise for the Beatles. John and Paul were hailed as "the greatest composers since Beethoven," and William Mann, the music critic of the *London Times,* said, "The outstanding English composers of 1963 must be John Lennon and Paul McCartney." The Beatles did not understand Mann's analysis of their music, but his critique was important to them because it made serious musicians who read the *Times* take notice of the group. Said Mann, "They have brought a distinctive and exhilarating flavor into a genre of music that was in danger of ceasing to be music at all."

Though their haircuts, wit, Liverpool background, and unusual name all had a role in the Beatle's acceptance in England, their music played a greater part. "I believe in songs," says Dick James. "I believe that the song invariably does more for the artist than the artist does for the song. A friend once said to me, 'Dick, I like the Beatles, but I can't see their songs.' I said, '*Schmuck!* It's the songs that are causing the great success!'"

Once regarded as a "nothing group in terms of national interest," the Beatles introduced sweeping changes in the British entertainment industry. The quartet changed the style of pop music and the appearance of pop performers, focused attention on the singer/songwriter, and changed the industry's attitude that groups were secondary to the solo artist. The Beatles were also responsible for stirring regional pride throughout the country, a fact acknowledged by the House of Commons. "The Beatles broke certain barriers in Britain," says Bill Harry. "Once they succeeded, talent emerged from all parts of the country: the Hollies, Freddie and the Dreamers, and Herman's Hermits from Manchester; the Animals from Newcastle; the Rolling Stones from Richmond; the Moody Blues from Birmingham; and the Paramounts, who evolved into Procol Harum, from Southend."

Beatlemania touched every level of teenage life-styles in Britain. While girls reacted hysterically to the group, teenage boys responded to the Beatles by growing their hair long and styling it in the "Beatle cut." Thousands more, such as Sting from the Police and Paul Rodgers from Bad Company, were inspired to pick up guitars and drums and either form or join groups, as Lonnie Donegan and Elvis Presley had done in the mid-1950s.

The *London Evening Standard* summed up the feelings of English teenagers then: "Nineteen sixty-three has been their year. An examination of the heart of the nation at this moment would reveal the word *Beatles* engraved upon it."

9

Within days after the Royal Command Performance, Brian Epstein began making plans for the Beatles' debut in America. Epstein was aware that no British pop performer had ever succeeded in the States, but he expected a more favorable response to the Beatles because they were unique in appearance and their music was not reflective of any one American artist. Epstein's optimism, however, was not shared by his English contemporaries. Since the late 1950s, the U.S. music industry had been notorious for rejecting British pop stars and their music, both of which were considered inferior imitations of American artists and their music. Since America was the originator of teen-oriented music, why bother to release foreign copies of American originals?

Dave Dexter, Jr., who was the director of the international artists-and-repertoire department at Capitol Records in Hollywood, recalls how in November 1962 he came across a record by the Beatles. "Every day I'd receive packages of forty-fives from all over the world. In one of these packages there was a record called 'Love Me Do.' When I first heard the recording, frankly I wasn't impressed. Compared to Sonny Terry and the other harmonica players who play that real earthy blues, I felt that John Lennon's was terribly superficial."

This particular package of singles, comprising a week's worth of new releases from HMV, Columbia, and Parlophone, did not, in Dave Dexter's opinion, provide one potential hit, and he rejected the entire shipment. Since the Beatles had yet to make an impression on England then, EMI did not pressure its American subsidiary to release the record and eventually placed the Beatles with an independent record label based in Chicago, Vee Jay Records, who agreed to distribute the group's records in return for an English outlet for one of their artists, the Four Seasons. Vee Jay released two singles, "Please Please Me" b/w "Ask Me Why" and "From Me to You" b/w "Thank You, Girl." Both records received heavy airplay to no avail.

The next record company to obtain the Beatles was an independent label based in Philadelphia, Swan Records, which acquired the single "She Loves You." Swan executives Bernie Bennink and Tony Mamarella were excited about the song, and in early September 1963 they persuaded a friend named Dick Clark, the host of the "American Bandstand" television program, to plug the record on his Record Revue segment. This was the group's first exposure on national television in America. The kids danced to the song and were shown a photograph of the Beatles. "Some of the kids snickered," says Dick Clark, "others laughed at the picture of the four shaggy-haired boys from Liverpool. The response was less than enthusiastic. I called Swan. Bernie got on the phone. 'You saw?' 'Yeah, I told Tony we may have a stiff,' said Bernie. 'Thanks for giving it a try anyway.'"

In mid-October 1963, Dave Dexter, Jr., traveled to London to preview records and met with Tony Palmer, EMI's artist-and-repertoire chief. "Tony kept insisting that I listen to this new Beatles record," says Dexter. "I told him, 'I don't want the Beatles. They've died on two other labels, why the hell should I bury them on Capitol?' Palmer said, 'Look, Lou Levy, the American publisher, was here last week and he bought this song. He says he's going to promote it; that the record's gonna be a hit.' Well, Lou Levy and I had been friends for nearly twenty years even then, and I had faith in him. So I told Palmer, 'Play the damn thing!' Tony lowered the cartridge to the disc and the music exploded! The record was 'I Want to Hold Your hand.' You'd have to have been deaf not to know that that record didn't have a hell of a chance in the market. So I grabbed the acetate and brought it back with me."

Before Capitol could acquire the rights to the Beatles, however, they had to agree to Brian Epstein's stipulation that they invest a substantial amount of time and money to promote the group in America in an effort to equal the group's British popularity. This time EMI pressured Alan W. Livingston, then president of Capitol Records, to commit $50,000 for the promotion of the Beatles.

Now that the Beatles were on Capitol, Epstein was confident that "I Want to Hold Your Hand" had a chance of succeeding in America. But the failures on Vee Jay and Swan, as well as the knowledge that British recording artists fared poorly in the States, worried him. In early November 1963, he flew to New York for a nine-day visit to meet with executives of Capitol's eastern office and hear their sales forecast and promotion strategy. "Brian expressed how he and the Beatles were happy to be with Capitol," recalls Brown Meggs, then director of Capitol's eastern operations. "But he was also apprehensive. He said, 'It's very important how we present them over here; I'm particular about that.' Epstein was the most particular manager I've ever dealt with. He was afraid that the Beatles would fall on their heads because of the failures on the other labels." Meggs assured Brian that Capitol would give the Beatles its maximum effort and support.

Epstein's most significant meeting was with Ed Sullivan, the New York columnist and host of the most widely viewed television variety show in America. After witnessing the hysteria at Heathrow Airport in October, Sullivan felt that the Beatles would be an interesting act to present on his program, but he did not believe they were going to be as big in America as Brian predicted. In order for the Beatles to have a chance in the United States, Epstein had to make bold demands of Sullivan. For two days they haggled over giving the Beatles top billing. Sullivan, knowing that British entertainers had a poor track record in America, felt it was absurd of Epstein to ask for top billing when the Beatles did not even have a record out in the States and were unknown to Americans. But Brian persisted, and in the end was able to secure three television dates for the group. Their network debut on February 9, 1964, coincided with Capitol's projected release date of "I Want to Hold Your Hand."

Brian knew that if the Beatles had been booked as a supporting act on "The Ed Sullivan Show," the American press most likely would have regarded them merely as one of the many novelty acts often presented on the program. Having top billing on three consecutive Ed Sullivan broadcasts, however, was interpreted by the news media as a sign of great importance. This alone had a significant bearing on the Beatles' success in the States.

Beginning in mid-November 1963, London-based correspondents from leading U.S. newspapers and magazines began reporting the hysteria the Beatles had created in Europe. The wire services made note of John's "rattle your jewels" remark because of its social content, and *Newsweek* printed a two-column feature, commenting, "They wear sheep-dog bangs, collarless jackets and drain-pipe trousers. One plays left-handed guitar, two have falsetto voices, one wishes he was a businessman and all four sing and sing and sing. They are the Beatles and the sound of their music is one of the most persistent noises heard over England since the air raid sirens were dismantled." Brown Meggs recalls: "By the time Capitol became involved with the Beatles, they were already a phenomenal act in Europe. Friends of mine on the staffs of *Time* and *Newsweek* were saying to me, 'Hey, I hear you guys are getting the Beatles. That's gonna be a fantastic thing, isn't it?' We knew to some extent what was coming. We'd seen photographs of police having trouble with crowds in London and Stockholm. You didn't have to hear their music to know that the Beatles must have something."

The momentum began to build in America with the announcement of the Beatles' appearance on "The Ed Sullivan Show." The sudden surge of media interest compelled Capitol to move the release date of "I Want to Hold Your Hand" forward from February 9, 1964, to January 26. By mid-December, television news programs began including the Beatles in their broadcasts. Walter Cronkite of CBS News reported on their success in Britain while a few bars of "I Want to Hold Your Hand" played in the background. Chet Huntley and David-Brinkley of NBC News reported that the Beatles were succeeding in Europe with Prince Valiant haircuts, and aired an interview with the group. Ed Sullivan plugged the group's appearances on his show, which led Jack Paar, the host of "The Tonight Show," to announce that he would scoop Sullivan by airing a film clip of the Beatles on his program. The excitement within Capitol intensified, and once again the release date of the single was pushed up, from January 26 to late December 1963.

All the brouhaha about the Beatles stirred the curiosity of America's youth. Everyone was raving about them, yet no one had heard much of their music or seen them as anything but pictures in magazines. Interest in the Beatles began to generate excitement reminiscent of Elvis Presley's early days. The Beatles mystique was brewing well before their single was heard on American radio.

On December 26, 1963, Capitol Records issued "I Want to Hold Your Hand" b/w "I Saw Her Standing There." Within hours after radio stations played the advance copies, the impact of the record was felt. New York City radio station WMCA was officially credited by Capitol as the first to play the disc. "The record was an instantaneous hit," says former WMCA disc jockey Joe O'Brien. "Seconds after 'I Want to Hold Your Hand' was played, the switchboard lit up like a Christmas tree."

The Beatles were emerging on a pop music scene that was in dire need of revitalization. (The Animals sang about the dismal state of American pop in the song "The Story of Bo Diddley.") By the end of 1963, *Billboard*'s list of number one singles for the year charted such songs as "Go Away, Little Girl" and "Blue Velvet," which were as far from rock 'n' roll as one could get. From 1959 to 1963, the music scene experienced the virtual or actual disappearance of many prominent rock figures, such as Elvis Presley, Chuck Berry, Little Richard, Jerry Lee Lewis, and Buddy Holly. Apart from the emergence of the folk scene, the most exciting music produced in America then came from Motown and Phil Spector. American teenagers were ready for a change, which is why they responded enthusiastically to "I Want to Hold Your Hand." It was a return to the rock 'n' roll of the 1950s, yet it was fresh to the ears of a younger generation.

At the outset of 1964, Capitol Records launched a massive publicity campaign to promote the Beatles' arrival in America. The label shrewdly concentrated its efforts in New York since success there would be noticed across the country. Disc jockeys and the music press were already creating an appetite for the Beatles. The biggest task that Capitol faced was responding to the inordinate requests from the press: 25,000 Beatle biographies, 15,000 photographs, and 1-million copies of a four-page newsletter published by Capitol called *National Record News* with the headline BEATLEMANIA SWEEPS U.S.

Capitol, however, wanted exposure on a larger scale. They were unsuccessful in persuading the cheering section of Washington State University to hold up placards saying "The Beatles are Coming" during the Washington State–Illinois Rose Bowl football game on New Year's Day, but Jack Paar gave Capitol an unintentional shot in the arm on January 3 when he aired a three-minute film clip of the Beatles singing "She Loves You." Trying for laughs at the group's expense, Paar ridiculed their haircuts and their screaming teenage fans. According to Dave Dexter, Jr., however, the Beatles' exposure on "The Tonight Show" did more to help the group than their debut on "The Ed Sullivan Show" because Paar's ridicule only served to make the group more appealing to American teenagers. Nevertheless, the following day the *New York Times* commented: "While trade papers of the U.S. entertainment world indicate that recordings by the Beatles should find favor among indigenous teenagers, it would not seem quite so likely that the accompanying fever known as Beatlemania will be successfully exported. On this side of the Atlantic, it is dated stuff. Hysterical screams emanating from developing femininity really went out with the payola scandal and Presley's military service."

The Beatles monitored the progress of their single on the U.S. charts during a three-week engagement at the Paris Olympia in France. When they arrived there, "I Want to Hold Your Hand" was listed at forty-five in *Billboard* magazine, and John commented to a reporter that he did not expect the record to be a hit in the States. However, the record began selling "at a fantastic rate," remembers Dave Dexter, Jr. "Capitol was forced to use the pressing facilities of rival companies to keep up with the demand." Dexter programmed twelve tracks culled from the group's two Parlophone albums into an LP called *Meet the Beatles*, and the LP and the single experienced a rate of sales never before known in the American record industry. By the end of January, "I Want to Hold Your Hand" and *Meet the Beatles* had each sold 1 million copies.

The success of these records led Vee Jay and Swan to resurrect their dust-gathering masters in an attempt to recoup their losses. All the tracks from *Meet the Beatles*, as well as from the albums *Please Please Me* and *With the Beatles*, which Capitol obtained from Parlophone and distributed to disc jockeys, inundated the radio airwaves, leading other record companies to protest, "Stations are playing our records like spot commercials between Beatles tunes."

The U.S. news media was covering a social phenomenon. Americans took to these appealing foreigners with their long hair, collarless suits, and sharp wit. The press was accustomed to hysterical reactions from "developing femininity," but the Beatles were unlike any pop stars they had seen before. Beatlemania was also harmless, humorous news at a time when America did not have much to smile about. The country had seen its most youthful president murdered a few months before, and indeed musicologists have theorized that Kennedy's assassination was a key factor in the Beatles' acceptance in America, since it created a mood of empathy. In any case, it was good for the American people to turn their heads from reality for a while and enjoy a bit of madness from across the pond.

On February 1, 1964, the Beatles were in their Paris hotel suite when Brian Epstein received a telegram from New York, saying BEATLES NUMBER ONE IN CASHBOX RECORD CHART WITH I WANT TO HOLD YOUR HAND. The single was number one in *Billboard* and *Record World* magazines as well. When Brian read the cable aloud, the boys were at first disbelieving; then they burst with excitement, jumping on each other and running around. With their arrival in America just one week away, the news that "I Want to Hold Your Hand" had topped the U.S. hit parade was welcome indeed, helping to ease their fears about succeeding there. "That was the single most important fact," says Brian Sommerville, "whether or not the American tour was going to be a flop or whether it was going to work." Paul later said that the Beatles had decided they would not travel to America unless they had a number one record there.

The Beatles left France and returned to England on February 5 to prepare for their visit to America. It was announced in the British press that a pair of concerts at the famed Carnegie Hall and a single date at the Washington Coliseum had been added to their schedule. Other groups, such as the Dave Clark Five and Gerry and the Pacemakers, made similar concert and travel announcements, but the Beatles were the first.

On Friday morning, February 7, 1964, John, Paul, George, and Ringo boarded a Pan American plane at Heathrow Airport for their flight to America, still more than a little uncertain of the reception that awaited them on the other side of the Atlantic, and afraid that they would fail. Harrison had traveled to St. Louis in mid-September 1963 to visit his sister and had walked into a record shop in New York City and asked if the store sold any records by the Beatles. The proprietor, who was shocked by the length of Harrison's hair, said he'd never heard of the group.

In New York, a local disc jockey kept a Beatle countdown. "It's now seven A.M. Beatles time," the DJ announced. "They left London one hour ago. They're out over the Atlantic Ocean, heading for New York. The temperature is thirty-two Beatle degrees."

Meanwhile, aboard Pan American Flight 101, the atmosphere was filled with apprehension and skepticism. It was a tense moment in their careers: They knew that if they failed in America, their popularity in England would suffer, as had Cliff Richard's.

Accompanying the Beatles to America was record producer Phil Spector, who had been on tour in England with one of his groups. He assured the boys that they would do well in the States, and emphasized this point by telling them he had changed his travel plans in order to fly back with them. "You guys are winners," said Spector, "so I know the plane won't crash."

While the Beatles worried about the reception that awaited them when their plane landed, many New York City radio stations interrupted their programming to broadcast an air traffic controller's conversation with the pilot of flight 101 as the plane neared JFK Airport. Outside the control tower, excitement had been building since the early hours of the morning. Thousands of hooky-playing teenagers had gathered to greet the Beatles at the International Arrivals Building, while hundreds of reporters, photographers, radio newsmen, and television camera crews waited on the tarmac. A journalist assigned to report the group's arrival commented that it was impossible for anyone there not to be affected by the emotion that filled the air.

At 1:20 P.M., flight 101 landed at Kennedy International Airport. John turned on his transistor radio, heard a newsman describing the hysteria outside, and turned it off in disbelief. Paul, George, and Ringo looked out the window, saw the crowds, and shuddered. Their plane taxied to a special area and waited for the ground crew to position the portable steps. The Beatles were the last to leave the plane. When they stepped out, the boys saw 3,000 teenagers standing four deep on the upper level of the International Arrivals Building, screaming and waving banners. Airport officials shook their heads in astonishment, commenting, "We've never seen anything like this before, not even for kings and queens." While many New York journalists noted that the reception topped that given for General Douglas MacArthur on his return from Korea, others found it amusing that the Beatles' entry visas permitted them to enter America "so long as unemployed persons capable of performing this work cannot be found."

From the chaos outside, the Beatles were taken to the press lounge for the biggest press conference they had endured thus far. "The conference was terribly ill-disciplined," recalls Brian Sommerville. "The room was inadequate to accommodate the reporters and photographers. They were scrambling on the floor with their tape recorders and microphones and were more concerned about their comfort instead of doing their job, which was to get an impression of the Beatles." Above the noise, Brian politely asked, "Would the photographers please be quiet so the reporters can ask their questions?" But the bickering and haggling continued until Sommerville demanded: "All right, shut up! Just shut up!" John Lennon came to the aid of the exasperated press officer: "Yeah, everybody shut up!" George Harrison recalls: "They started asking us all funny questions, so we answered them with stupid answers."

REPORTER: Will you sing for us?
BEATLES: No!
REPORTER: Is it because you can't sing?
JOHN: We need money first.
REPORTER: Why do you sing like Americans but speak with an English accent?
JOHN: It sells better.
REPORTER: Are you in favor of lunacy?
PAUL: It's healthy.
REPORTER: Do you ever have haircuts?
GEORGE: I had one yesterday.
RINGO: It's no lie; you should have seen him the day before.
REPORTER: How do you account for your great success?
JOHN: If we knew, we'd form another group and be managers.
REPORTER: How about the Detroit campaign to stamp out the Beatles?
PAUL: First of all, we have a campaign of our own to stamp out Detroit.
JOHN: How big are they?

The Beatles' brash wit at this first press conference set the tone for this and subsequent tours. After the press conference, each of the boys rode in a separate limousine from the airport into Manhattan. The motorcade was followed by carloads of reporters and by fans who honked car horns, screamed, and waved. The Beatles were amazed by the reception. Each turned on his transistor radio and listened to stations playing their music and broadcasting up-to-the-minute reports on the progress of their motorcade.

When they arrived at the Plaza Hotel, they found thousands of teenagers blocking traffic on Fifty-ninth Street and Fifth Avenue. Geoffrey Ellis, a close friend of Brian Epstein's, was then living in New York and he met the group at the Plaza. Ellis remembers the chaos: "There were crowds of teenagers and mounted police during their stay in New York and the shocked faces of the Plaza Hotel staff, who'd been conned into reserving rooms for the Beatles, not realizing who they were. I could hardly believe it! I went up to the corridor where their suites were, and it was packed with people, security and business people, clamoring to get in. It was very astonishing." In November 1963, when Brian had made the reservations at the posh hotel, the Beatles had been unknown in America and the management had not thought it necessary to inquire into the backgrounds of the four English "businessmen" booked into suites 1209 to 1216. Now, after seeing the hotel practically demolished in one day by crowds of teenagers, the manager decided to ask them to find other accommodations. He mentioned this to his wife during dinner, but relented when his teenage daughter began to cry.

The Beatles, of course, were thrilled to be accepted by the country that had given birth to their musical influences. Paul described this feeling as "a very up buzz from the word go."

In the days following their arrival, they rehearsed for their first television appearance—"The Ed Sullivan Show," broadcast from the Hammerstein Theater (now called the Ed Sullivan Theater). The theater's 728 seats were sold out soon after the group's appearances were announced. By air time, ticket requests reached 50,000. "I've never seen anything like it in the fifteen years of our show," said Ed Sullivan.

The boys astonished the show's production staff with their professionalism during rehearsals, though George Harrison, who became ill on the plane flight over, was absent.

That afternoon it appeared that George would miss the broadcast. Ed Sullivan was in a panic and vented his nervousness on Neil Aspinall, who took Harrison's place during the final rehearsal for the cameramen. A doctor examined George at the Plaza and said that the ailing Beatle had a sore throat but would be well enough to perform. Sullivan was relieved, but still edgy because an enormous number of viewers would be tuning in for this show. An astute showman, Sullivan did not tolerate interference from anyone, and by air time he had had enough of Brian Epstein's demands and arrogance. "I would like to know the exact wording of your introduction," Brian demanded. Sullivan replied, "I would like you to get lost!"

That evening, an estimated 73 million viewers tuned in to watch "The Ed Sullivan Show." Sullivan, who had wisely scheduled the Beatles to open and close the program, instructed the studio audience to behave themselves during the introduction and show enthusiasm for the other performers on the bill. At seven o'clock, the show went on the air and Ed Sullivan announced, "Yesterday and today our theater was jammed with newspapermen and photographers from all over the nation, and these veterans agree with me that the city has never witnessed the excitement stirred by these youngsters from Liverpool who call themselves the Beatles. Now tonight, you're going to be twice entertained by them. Ladies and gentlemen, the Beatles!" The group appeared on a stage with huge arrows pointing at them—set designer Bill Bohnert's way of symbolically saying "The Beatles are here!" The group opened with "I Want to Hold Your Hand" and went on to do "All My Loving," "She Loves You," "Till There Was You," and "This Boy" during the show.

It was the moment the teenagers had been waiting for—and they were not disappointed. During the hour that the program was on the air, not one major crime committed by a teenager was reported in the country. The Beatles brought Sullivan the highest ratings in television history. It was the most exciting thing Sullivan had ever seen—"bedlam."

The following day the Beatles traveled to Washington, D.C. for their first American concert appearance. On February 11, 10,000 fans filled the Coliseum, the largest audience the group had entertained. The Beatles performed in the round, and the concert was perhaps one of their most unusual dates since backing beat poet Royston Ellis in Liverpool four years earlier.

As John, Paul, George, and Ringo walked on stage, they saw four middle-aged men in suits, each standing at a corner of the platform and wearing a Beatles wig. The group opened with "Roll Over, Beethoven" and performed for thirty-five minutes.

After every fourth song, their road crew came on to turn the amplifiers and Ringo's platform so that the Beatles could face another section of the audience. Screaming teenagers bounced in their seats; one policeman was seen using bullets as earplugs.

After the concert, the Beatles attended a civic reception at the British Embassy. They spent twenty minutes talking privately with Ambassador Sir David Ormsby-Gore, who was having a hard time figuring out which Beatle was which.

"Are you John?" asked the ambassador, speaking to John.

"No," said Lennon, pointing to George, "He's John."

"Hello, John," said the ambassador, speaking to George.

"I'm not John. He's John," said Harrison, pointing to Ringo.

The boys kept this game going until the ambassador was thoroughly confused, much to Brian Epstein's consternation. At the end of their conversation, Ringo turned to the ambassador and asked, "And what do *you* do?"

The reception, attended by embassy employees and upper-class expatriates, lost its appeal for the Beatles as the evening progressed. An intoxicated woman took a pair of scissors from her purse and snipped off a lock of Ringo's hair, which infuriated him. Embassy officials pushed and hustled the boys from one place to another and forced them to meet people and sign autographs. Before the reception was over, John stormed out and went back to the hotel in a temper. This was the last time that the Beatles attended a civic reception.

They returned to New York the next day for two concert performances at Carnegie Hall. Promoter Sid Bernstein received 2,000 ticket requests for each of the hall's 3,000 seats, turning down requests from actor David Niven and actress Shirley Maclaine. Bernstein, though, was pressured to place 150 seats onstage to cater to the "big shots" unable to purchase tickets.

While the Beatles were performing inside, the police outside narrowly averted a confrontation between hundreds of girls and about a hundred boys, who carried signs with anti-Beatle slogans, protesting that their girlfriends had fallen in love with members of the group. Throughout the Beatles' stay in New York, the police had a rough time controlling the fans. They fought back crowds of hysterical teenagers every time the Beatles' limousine pulled up or drove away, but had to be careful not to manhandle the kids for fear of bad publicity, though the crowds sometimes became uncontrollable. In desperation, the police accused Capitol Records and Brian Epstein of hiring hundreds of fans to incite teenagers by screaming and acting hysterically. The cops assigned to protect the Beatles were in no less danger than the group, as one newspaper reported: "One group of girls asked everybody who came out, 'Did you see the Beatles? Did you touch them?' A policeman came up and one of the girls yelled, 'He touched a Beatle! I saw him!' The girls jumped on the cop's arm and back."

After the Carnegie Hall concerts, the Beatles became bored with the novelty of being in America. Though they knew that the purpose of the tour was to promote their records and introduce themselves to the American public, the boys felt like show-business freaks. They were irritated by the inane and condescending questions that the press asked about their hair, name, and what each ate for breakfast; tired of meeting patronizing disc jockeys who attached themselves to the group and would not let go; and fed up with the countless photo sessions. "They had so many," says Brian Sommerville. "Photographers would say, 'Do this' and 'Do that.' All these things are terribly boring. They'd say, 'Why can't they print the last one? They took a thousand photographs, why do they need another one?'"

The boredom was compounded by a twelve-to-sixteen-hour-a-day work schedule that left them physically and mentally exhausted. On February 13, the Beatles flew to Miami, for their second "Ed Sullivan Show" appearance, scheduled to be broadcast from the Deauville Hotel's Mau Mau Club. They were supposed to travel first-class, but someone called the airline and changed their reservations as a joke, forcing the boys to sit in the tourist section. In addition, for some reason more tickets had been issued than there were seats in the Deauville. The boys had been dissatisfied with their television debut the week before when two microphones went dead on them during the last half of the show. This time they were upset that hundreds of fans had purchased bogus tickets and were turned away. The Beatles performed "I Saw Her Standing There," "I Want to Hold Your Hand," "From Me to You," "Twist and Shout," "Please Please Me," and "She Loves You" for the hour-long program.

The American tour was supposed to end the following day, but Brian Epstein, who knew that the boys needed time to rest, extended their stay to give them a five-day holiday in Miami. They spent time water-skiing, swimming in a private pool, sunbathing, and clowning with Cassius Clay (Muhammad Ali), who was in training for his second bout with Sonny Liston. Their five days in the Miami sunshine instilled new life and vigor into each of them.

On Friday, February 21, the Beatles ended their American visit. Financially, the tour was a failure, but the group had accomplished exactly what they had set out to do: They had stirred up a whirlwind of interest in the Beatles. Their stay in America could have been profitably expanded into a barn-storming, nationwide tour of one-night stands. Brian Epstein had received hundreds of offers from promoters across the country for concert appearances, but he rejected them all because the Beatles were committed to begin work on their first motion picture—*A Hard Day's Night.*

PART THREE

PRISONERS OF FAME

Circa March 1964 to August 1967

10

To Brian Epstein, *A Hard Day's Night* was more than a motion picture starring the Beatles. He knew that the movie would be distributed throughout the world and be seen by millions of teenagers, which would increase record sales; showcase the talents of John, Paul, George, and Ringo; and entice a new audience of fans. He also thought that a film would broaden the group's appeal and help change the opinions of the many critics who still believed that the Beatles were merely show business freaks.

The idea for a movie starring the Beatles was first proposed to Brian Epstein by Noel Rodgers, an English executive from United Artists Records, following the group's appearance at the London Palladium in October 1963. Before Rodgers met Epstein, he had persuaded the film division to finance a motion picture so his floundering record label could retain the distribution rights to a sound-track album and share in the huge profits that Beatles records were generating in England then. Rodgers assured the film executives that the revenues from a long-playing disc would cover their investment if the movie was a box-office failure.

United Artists Films agreed to commit $500,000 to the production and asked an American filmmaker named Walter Shenson, who had made two successful films for UA within this budget range (*The Mouse that Roared* and *The Mouse on the Moon*), to produce the film. "This was one of those rare occasions where a movie is made for a very unusual reason," says Shenson. "It happens today, but in 1963 no one ever said, 'Let's make a movie so we'll have a sound-track album.'

"The Beatles and Brian Epstein were eager to make a movie, but they didn't know anything about filmmaking. I met Epstein and he thought I'd be okay with the boys, but he said I'd have to meet them. So I met them and we seemed to get along at this one meeting. They asked me if I had a director in mind, and I mentioned Richard Lester. They liked the idea that I had produced a picture with Peter Sellers, and I said that Dick was someone who had worked with Peter in British television and had directed 'The Goon Show.' The Beatles knew who Dick was and said, 'Why don't we meet him, too?' So I arranged for the six of us to get together."

The meeting took place upon the group's return from Sweden in October 1963. When the filmmakers met the Beatles, they did not have a specific story line in mind for the film, but one emerged through John Lennon's response to a casual question. "Did you like Sweden?" Lester asked him. "Yes, very much," said John. "It was a room and a car and a car and a room and a concert, and we had cheese sandwiches sent up to our hotel room." The director suddenly saw the outlines of the plot. The Beatles expressed their concern about the script, telling Shenson and Lester that they knew the types of movies in which they did and did not want to appear, and having already turned down a lot of offers, they were also uncomfortable about appearing in a movie without any acting experience.

The filmmakers knew that the typical teenager pop movie with its hackneyed boy-meets-girl story line would not be right for the Beatles. They had to create an entirely different theme. At the group's request, playwright Alun Owen was commissioned to write the screenplay. They felt that he was qualified to write dialogue for them because of his Liverpool background and the numerous television and stage plays he had written about the working class of northern England. "Alun Owen said to me," recalls Walter Shenson, " 'Now that you're hiring me to write a script for the Beatles, what's the story about?' and nobody had any idea at the time. I said, 'We want to make a movie that's an exaggerated day in the life of the Beatles, because a lot of people don't know what a day in the life of the Beatles is like.' Alun asked, 'What's a day in the life of the Beatles?' They were playing in Dublin then. I said, 'You go to Dublin, and when you come back, *you* tell me.' "

The Beatles were then performing on their most extensive tour of Great Britain. Shenson arranged for Owen to move into the hotel where the group was staying and attend the concerts at the Ritz Theater in Dublin. Owen returned to London two days later and told Shenson, "I know what it's like now. They're prisoners of their success. They go from the airport to the hotel to the theater, back to the hotel, then back to the airport. That's all they see, because they'd be mobbed if they got out of the car or out of the hotel or away from the concert hall. I see the story as them being prisoners of their success. And now I've got an idea about one of them having a grandfather. It'll give me some plot things. I also see a scene where they break out from backstage and they just sort of walk about."

Originally intended as an exploitation film for the English theater market, and after the success of the group's American tour, United Artists was particularly anxious to have the movie made quickly, believing, as did many, that the Beatles' popularity would be short-lived. To United Artists, the film was no more than a ninety-minute commercial for a sound-track album—all that was required were images of the group, shot and sequenced in any way. The filmmakers were told they had two months to complete the picture.

Production of the Beatles' first film, which was then titled *Beatlemania No. 1*, began on March 2, 1964, at the Paddington Railway Station in London. The camera followed John, Paul, George, and Ringo as they were chased by hundreds of teenage fans in the streets, through the railway terminal, and onto a

British Railways train. For this sequence John, Paul, George, and Ringo had been ordered to wear matching black suits, but each showed up in street clothes. The continuity director, who was responsible for consistency in such matters from one scene to the next, expressed her annoyance in a memo to the film editor: "I trust this is not the way we intend to go on. God help us!"

Shenson and Lester wanted the film to capture the reality of the Beatles' daily lives. Events had to seem to be unfolding before the camera, and each of the Beatles had to emerge as a distinct individual. This was difficult at first, says Walter Shenson, "because we didn't know very much about them. All of us wanted to make sure that we didn't write a movie for one four-headed monster—we wanted four personalities. At first we guessed that their personalities were interchangeable, but as we went along, they were not interchangeable but four distinct men, and we began to rewrite. When we saw the daily rushes each day, we said, 'My God, we don't know anything about George, but he's funny. Let's give George more to do.' We knew that Paul was the best-looking—let's give him a little romance. We knew that John was the wittiest—let's give him the big jokes. And Ringo's got to be the butt of everything because he's the drummer and sits four paces behind them. Well, those were natural things, and we began to develop them as we went along."

The Beatles spent three weeks filming at the Twickenham Film Studios, ten miles west of Central London. They were intrigued by the art of filmmaking and enjoyed themselves on the set. In fact, one particular scene, in which a closet door was opened to reveal an elderly, timid hotel bellman (played by Eddie Malin) standing in his underwear, had to be filmed numerous times because the boys kept bursting out laughing. But the group earned the respect of the filmmakers for the professionalism and courtesy they displayed on the set. "They said, 'Yes, sir' when you said, 'Do you mind doing this?'" recalls Walter Shenson. "Brian Epstein told me how pleased he was with the whole working relationship because it made his life easier. He said, 'If you turned out to be a difficult man and the director turned out to be somebody who pushed them around, *I* would have caught hell from them for getting them

The classic early Beatles at the Prince of Wales.
(Courtesy Dezo Hoffman/ Rex/RDR)

On the set of *A Hard Day's Night*, March 1964. (Courtesy Walter Shenson)

The '66 tour. (Courtesy Bob Bonis)

Director Dick Lester and Paul McCartney on the film set of *A Hard Day's Night*, March 1964. (Courtesy Walter Shenson)

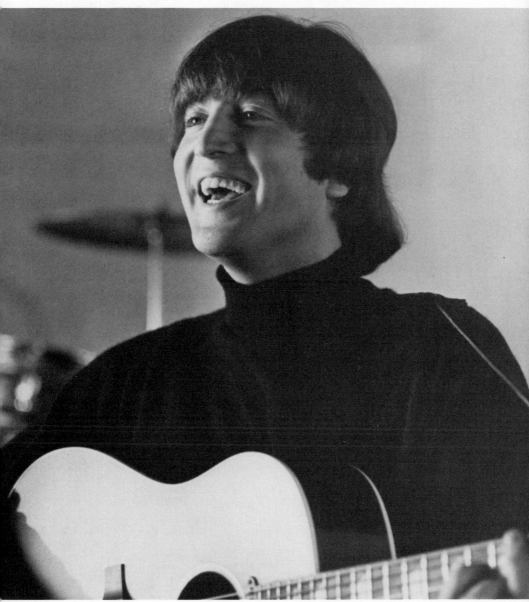

John Lennon, 1965. (Courtesy Walter Shenson and Suba Films)

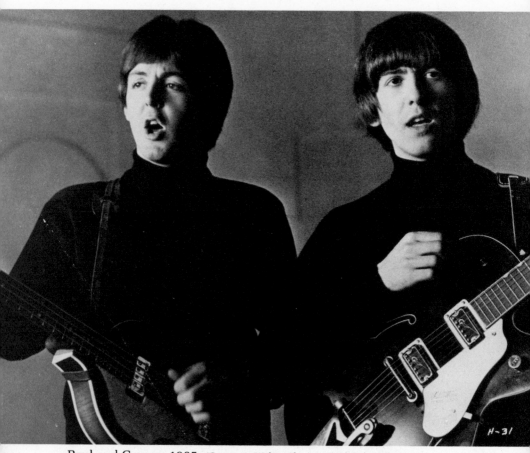

Paul and George, 1965. (Courtesy Walter Shenson and Suba Films)

John Lennon and Victor Spinetti practicing for
the mad scientist scene in *Help!* (Courtesy Walter Shenson and Suba Films)

Clowning with Dick Lester on the set of *Help!* Bahamas, 1965.
(Courtesy Walter Shenson and Suba Films)

George with Patti during his first sitar lesson at the Asian Music
Circle. London, 1965. (Courtesy Camera Press)

Brian Epstein with Ringo and Maureen Starkey on their wedding day. (Courtesy Camera Press)

Mick Jagger and Lennon having a laugh. London, 1965.
(Courtesy RDR Productions)

Always protective, Malcom Evans and Neil Aspinall oversee matters during a concert for the 1966 tour. (Courtesy Bob Bonis)

Brian strikes a tourist's pose on the Beatles' last tour, one year before his death. (Courtesy Bob Bonis)

The Beatles and Brian Epstein in their suite at Paris's Hotel George V on the night "I Want to Hold Your Hand" hit the top of the charts in the United States. (Courtesy Dezo Hoffman/Rex/RDR)

Crowds await the presence of Princess Margaret at the royal premiere of the Beatles' film. (Courtesy Camera Press)

into this thing.' Brian was grateful that there were no midnight phone calls from the boys saying, 'I don't want to go to work tomorrow morning.' "

The only aspect of the production that the Beatles disliked was having to wake up early in the morning to be on the set at Twickenham. The early calls interfered with their social life at night, which was usually spent at the exclusive Ad Lib Club in London. With other musicians, such as the Rolling Stones and the Animals, they'd party into the early hours of the morning, arriving at Twickenham at 8:00 A.M. half asleep and hungover. Paul missed the second day of filming because he was "sick" in bed with a headache.

In late March the production moved from Twickenham to the La Scala, a dilapidated theater in London that Richard Lester had remodeled to look like a television studio. Lester recruited hundreds of teenagers to sit in the studio audience and scream hysterically during the filming of a Beatles' television-performance scene. Though many teenagers did not need an incentive to scream at the group, the British Film Union stated that the filmmakers had to pay a daily wage to the "fans" who participated in the movie. (One of the extras in the La Scala sequence was a twelve-year-old actor named Phil Collins, who later became the drummer and lead singer for the group Genesis.) During the filming at the La Scala, thousands of girls converged outside the theater hoping to see the Beatles, and one day a large group sawed through a set of iron bars and made their way onto the set.

Fans made it not only difficult to film but dangerous for the cast. Victor Spinetti, one of the actors in the film, recalls: "I was in the car with [the Beatles] once where we couldn't move. When we arrived at the La Scala, we couldn't get out of the car because the street was blocked. Some girls grabbed hold of the back fender of the car and were dragged along the street and their legs were scuffed, but they didn't care because it was done by the Beatles' car. George was the first one to make a run for it. A girl grabbed him by the head and tore it and blood just ran down his face. I mean, Beatlemania was an extraordinary occurrence."

Among the actors on the set, discipline was loose, but the Beatles were professional enough to keep their clowning

within limits and their impromptu comedy routines contributed to the film. By observing the group, Richard Lester and
Alun Owen developed new ideas for the screenplay.

"Dick Lester had five cameras going at once," says Victor
Spinetti, "because they never kept to the script; you didn't
know what they were going to say. I remember walking on the
set and I was meant to be this television director, saying,
'You're late! You should have been at rehearsal ages ago!' John
said, 'You're not a television director, you're Victor Spinetti
acting a television director.' And I continued with my lines. 'I
am from the BBC. I have on my wall a certificate saying I'm
from the BBC. I am a director!' As I did that, I knocked the
cymbals of Ringo's drums and Ringo said, '*Eh*, he's fingering
me cymbals.' John said, 'Well, he's a famous cymbal fingerer.' I
went up to Paul and said, 'Well, you're late!' and Paul said,
'*Oh*, I'll give you such a kiss in a minute,' and they were
sending me up or putting me down. Because they had five
cameras going all the time, four or five at once, they got the
essence of the Beatles, and that was the cleverness of that
film."

At lunchtime each day, Shenson, Lester, and a few members of the production staff disappeared from the set to view
the rushes from the previous day. One afternoon the Beatles
followed them and burst into the screening room. "They came
in screaming and yelling," remembers Shenson. "They said,
'Why didn't you let us come and see?' I'll never forget the four
of them walking in and [seeing] themselves for the first time,
huge, up on the screen. They were funny because they were
saying, 'It's a movie! It's a movie!' and there was just a day's
work. There were images that moved and spoke. There was no
holding them back after that. The reason we kept them out was
we thought they'd be distracted or depressed. They might
have lost the spontaneity we wanted and started to be actors,
which we didn't want. Well, we were wrong. They loved the
idea and they improved."

Although *Beatlemania No. 1* had been the film's working
title up to now, United Artist was pestering the filmmakers to
decide on a more suitable name so they could begin publiciz-
ing the picture. Finally, after forty-three days of filming, they
came up with one.

"We were sitting around at lunch one day at Twickenham," says Walter Shenson, "and I was eating with John Lennon, and just in conversation he asked, 'Have you ever heard Ringo misuse the English language?' I asked him for an example. John said, 'Well, if we worked all night on a recording session, the next day he would say, "Boy, that was a hard day's night." He uses those kinds of expressions.' I said, 'That sounds like a terrific title for the movie.' So we canvassed the others in the dining room and we all thought it was pretty good. I called United Artists in New York and said, 'This is your title,' and got dead air for a moment. They called back and said, 'Oh, everybody likes it!' "

Walter Shenson had told the Beatles that he needed six original tunes for the film—two ballads and four fast songs—and the group had recorded and delivered them to him before the first day of filming. "We were wrapping up to go home," remembers Shenson, "and I said to John, 'You know, everybody's agreed to A Hard Day's Night for the title. Do you know, we don't have a song called "A Hard Day's Night." It'll help sell the picture and you guys will have another record. Do you think you and Paul could write me one?' John said, 'Where will it fit in the movie?' I said, 'Over the titles—everything else is spotted in the picture—just over the titles.' "

Shenson explained that the opening segment of the film was the scene in which fans chased the Beatles onto a train, and that John did not have to write a song that told the story of the movie. "We got into the car and started to drive to London," says Shenson. "John said to the driver, 'Would you please hurry up and drop me off and then take Walter home because I want to get home and do something.' He looked at me and said, 'I think I've got an idea for the song.' Now this was at ten o'clock at night. At eight the next morning, we were in the studio and the assistant director tells me that John wants to see me in his dressing room. I went in and John had a matchbook cover propped up against the mirror and there were some words on it. Paul was standing next to him; they both had their guitars at the ready. John said, 'How will this do?' and they played and sang for me 'A Hard Day's Night,' which they had written that night or that morning."

On April 24, the production of A Hard Day's Night concluded. By the end of the month, United Artists had recouped its investment from the advance sales of the sound-track album, which had earned $700,000 for the company.

Midway through the filming, the Beatles had previewed one of the songs from the movie on a single, "Can't Buy Me Love" b/w "You Can't Do That," which was the first record by an artist to register advance sales of 1 million copies in England and America. With the single—the group's first disc to be number one on both sides of the Atlantic simultaneously—a system developed between John and Paul in which the main composer of the song sang lead vocal.

The commercial success of the Beatles took John Lennon's first book, *In His Own Write*, to the top of the American best-seller list. The book—the first nonmusical creative venture by an individual member of the group—was comprised of offbeat stories, poems, and sketches that John described as "the Beatles' sense of humor on paper." Its publication was more than proof of the group's versatility; John had dreamed of being a beat poet since the time he and Stuart Sutcliffe had shared quarters at Gambier Terrace. Many American and English book reviewers, who did not understand Lennon's sense of humor, dismissed the work as mere nonsense, but a few compared *In His Own Write* to Joyce's *Finnegans Wake*, a novel that combined words from various languages to form new words.

The highest tribute the book received came from the Christina Foyles Literary Guild, whose members chose to honor John at an award luncheon on April 23 at the Dorchester Hotel in London. John and Cynthia arrived at the Dorchester tired and slightly hung over from having spent most of the previous night drinking and dancing at the Ad Lib Club. The publisher of Jonathan Cape escorted the Lennons into the hotel's banquet hall, where hundreds of people in formal attire applauded John as he walked to the main table. Lennon was under the impression that the luncheon and the presentation of the Christina Foyles Literary Prize was a formality, and that all he had to do was eat and then walk away with his award. After lunch, however, the emcee toasted and introduced the guest of honor, and upon accepting his prize, John was asked to give a speech about his work. Paralyzed, all John could do was mumble "thank you very much" and sit down, which angered the crowd, who had expected a performance of some kind.

By the summer of 1964, the Beatles had performed on tour in only three countries outside of Great Britain: Sweden, France, and the United States. Their albums and singles were being sold throughout the free world and had tremendous success on the charts, but Brian Epstein was eager to expand the scope of their popularity and stimulate world record sales through concert performances. Thus, during the spring of 1964, he had been organizing a world tour for the Beatles. They would appear in sixty-two cities on four continents and give 110 performances.

On the eve of the tour, however, Ringo Starr collapsed during a photo session in London and was rushed to the University College Hospital, where doctors diagnosed tonsillitis and ordered a week's rest. The group was in a dilemma: Should they postpone the tour? After a violent disagreement between John and Paul on the one side, who felt they should get a replacement, and George on the other, who felt Ringo was essential, a session drummer named Jimmy Nichol was hired to stand in for Ringo, who rejoined them two weeks after the tour began.

The first leg of the Beatles' 1964 world tour lasted twenty-eight days and took the group to Denmark, Holland, Hong Kong, Australia, and New Zealand. Wherever they appeared— at airports, concert halls, and hotels—there were massive demonstrations of hysteria, but they were used to this by now, and the excitement of traveling to the faraway places they had read about in high school heightened their enthusiasm.

The tour opened on June 4 in Copenhagen, Denmark, where the group rehearsed with Jimmy Nichol prior to a performance at the Tivoli Gardens. The following day they arrived in Holland. During the Beatles' first day in Amsterdam, 50,000 people cheered them as they took an afternoon sightseeing excursion through the canals of the city. In the evening the police escorted John, Paul, and George into the Walletjis,

Amsterdam's red-light district, where they spent the night in a brothel. John, too drunk to walk, was supposedly photographed leaving the brothel on his hands and knees.

From Holland they flew back to London, where they held an airport press conference before boarding a BOAC jet bound for Hong Kong. Then on to Australia, the highlight of the tour. The group arrived in Adelaide on June 12 and was greeted by nearly 300,000 people lining the entire route of the Anzac Highway from the airport to the hotel. Ringo Starr joined the Beatles onstage four days later in Melbourne, sending Jimmy Nichol, who'd experienced twelve days of stardom, back to England. The music world never heard from him again.

The tour thus far had been literally a roaring success. But when the Beatles arrived in New Zealand, they experienced the unpleasant side of their popularity for the first time. In Wellington jealous boys broke into the group's hotel room and hid in a closet, hoping to jump the four and cut off their hair when they returned. A chambermaid discovered the boys, who fled down a fire escape and into the arms of the police. In Brisbane a crowd of boys threw rotten eggs, pies, and pieces of wood at the Beatles while they were performing. Police had to keep angry fans from tearing the troublemakers apart. When they were brought to the group's dressing room after the show and were asked to explain their behavior, one boy said they were tired of listening to Beatles music every time they turned on the radio and jealous that their girlfriends talked about the Beatles instead of them.

By the time the first leg of the tour ended on July 2, the Beatles realized that their popularity would not be short-lived. They'd never dreamed that fame could incite the kind of madness they'd experienced in New Zealand.

Brian Epstein and John Lennon had worked together to achieve the kind of stardom they dreamed of. They concerned themselves with solidifying the group's visual image, with a phenomenon that would outshine Elvis's fame. But there were external factors that contributed to Beatlemania. Census reports for 1964 indicate that there were more teenagers in the world then than at any other time, and music was more accessible as affordable transistor radios flooded the market from the Far East. The Beatles emerged on the international music scene at a time when teenagers were without an idol, and the group seemed to have the qualities that kids admired. The four distinct personalities of John, Paul, George, and Ringo, together with the quality of their music, coalesced into a unique package that was marketed to youth.

The Beatles were anxious to see how *A Hard Day's Night* had turned out, not only to satisfy their own curiosity but to help them gauge how the public would respond to their first motion picture. On the eve of the film's world premier, Brian Epstein asked Walter Shenson if they could screen the movie. The producer arranged for them to preview it at a film studio near the Dorchester Hotel in Mayfair, London. "Dick Lester was chicken," says Shenson. "He didn't want to come. He thought that they may not like it. I said, 'Don't be silly. It's a marvelous film.' I sat there with the four of them and ran the film. When the lights went on, I turned around and looked at them and said, 'Well, that's it.' The first line that came out came from George. 'Well, Walter, whatever they say about it, I'm sure glad we made this film—it's so good.' It took a lot of guts and self-confidence to say that, not waiting until the world says it's good. The others agreed and didn't go into a huddle to discuss whether or not they liked it."

On July 6 the city of London closed Piccadilly Circus to traffic for the world premiere of *A Hard Day's Night* at the Pavilion Theatre. Asked how he felt about the group's performance in the picture, John Lennon told a reporter, "Well, it's as good as anybody that makes a film and can't act, you know." Film critics had eagerly awaited the release of the movie, hoping to prove that the Beatles were long on hair and short on talent. To their surprise, they found the film good and the Beatles competent actors.

A Hard Day's Night personifies Beatlemania and portrays the group the way fans want to remember them today. The film drew crowds of adults as well as teenage fans, and parents whose kids had been driving them crazy with Beatles music day and night began to see the group differently. "When the film came out, a lot of older people became converts," says Walter Shenson. "The Beatles were so appealing on the screen that parents began to say, 'Aren't they adorable?' or 'Aren't they funny?' and 'That music is nice.' There's just no way that you're not caught up by the Beatles. I know of famous people, like Leonard Bernstein, who went back five or six times to see the movie because they began to realize that the young people were right, that there was something there."

Film critics compared the group's performance in *A Hard Day's Night* to the Marx Brothers. "The Beatles asked me if I could get them some Marx Brothers movies to show them," says Shenson, "because they had never heard of them. They weren't naïve, just too young to know about the Marx Brothers. We ran some pictures and they fell all over the place laughing at them." After the premiere, Richard Lester worked with Groucho Marx, who had seen *A Hard Day's Night* and hated it. He told Lester he couldn't tell them apart.

The Beatles' first extensive tour of America coincided with the release of the film. This time, of course, there was no anxiety about their reception in America. Their records were selling at a phenomenal rate, and *Variety* predicted that this would be the first transcontinental tour to sell out before the first date was played.

It was. In early spring 1964, Brian Epstein had hired a New York management firm, the General Artists Corporation, to represent the Beatles in North America. GAC executive Norman Weiss spent six months organizing the tour. "Every promoter in the country wanted to do dates on the Beatles," says Weiss. "Brian wanted to do a tour because of the money, and Capitol Records wanted them to do one as well. We started working on it in March, but we were working in the dark because none of us knew the extent of their popularity. We didn't know the kinds of problems we were going to run into with crowd control because nothing like this had ever happened before."

The Beatles opened their U.S. concert tour at the Cow Palace in San Francisco on August 19. Upon their arrival the day before, they'd been mauled by thousands of fans at the airport. Promoters of the Cow Palace date wanted the Beatles to participate in a ticker-tape parade through the city, but the group adamantly refused, fearful of people being shot.

On the recommendation of the Rolling Stones, Epstein hired Bob Bonis, a 230-pound six-footer, to help road-manage the tour. (Bonis had road-managed the Stones' first American tour in June 1964.) "It was a bit of a fight every time getting them in and out of venues," says Bonis. "We all lost watches and pieces of hair. Frankly, on their first two tours, it was damn frightening. The Beatles were told, 'The minute you're through, put your guitars down and run like hell.' The orders were to follow me no matter where I ran. Sometimes we had to change exits in midstream because kids somehow caught wind of our plans. Fans in Seattle destroyed a Cadillac they thought we were in."

The Beatles' stage show consisted of twelve songs: "Twist and Shout," "You Can't Do That," "All My Loving," "She Loves You," "Things We Said Today," "Roll Over, Beethoven," "Can't Buy Me Love," "If I Fell," "I Want to Hold Your Hand," "Boys," "A Hard Day's Night," and, as a closer, "Long Tall Sally." They seldom deviated from this set of songs, but occasionally changed the opening and closing numbers to break the monotony. Though they'd expected to be well received, they were nevertheless astonished by the receptions they received on the tour. "By the time the first few dates were played," says Bob Bonis, "the Beatles were euphoric. They were so happy about what was going down." The music, however, was rarely heard above the jetlike roar of 15,000 to 20,000 fans.

At each stop on the tour, the Beatles held a press conference at the airport, hotel, or venue. It was easier to meet the press en masse rather than accommodating each reporter or photographer with an interview or photo session. "In the airplane we'd carry roughly sixty people, and about ten of these people were press," says Bob Bonis. "Brian charged them a thousand dollars a week to come on the plane because we were giving them transportation and food. We'd prepared a bunch of questions for the press because the questions [the Beatles] got asked locally were so stupid. In order to keep things interesting for the Beatles and keep them awake, instead of the 'Do you sleep in your pajamas?' routine, we planted questions. To me, the highlight each day was not the concert but the press conference, where they were really at their best. They said the most outrageous things."

The Beatles were masters at handling the press, especially

American reporters. They knew how to be provocative without being offensive and learned how to brush aside serious questions with a joke or smart remark, and if one couldn't answer, there was at least one other Beatle who could. Nearly everything the boys told the press was accepted as gospel. According to Bob Bonis, they would tell reporters the most farfetched stories about themselves and return to their hotel suite and say, "What an asshole! That guy actually believed that story!" Despite the Beatles' fame, the American press corps did little to research the group's background and rarely asked about their musical influences, their opinions about music, the direction of rock 'n' roll and its future. The boys were seen more as show-business curiosities than as artists.

The Beatles traveled to each city on the tour in an Electra turbojet chartered by Epstein from American Flyers Airlines. At the start of the tour, an American psychic named Jean Dixon predicted that their plane would crash, which made the group very nervous because they knew Dixon had accurately predicted President Kennedy's assassination the year before. Flying into Denver on August 26, it appeared to George Harrison that the prophecy would come true when the pilot banked steeply during the final approach to Stapleton Airport. George panicked and began yelling, "We're gonna crash! We're gonna crash!" but calmed down after several people assured him that everything was all right.

The Beatles' one-day stay in Denver illustrates the "madness" the group experienced in every city on the tour. "We arrived in Denver and put the Beatles in a limousine," says Bob Bonis. "The Beatles waved and did the whole number for the press so they could get their footage. Then a cameraman hopped into the front seat and started filming them sitting there trapped in the back seat. I grabbed the guy and gave him a yank and yelled 'No!' I guess I yanked him too hard and threw him onto the tarmac and the camera went flying. Another cameraman filmed that and we saw it on the news that day. So when I arrived at the stadium, the boys were lying on cots, and as soon as they saw me they screamed, 'Oh, no!' and started diving for cover under the cots, saying, 'The terror is here!' "

Before the group left Stapleton Airport for the Browns Hotel, the mayor of Denver persuaded them to tour the perimeter of the airfield to see it ringed by fans. When the entourage arrived at the hotel, thousands of fans were waiting to greet the Beatles. GAC security men had arranged for a limousine to pull up in front of the hotel with four people disguised as the Beatles, while John, Paul, George, and Ringo entered safely through the back entrance. It didn't quite work. A dozen reporters and photographers were not fooled by their diversion and chased the group through the kitchen, knocking over pots and pans. Epstein, the Beatles, and George Martin ducked into a service elevator, but before they could shut the door, a handful of reporters and photographers squeezed in with them, overloading it and forcing them to leave through the emergency door on top.

The Beatles knew they couldn't avoid the massive crowds that greeted them at airports and hotels, and though the surging, screaming throngs were often truly frightening, they each realized that these receptions weren't meant to harm. Throughout the tour, Epstein and GAC agents could not figure out how the fans knew the time of the Beatles' arrival at airports and the names of the hotels in which they were booked. This information was kept a secret to reduce the possibility of someone being hurt, particularly the members of the group. Later in the tour, Epstein and GAC discovered that an American disc jockey who was traveling with the entourage was selling this information to the press. The press passed it on to the fans and encouraged them to be at the airport and hotel, supposedly to show the Beatles how much they cared for them, but really to give the media a story for the evening news and the morning paper.

In fact, one of the many aspects of touring that annoyed the Beatles was the press's treatment of the band—as though the circus had come to town. John, Paul, George, and Ringo thought they were simply performing a concert, but they grew cynical over the theatrics they felt subjected to. George Harrison remembers the Beatles arriving in Chicago and being escorted to their hotel by overenthusiastic policemen on motorcycles with sirens blaring.

All of those who worked with the Beatles on this first major tour of America were stunned by the things they saw going on around the group. GAC agents Norman Weiss and Bob Bonis were veterans of many concert tours prior to the Beatles and were not easily impressed, but nothing they had experienced before could compare to the Beatles' American tour.

"We played Forest Hills, and after a lot of hassling we got permission to land a helicopter on the field," says Weiss. "The tennis stadium is in a residential area, and if we had tried to drive through there, we never would have made it. You know how noisy it is inside a helicopter? We were coming down to land in the middle of the stadium and there were about fifteen thousand people there. As we were coming down, the noise of the screams was louder than the noise inside the helicopter, and all we could see were all these faces looking up. It was like God was descending. Every kid had a camera with a flash, and all of a sudden, all the flashbulbs started going off."

As portrayed in the film *A Hard Day's Night*, the Beatles had become prisoners of their fame. The group passed the time by watching television, playing games or their guitars, and meeting show-business personalities they admired. On several occasions, obnoxious people tried to force themselves on the Beatles. "There was a real drunk guy saying he was the mayor of Toronto," recalls Bob Bonis. "He said, 'Wake them up!' This was at three in the morning, and he brought up four other drunks with him. He easily went past the security guards because they said, 'He *is* the mayor!' He said, 'Wake them up!' to Neil Aspinall and me, who happened to be chatting out in the hall. Then he really got outrageous.

"Every celebrity who was anyone wanted to meet the Beatles. I remember Pat Boone throwing a fit in Las Vegas because they wouldn't meet his kids. They didn't like Pat Boone anyway. There were all kinds of people who *had* to meet the Beatles."

Once in a while, one of the boys would sneak out of a hotel in a disguise. Sometimes they would get away unnoticed, but more often they had to run for their lives. For their protection, Epstein prohibited them from going out at night. "By the time they got to America," says Bob Bonis, "they were used to this kind of life-style. They were uncomfortable with it, but they resigned themselves to it. George was the one who continually wanted to go out. There was a period in Dallas where we had a few days off and George wanted to fly to New York to see his sister, but Brian wouldn't let him. Brian pretty much kept them together and kept telling them not to run out. What surprised me was how little they played their guitars inside the hotel room. They had acoustic guitars and they'd play them quietly. They were conscious of their image and wanted to maintain it. For example, we were playing Monopoly in the suit—the four boys, Jackie DeShannon, Neil, and myself—and it got a little rowdy; fun rowdy, like 'All right, goddamn it, I'll take my property,' and it was the Beatles who'd say, 'Shh, relax, we're in a hotel.' "

Stories about orgies taking place on tour or prostitutes being brought to their hotel suites after a performance are largely exaggerated. Bob Bonis recalls only one occasion, in Atlantic City, where hookers were present in their room. "They were a gift from a local Mafia guy," says Bonis. "He wanted to show them what a nice guy he was. It was like saying, 'Guys, we really appreciate what you've done for the city. Here, have a good time.' The boys didn't react too well. In fact, I can think of two disc jockeys who grabbed two of the hookers right away."

John, Paul, George, and Ringo were well aware that reporters and photographers followed their every movement, waiting for them to make a mistake. Even the utmost discretion was no guaranty of safety. "I would go downstairs in the hotel lobby," says Bob Bonis, "and one time I heard a mother briefing her daughter—a real gorgeous little girl—saying, 'Try and sneak into their room and let one of them get you in bed and then yell "Rape!" ' "

The Beatles made one unscheduled stop, in Kansas City on September 17, which was supposed to have been a rest day for the group. Charlie Finley, the owner of the Kansas City Athletics baseball team, offered Brian Epstein $50,000 for one twelve-minute performance and sent the Beatles three boxes of baseball bats painted Kelly green, one of the team's official colors. Brian refused the check, telling Finley that it was the group's day off. Finley, however, had gone to great lengths to assure the teenagers of Kansas City that he would bring the

Beatles to their city. He tore up that check and doubled the offer, but Epstein again refused. Then Finley wrote a check for $150,000—which came to $12,500 per minute. Epstein saw the publicity advantages in accepting it because the fee was the highest ever offered to a performing artist. The final decision was made by the Beatles, who agreed to play the date.

The day before the tour ended, Mr. Pigman, the owner of American Flyers Airlines, invited the Beatles to spend a day of rest on his ranch in the Ozark Hills in southern Missouri. Pigman flew the group and their entourage from Dallas in his private plane, which was so old that it reminded the Beatles of the one in which Buddy Holly had died.

The last date on the tour was a charity performance for cerebral palsy at the Paramount Theater in New York. The benefit brought out New York's social elite, who paid $100 a ticket to see the Beatles, Steve Lawrence, and Eydie Gorme. "I don't know how so many kids got in," recalls Bob Bonis. "I guess they got the tickets from their parents, but over half the audience was kids and the others were the usual charity crowd with tuxedoes and gowns. Those kids were climbing all over the seats, ripping people's gowns by accident. It was just chaos out front. And poor Steve and Eydie came out and the kids were yelling, 'We want the Beatles!' The boys didn't know what was going on, because they were stuck upstairs in their dressing room. I'd run upstairs every ten minutes with a hilarious story or two. John loved this and he came down to have a look around."

During the Beatles' performance at the Paramount, security guards kept throwing a "skinny kid" off the stage. The kid was later identified as Bob Dylan, and when Bonis recognized him, he took him backstage to see the group. The Beatles had met Dylan in February 1964 and were familiar with his music; indeed, throughout their three-week engagement at the Paris Olympia, they'd repeatedly played two of his albums, *Bob Dylan* and *The Free-Wheelin' Bob Dylan*, which the group enjoyed. After the Paramount show, Bob Dylan returned to the Beatles' hotel, where they talked about music. Sometime during the night, the folk singer introduced John, Paul, George, and Ringo to marijuana.

Bob Dylan's influence on the Beatles can be heard on the group's fourth Parlophone album, *Beatles for Sale*, which was released in late November 1964. The LP featured "I'm a Loser," one of John's first compositions to be based on personal feelings. Lennon acknowledged that Bob Dylan had changed his approach to songwriting, convincing him to pay more attention to the words.

From the start to the end of the one-month tour (on September 20), every existing American show-business record for attendance, box office, and fees was broken. The Beatles grossed over $2 million, performed for over 500,000 people in 25 cities, and gave 32 concerts. They logged nearly 40,000 air miles and spent 60 hours traveling in a plane. Never again would the group undertake such an extensive tour of America.

11

By the beginning of 1965, the Beatles were disenchanted with their fame, which they knew would disappear if the group broke up, stopped touring, or released a string of unsuccessful recordings. They were not considering any of these alternatives then, but they did decide to reduce the number of performances on their next world tour to half those of the previous one.

John, Paul, George, and Ringo were caught in the middle of an extraordinary experience they did not understand. Initially, fame had been a novelty—they'd enjoyed the attention, the notoriety, the success, and the wealth it brought to them. But in the fourteen months that had passed since October 1963, they had been forced into a life-style for which they were not prepared. They had seen their freedom and privacy decrease as the group's popularity increased. Each began to wonder whether the financial rewards were worth such a sacrifice. In desperation they turned to drugs to cope with the demands and the speed of their fame.

The Beatles had begun using drug stimulants while they were performing in Hamburg in 1960, and continued to use them until they tried marijuana. John Lennon, who was introduced to Benzedrine at the art school, used to send people to buy speed for him between sets at the Cavern Club so he could survive the grueling hours. Since the time that Bob Dylan introduced them to their first marijuana cigarette, the Beatles frequently smoked pot to relax.

According to Cynthia, the rot began to set in among the Beatles the moment marijuana and LSD entered their lives. John and George were the first to be introduced to LSD. In early 1965 they unknowingly ingested the drug while dining with a friend of Harrison's, who mixed it into their coffee. They went to the Ad Lib club and started going crazy, having a wonderful, if terrifying, time. John and George did not become frequent users of LSD then, but the experience was eye-opening.

Following a two-week Christmas booking at London's Hammersmith Odeon, which ended on January 16, 1965, the Beatles began a one-month rest period. John and Cynthia traveled to St. Moritz with George Martin and his wife for a ten-day skiing vacation. Paul and Jane Asher took a three-week holiday in Tunisia, and George and Patti Boyd visited the Harrison family in Liverpool, where they attended the wedding of George's brother, Peter. Ringo, who had been singled out as the key subversive figure in an absurd book called *Communism, Hypnotism and the Beatles*, remained in London with his girlfriend of three years, Maureen Cox. In early February Maureen learned that she was two months pregnant with Ringo's child. The couple obtained a marriage license and were quietly wed at 8:15 on the morning of February 11 in London. The ceremony was attended by John, George, and Brian (Paul was still vacationing in Tunisia).

In late February the Beatles began working with producer Walter Shenson and director Richard Lester on the motion picture *Help!* The movie was the second of a three-film contract the group had signed in November 1963 with United Artists.

"We all agreed—the Beatles, Dick Lester, and I—that we would not make another day in the life of the Beatles," says

Walter Shenson. "So we came up with *Help!*, which was sort of a cartoon movie—a movie-movie."

Again, the filmmakers did not want to make the standard pop film. An American writer named Marc Behm, who had what Walter Shenson considered a wild sense of humor, was commissioned to write the script. "Dick, Marc, and I sat around for a weekend," recalls Shenson, "literally ad-libbing and inventing this crazy plot line of Ringo and the ring, and this silly Far Eastern cult that wanted to sacrifice a maiden, but they can't sacrifice her unless she's wearing the ring. Whoever's wearing the ring is gonna be sacrificed. Marc wrote this wild script, and then an English writer, Charles Wood, was assigned to do some more work on it. Between the two of them, we came up with that screenplay."

Confident after the box-office success of *A Hard Day's Night*, United Artists provided a budget of over $2 million for *Help!* and this time Shenson and Lester were not pressured to rush the production; UA felt that if the Beatles' popularity waned slightly, there would still be a ready-made audience for a second film. The filmmakers surrounded the group with a superb cast of British actors, including Leo McKern, Victor Spinetti, and Roy Kinnear, and decided to film the movie in exotic, picturesque locations, such as the Bahamas.

The cast spent the first two weeks filming in Nassau. "The first day was on the yacht," recalls Victor Spinetti. "I was playing the mad scientist. Ringo escapes me and dives into the water. People helped Ringo out of the water, then Dick Lester said, 'Let's do another shot.' After the shot, Ringo is shivering and everything because it was bloody cold, and then Lester said, 'Could we do another shot?' The third time, Ringo said, 'Do we have to do it again?' Dick Lester said, 'I'd like another one. Why?' Ringo said, 'Well, 'cause I can't swim.' And the director went white and said, 'Why on *earth* didn't you tell me?' He said, 'Well, I didn't like to say.'"

Ringo was slightly injured during the filming of one sequence when he was overcome by a smoke bomb. Richard Lester and the camera crew were unaware of Ringo's distress and continued to film.

The scenes shot in the Bahamas eventually appeared in the final version of the film. The Beatles had been asked to sit in the shade as much as possible to avoid being sunburned, so their facial tone remained consistent for the sequences filmed in Obertourn, Austria. "*Help!* was a more difficult picture to make," says Walter shenson. "We went to the Bahamas, Austria, and we dragged the Beatles out to Salisbury Plain in the cold weather. It was a tougher picture to do, so being human they had every right to complain. But they were never pampered. They didn't demand individual dressing rooms—none of that nonsense. There were many nights up in the Austrian alps, cold as hell in March, when they wished they were somewhere else. It was no fun spending three weeks in a little village, no place to go. We all had to make our own fun after a day's shooting. They had early calls in the morning, and the Beatles in those days were night people, and there was nothing to do at night. They had to get out in the snow and do certain stunts."

The skiing sequence was an actual depiction of the Beatles teaching themselves how to ski. They wanted to learn and were determined not to be beaten by the unwieldy slabs of wood on their feet. The boys, particularly John, assaulted the slopes of the Obertourn Ski Resort, where the cast was staying. The segment in which the group played the ice game known as curling was delayed for several days when Victor Spinetti became ill.

"I was in bed and the Beatles visited me," Spinetti recalls. "Each one of them visited me separately, and the way they visited me when I had the flu is really what they're like. Knock at the door, Paul McCartney opens the door and looks around and says, 'Is it catching?' I said yes and he closes the door.

"George Harrison walked in and said, 'I've come to plump your pillows, because whenever you're ill, people plump your pillows.' So he came in and plumped me pillows and tidied the sheets and made me feel comfortable.

"John Lennon walked in and said, 'You are in die ztate of Austria; you are going to be experimented upon by ze doktors, and your schkin vill be made into lampshades. Heil Hitler!' and walked out.

"Ringo walked in, didn't say anything, sat down by the side of the bed and got the menu that's always there, opened the menu, looked at me, and said, 'Once upon a time, there were three bears—momma bear, daddy bear, and baby bear.

"That's the essential difference between the four of them. John, the realist. Paul, the one who thinks that if it's catching, he might not be able to do the shot tomorrow. George, the caring. And Ringo, the fantasist."

The movie's working title was *Eight Arms to Hold You*, which was inspired by a forty-foot statue of the goddess Kali, a prop in the film. "As I recall," says Walter Shenson, "I think we all liked [that title] but hadn't tied it down. Then word got out that that was what the film was going to be called, though it wasn't official. Then we hated it. It was Dick Lester's wife who came up with the title *Help!*"

On April 1 the production of *Help!* moved from Austria to the film sets of Twickenham Studios, where the actors and film crew nervously expected the Beatles to spring an April Fool's Day prank. To their bewilderment, the boys acted as though they did not know what day it was. Many of these technicians and cameramen had worked on the group's first motion picture, and they noticed that the Beatles lacked the vitality they'd displayed in *A Hard Day's Night*. Though John, Paul, George, and Ringo were a year older and had been changed by the events they'd experienced in that time, their belief that they were "guest stars" in their own film, as well as their dope smoking on the sets, made them less enthusiastic about making the picture. John Lennon later commented that the Beatles were puppets in the movie, and that the strings were being pulled by the experienced actors.

The group's disillusionment, which had started toward the end of 1964, began to invade their personal lives. Though Paul seemed happy with his life and Ringo was excited about the child his wife was expecting, John was experiencing a mild depression about his physical appearance and the direction that his life had taken since the Beatles became famous. He expressed these feeling in the song "Help!," which he wrote three days after the group returned from Austria.

George's love for Patti Boyd was the most positive feeling in his life then. She was the inspiration for the song "I Need You," which Harrison wrote for the movie when the group was in the Bahamas. Though success had given him all the material things he wanted, George was not thoroughly happy with his life with or without the Beatles. During the filming, however, Harrison became influenced by the production's Far Eastern theme. He was introduced to the culture of India on his twenty-second birthday. While the group was in Nassau waiting to film a scene in which they follow a trail of painted footprints made by a man suspended from a dirigible, a swami walked up to them and gave each a book about East Indian philosophy. John, Paul, and Ringo were not interested in the literature, but George began reading the book and was fascinated by the Hindu concept of man's purpose in life. He read the book throughout the Beatles' stay in Nassau and Austria, and wondered if Indian philosophy could restore a sense of order to his life.

George was drawn closer to the East Indian culture on the film sets at Twickenham Studios. Director Richard Lester had hired four musicians to play Beatles songs on Indian instruments, one of which was the sitar. During a break in the filming, George talked to the musicians, who showed him how the instrument was played. He was initially intrigued with the technical aspects of the sitar, but he later learned that the instrument and Indian music were an expression of Indian philosophy. He purchased an inexpensive sitar and began learning to play with the help of the Indian musicians in the movie.

In early May the last major scenes were filmed on Salisbury Plain. The British War Office provided Dick Lester with armored tanks and hundreds of soldiers to participate in a mock battle against the Far Eastern cult. On May 12, the production of *Help!* concluded.

By June 1965, the Beatles had sold an estimated 100 million records worldwide. In addition, nearly 1,400 versions of Lennon/McCartney compositions had been recorded by various artists. The tax that the group and EMI Records were paying to the British government from global record sales was so substantial that it had stimulated the British economy. Prime Minister Harold Wilson, who was well aware of the Beatles' contributions to the export market, persuaded the queen to include John Lennon, Paul McCartney, George Harrison, and

Richard Starkey on her Birthday Honors List and award them the Members of the Most Excellent Order of the British Empire medal. The MBE ranked 120th out of 126 titles that a British subject could receive for distinguished service to the crown and country, and was usually given to civil servants. The Beatles were the first English pop group to be awarded the MBE since the honor's inception in 1917.

The announcement immediately drew vehement outcries from retired soldiers, many of whom returned their medals to the queen in protest. "On behalf of all the men and women who served beyond the call of duty," one letter said, "now its meaning seems worthless." The public and press directed its heaviest criticisms at Prime Minister Wilson for having sanctioned the award, accusing him of undermining the honors system. The only support Harold Wilson received came from six Liverpudlian members of Parliament, who said: "Being the first entertainment group that has captured the American market and brought in its wake great commercial advantages in pound earnings to this country, this House strongly appreciates the action of Her Majesty in awarding the Beatles the MBE."

The Beatles reacted to the news of their award with surprise and amusement, but John wasn't particularly flattered by the honor, feeling that he had compromised himself too much since 1962 in order to publicly maintain an image he had come to loathe. As far as he was concerned, the MBE was the last straw, and his initial reaction was to reject it, until Brian convinced him otherwise.

Paul, George, and Ringo felt it was unthinkable to refuse the honor, but John felt strongly that to accept would be hypocrisy—particularly in light of the British government's support of the Vietnam War. This was the blossoming seed of radical individuality—restrained, at least for the moment, by Brian Epstein's obsession with what was and was not proper. Lennon had no right, Epstein felt, to alter the group's image by voicing his personal opinions. Though John despised the MBE award, he later defended the Beatles' moral right to the title, explaining that they got theirs for entertaining people, not killing them like other recipients.

The MBE award initiated a change in England's attitude

toward the Beatles. A country rich in history, culture, and tradition was now acknowledging itself for the rock 'n' roll music it produced. Although there were other performers who were part of the British Invasion and had helped stimulate the British economy, the Beatles were singled out because they had sold more records. The English Establishment, however, was appalled by the idea of four anarchistic musicians being honored as England's new national heroes. The Beatles knew that the MBE had maneuvered them into a catch-22 position: They were damned for accepting the honor and would have been subjected to greater damnation for refusing. The Beatles also lost a small portion of their following when they accepted the award, although these rebellious teenagers were already switching their allegiance to the more anarchic Rolling Stones.

Following the world premiere of the film *Help!* on July 29 at the London Pavilion, the Beatles decided that they would not appear in another motion picture that cast the group as themselves. The fact was that all four of them, and their music, had matured appreciably since 1962, yet the image they were asked to project remained the same. They were still perceived as the Fab Four, but their music had gradually begun to project a totally different image of the band. These musical changes were evident on the group's fifth Parlophone LP, *Help!*, which was released in early August 1965.

John had begun to compose tunes subjectively rather than objectively, which was apparent in the tracks "Help!" and "You've Got to Hide Your Love Away," both of which Lennon said were written in his Dylan days. Paul composed many of his songs in the standard pop/rock style, though his love for Jane Asher inspired him on occasion to express his feelings in such songs as "All My Loving" and "And I Love Her." "Yesterday," one of Paul's compositions on the *Help!* album, is regarded today as a classic. The song was one of three written by McCartney in 1965 after an argument with Jane led the couple to separate for a while. He felt it was "the most complete" song he'd ever written.

"Yesterday" was the group's first recording to be scored for orchestral strings and the first track to feature musicians other than the Beatles, or George Martin, who had played the piano on tunes such as "Money" and "A Hard Day's Night." At first Paul was hesitant about the strings, fearing a Mantovani effect, but when Martin suggested a simple string quartet, Paul went along.

The song marked the beginning of a new musical direction for the Beatles, which was initiated by George Martin. They now made efforts to break out of the four-instrument mode and became much more experimental. Many critics began to regard them as serious artists.

On August 15, 1965, the Beatles embarked on a sixteen-day American concert tour guaranteed to net them $2 million. They were booked to perform in outdoor sports complexes that held audiences of 50,000. Before leaving England, John, Paul, George, and Ringo were each insured for $1 million by Lloyds of London.

The tour opened in New York at Shea Stadium, where the Beatles performed for two consecutive nights before 56,000 fans, which was then the largest audience to attend a rock concert. The teenagers' excitement rose to the point of hysteria, which only subsided during the playing of the national anthem. When disc jockey Murray ("the K") Kaufman, who emceed the show, announced that the Beatles were in their dressing room, fans screamed throughout the performances of King Curtis, Brenda Holloway, Sounds Incorporated, and the Discotheque Dancers.

The Beatles had arrived at Shea Stadium hours earlier. They sat in their dressing room listening to the screams and tried to overcome their fear that fans would rush the stage and mob them. Before the show, John and Paul made a bet with each other as to which side of the stadium would break through first. During the Beatles' thirty-minute performance, which was filmed and later broadcast on American and British television, fans tried to get past police lines and reach the stage in the middle of the ballpark, but security was well organized and no one got close to the group.

They wound up enjoying their dates at Shea. There was one sour note, however. That first night, they returned to the Warwick Hotel to watch the news reports on television, and were appalled by what they saw. Ed Lefler, an agent from GAC in charge of security on the tour, recalls: "It was the night rioters burned down Watts. Just think, here the Beatles are creating all this fun and excitement—remember, they were from another country and didn't know about all this—and after this incredible evening, they came back and saw the decay on television. They felt strange . . . it was something they found hard to comprehend." During the tour, Paul shocked the American press by saying, "I believe Negroes will be in control one of these days. Then they'll make the white people suffer as they've suffered. It may sound cruel, but it's only natural, isn't it?"

After the dates at Shea Stadium, the Beatles performed in Toronto, Atlanta, and Houston. The intensity of Beatlemania had doubled since 1964, as had the unpleasant aspects of their popularity.

"We arrived in Houston about two o'clock in the morning and there were about ten thousand fans at the airport," remembers Ed Lefler. "We taxied up to a special place and all hell broke loose. Kids broke through the police barriers and swarmed all over the plane. We couldn't do anything; we were stuck in the plane because they couldn't start the engines. A lot of guys were there because they figured a lot of girls would come out to the airport, and it got violent. The photographers were there and they egged the crowd on more and more.

"I went into the cockpit and asked them to send a fire truck over to hose down the kids so no one would get hurt, but they refused to do that. What they finally did was send one of those catering trucks, which was about ten feet high, but it was open on both sides. We decided to chance it and got out. The Beatles, Neil, and Mal Evans and myself went out on this open van, and the guys started throwing rocks at us and one hit Mal on the side of the head, knocking off his glasses. It was frightening."

After appearing at Comiskey Park in Chicago, the group's flight to Minneapolis provided more anxious moments for the Beatles. "The plane was about to land," recalls Ed Lefler, "and one of the engines caught fire. I saw the fire first and tried to keep everyone calm. To give you an example of John Lennon's humor under duress, as I walked down the aisle, John stood up and screamed, 'Women and children and Beatles off first!' It just got everyone laughing and relaxed."

On August 21 the Beatles performed at Metropolitan Stadium in Minneapolis. After the concert, the group returned to the Lemmings Motor Inn—an appropriate name, since thousands of fans converged there, and stayed well past midnight. The police started clearing the kids away around one o'clock, but one girl remained. When Assistant Police Chief Ronald Dywer asked why she had not gone home, she told him that her girlfriend was in Paul's room. Dywer, who was also an inspector with the vice squad, began banging on the door, ordering McCartney to let him in under threat of arrest. When the police walked in, they found Paul alone with the girl. He said she was twenty-one years old and the president of one of their fan clubs, but after questioning, Dywer learned that she was fourteen. The situation looked bad for McCartney: It was after 1 A.M. and Paul could have been arrested for contributing to the delinquency of a minor. But the girl's parents decided not to press charges.

The fact remained, however, that even the most innocent connection between Paul and a fourteen-year-old girl could have been devastating to the Beatles had the press decided to distort the story. It was yet another reminder of the need to be discreet because they were being watched day and night by reporters and fans, who deemed everything the group did newsworthy. Dave Dexter, Jr., remembers how a cynical John Lennon reacted to being under the microscope at a private party hosted by Capitol Records in Beverly Hills.

"The booze flowed, the inane small talk of close to hundred guests had gradually increased to a roar. Dozens of nicely dressed, courteous little neighborhood boys and girls assembled at nearby residences, politely calling for John, Paul, George, and Ringo to step outside for a moment. George couldn't; he was visiting his sister. John, Paul, and Ringo wouldn't. I asked Lennon why. 'Bloody little bastards,' he answered almost viciously, 'try to interfere with us constantly, trying to deprive us of our privacy. We've had it with 'em, mate!' "

The 1965 American tour brought the group's distaste for performing to its highest level. John and George, in particular, felt that Beatlemania had gone too far; that it had reached a momentum impossible to stop. Depending on the group's mood and whether or not they liked a venue, a show would last thirty-five minutes or the boys would rush through their performance.

The physical exhaustion of touring was less of a factor in 1965; more important were the pressures to which the Beatles were subjected. Wherever they performed, threats were made on their lives by teenage boys whose girlfriends had fallen in love with one or another of the Beatles. "Threats on their lives couldn't be shrugged off, nor could we accept the reality of them either," says Ed Lefler. "We just checked and double-checked the security and felt confident it was the best it could be." Though Brian Epstein and GAC agents did not mention the death threats to John, Paul, George, and Ringo, all four were haunted by one fear every time they performed before 50,000 fans: "If the audience rushes the stage, we'll be helpless."

Following a performance at Dodger Stadium in Los Angeles, the Beatles spent five days relaxing in California. They rented a house at 2850 Benedict Canyon in Beverly Hills, where they were visited by movie stars and such music personalities as Jim McGuinn of the Byrds. During this break, all except Paul experimented with LSD. They'd smoked marijuana throughout the tour, but were so afraid Brian Epstein would catch them that they posted guards outside their hotel suite and smoked in the bathroom.

Four days before the tour ended, the Beatles met Elvis Presley. The group's admiration for Elvis had not diminished since their schoolboy days, and during the February 1964 tour they had Capitol Records employees running all over New York acquiring Presley's entire record catalog. Elvis, though, was not eager to meet the Beatles. Those close to him said he was jealous of their success and viewed the quartet as his rivals. Brian Epstein had tried to set up a meeting the year before at the boys' request, but Elvis told his manager, Colonel Tom Parker, to make up an excuse to avoid it. Parker eventually persuaded his star to see the group, though Presley insisted that they come to him. The Colonel told Epstein, "Elvis is dying to meet the Beatles!"

The meeting was arranged for August 27 at Presley's home on Perugia Way in Bel Air. "The boys were scared to death," recalls Bob Bonis. "They were nervous wrecks. The biggest nervous wreck was Mal Evans. He was the president of the Elvis Presley Fan Club of England, and they were laughing at him, trying to cover their nervousness."

When the Beatles arrived at Presley's mansion, they were greeted at the door by Elvis himself. He led them into the living room, where John, Paul, George, and Ringo sat together on a couch, not saying a word, merely staring at their boyhood idol in awe. After five minutes of this, Presley became annoyed and said, "Well, look, if you guys are gonna sit there and stare at me all night, I'm gonna go to bed! I just thought we'd sit around and talk. We can talk about some music and maybe play a little, jam a little."

The awestruck Liverpudlians snapped back to reality. Paul said, "God, we'd love to play with you!" Lennon and McCartney talked with Elvis on one side of the room. He told them how much he liked their music, and John jokingly said that they did not like his anymore. "You should go back to your original sound," John said. "It was the greatest sound you ever had." Ringo played pool with one of Presley's roadies, and George hardly said a word all night.

Normally, celebrities were eager to meet the Beatles. But though the boys enjoyed talking with Bob Dylan, Joan Baez, and Mike Love of the Beach Boys, Elvis was the one person in America they'd really wanted to meet. "We can't tell you what a thrill it was," said John as they left. Presley later denied that the meeting ever took place.

Some celebrities actually forced themselves on the Beatles, and the boys became disgusted with such people who had become attached to them and were making a career out of their association with the group. "Murry the K was a pet peeve of the Beatles," says Bob Bonis. "They hated him with a venom. If you wanted to get the Beatles uptight, just show them a story about the 'fifth Beatle.'" Kaufman had awarded himself this "honorary" status during the February 1964 tour and continued to use the title until Brian Epstein threatened him with a lawsuit.

*   *   *

The American tour ended in San Francisco on August 31 with matinee and evening performances at the Cow Palace. During the first show, there was inadequate security and a riot erupted causing the matinee concert to become known in San Francisco as "the battle of Cow Palace." Teenage girls hurled themselves toward the stage into a line of security men. Keith Power, writing in the *San Francisco Chronicle,* said, "Most of the teenage girls who broke through the police lines and reached the stage appeared overcome with the nearness to the Beatles and simply swooned onto the floor. The four young men from Liverpool, who returned to San Francisco guarded like royalty, reacted to the wild reception with gracious aplomb. A year older and still slightly amused by their success, they ritually belted out songs and music their thousands of subjects had paid not to hear."

At the height of the pandemonium, fans rushed the stage, running over chairs and trampling people in their path. Security men dragged twenty girls off the stage, two of whom held John and Paul in a bear hug. Several teenage boys also made their way onto the stage. One boy stole a hat that John was wearing, and another tried to punch Lennon in the stomach. All during the performance, the Beatles were pelted with class rings, stuffed animals, and whatever else fans could throw. One security guard was knocked unconscious by an empty soda bottle. Paul stopped the concert twice—once so security guards could remove a pregnant woman from the audience, and another time to restore order. "Listen! Listen!" said McCartney. "All right now, don't push. Things are getting out of hand!" Despite Paul's plea, the fans persisted. A reporter from the *Chronicle* said, "At no time did one single Beatle note penetrate the jetlike screams."

On October 26, the Beatles presented themselves in the Great Throne Room at Buckingtham Palace to receive their MBE medals. The boys were nervous about the ceremony, and John Lennon recalls that the group smoked marijuana in one of the palace washrooms to relax before the investiture. (George Harrison remembers smoking only a cigarette.) An hour before the presentation, the Beatles were instructed by a palace guardsman on how to walk and behave when acceping their honor from the queen. "Every time he read out the names and got to Ringo Starr, he kept cracking up," said John.

They could not help but be impressed by the display of pageantry in the palace. There were 180 people receiving awards that day, and as the group stood in line, awaiting their cue to walk toward the throne, musicians from the Coldstream Guard solemnly performed selections from *Bitter Sweet* and *Humoresque*. Their names called, the boys walked four paces, bowed, and shook hands with the queen, who pinned the silver medals on their left lapels and said a few words to the group:

HER MAJESTY: How long have you been together?
PAUL: Oh, for many years.
RINGO: Forty years.
HER MAJESTY: Are you the one who started it all?
RINGO: No, ma'am. I was the last one to join. I'm the little fella.

John, Paul, George, and Ringo took four steps backward and bowed again.

After the investiture, the Beatles held a press conference, where they displayed their medals and talked about the ceremony. Each of the Beatles also received a framed letter signed by the queen proclaiming that they were members of the Most Excellent Order of the British Empire. John destroyed his letter by scratching out each line of the proclamation with a knife, and gave his MBE medal to Aunt Mimi, who placed the honor on top of her television set, where it rested for four years.

From mid-October to early November, the Beatles worked in the Abbey Road Studios recording the songs for their sixth Parlophone album, *Rubber Soul*, which was issued in the U.K. on December 3. The title was suggested by Paul and was meant to be a pun about England's infatuation with soul music. The LP heralded the beginning of the group's studio years, which are regarded as their most creative period as a band.

Rubber Soul was an artistic breakthrough for the Beatles. The change in the group's musical direction, which was inspired by "Yesterday," led them to begin experimenting on a minimal level with nonrock musical styles, which in turn influenced Lennon and McCartney's approach to songwriting. Furthermore, the Beatles brought into the studio the knowledge that many of their English and American contemporaries were releasing records that introduced unique sounds to pop/rock, such as the Rolling Stones' use of the fuzz box on "Satisfaction."

George Martin's role as the group's producer had begun to change from master and his pupils to servant of four masters. The Beatles—mainly John and Paul—started to produce the albums, and they kept gaining expertise.

On this album the compositions of John Lennon and Paul McCartney are sensitive and cleverly phrased, but there is a noticeable difference in their styles, indicating that the two were beginning to drift apart.

Rubber Soul featured six Lennon songs, three of which he said were autobiographical. "In My Life" was originally conceived as an imaginary bus journey from Menlove Avenue through Woolton, during which Lennon remembered the people and the places he had known and loved as a child and teenager growing up in Liverpool. The song "Nowhere Man" was inspired by John's unsuccessful attempt to compose another tune. He had sat at a piano for several hours trying to think of lyrics to accompany the chord combinations he was playing, but got nowhere. "Norwegian Wood" told the story of an affair he'd had but he phrased the lyrics in such a way that his wife would not know.

Paul McCartney composed four tunes for the album, including "I'm Looking Through You," which he wrote during and about his brief separation from Jane Asher; and George Harrison contributed two songs to the album: "Think for Yourself" and "If I Needed Someone." He also wrote the bass line to "Drive My Car" and played the sitar on "Norwegian Wood," which introduced raga-rock to pop music and inspired other groups to use the instrument on their recordings. Harrison had begun to assert himself as a songwriter on the Beatles' last album, but his efforts were stifled by John and Paul, who showed little interest in his writing and gave him little encouragement.

The release of the *Rubber Soul* album coincided with the Beatles' fifth national tour, which opened on December 3 in Glasgow, Scotland, and closed nine days later in Cardiff, Wales. It was the group's shortest tour of England, and their last.

12

Before the year 1966 had begun, the Beatles decided that they no longer wanted to present themselves as the Fab Four. Though this concept had proved lucrative in 1963–64, the group had outgrown the image by 1966 and saw no reason to maintain the pretense.

While many less successful pop stars envied the Beatles' youth, fame, and glamorous life-style, the group was half hoping for a decline in their popularity, which they referred to as the Downfall. They had endured Beatlemania for over two years, and during this time they had learned that fame meant living like prisoners, perpetuating an image that the public liked no matter how condescending it was to the musical and intellectual growth they had experienced, and controlling their anger when subjected to the indignities of rude and ignorant people.

Paul McCartney, whom the other Beatles had nicknamed "the star" because he loved the adulation and touring, was the last member of the group to realize fame's shortcomings. Being a Beatle was not, as George Harrison said then, "the living end!" The irrationality of Beatlemania had forced John, Paul, George, and Ringo to mature far beyond their age to survive the madness and absurdity going on around them.

The Beatles' attitudes toward themselves had changed so markedly that their third motion picture, A Talent for Loving, did not see fruition. The film, based on Richard Condon's novel, would have cast John, Paul, George, and Ringo in a cowboy comedy set in Mexico. The group was supposed to begin filming in April 1966 and record a sound track of western music. Producer Walter Shenson, who met with the Beatles during their last tour of England to discuss the movie, recalls: "They said to me, 'We don't want to play the Beatles anymore!' I said, 'Well, you are the Beatles! I didn't create you; you created yourselves. I don't know how I can make a movie with four guys and call them Joe, Walter, Sam, and Charlie. You're always going to be the Beatles!' John pointed out, 'We've been talking for twenty minutes and I haven't called you by your first name and you haven't called me by my first name, so why do we have to be named anything?' I said, 'Any movie you make, you're always going to be the Beatles.'"

The conflict between their individual identities and their joint identity as Beatles led them to begin ridding themselves of anything that perpetuated or projected the Fab Four image. By early 1966 they began taking steps to regain control over the direction of their careers. Having decided that they would not appear in any film as the Beatles, the group also tried to put an end to touring, which they felt inhibited their creativity. "The Beatles said that they didn't want to do the 1966 dates," says Tony Barrow, "but Brian Epstein was able to persuade them to do so. I don't think Brian believed that the 1966 dates would be the last, but the Beatles did. Brian was convinced that he would be able to talk them around for another year when the time came."

The Beatles wanted to devote the time and energy they invested in touring and filming each year to something more artistically meaningful to them. Following the release and critical acclaim of Rubber Soul, the group just wanted to grow musically.

In late March 1966, the Beatles began recording the selections for their seventh British LP, *Revolver*. The sessions lasted two and a half months, the longest time the group had ever devoted to producing an album. They also recorded the songs "Paperback Writer" and "Rain," both of which were issued on a single on June 10 by Parlophone. "Rain" was the most significant of the two tracks. Composed by John Lennon, it was the first pop/rock recording to use backward masking with the line "Can you hear me? Can you hear me?" After recording the song one night, John stumbled home at five A.M. and put on the tape, but it came out backward. He liked it so much he wanted to release the whole song that way, but of course that wasn't feasible.

Drugs were a staple of the Beatles' diet then. Though Paul was still afraid to use LSD, and Ringo, after one psychedelic experience, stopped taking the drug because the effects had shocked him, Lennon and Harrison ate LSD like candy, and had "thousands of trips," according to John.

Toward the end of June 1966, the Beatles embarked on their last world tour—a total of twenty-two dates in West Germany, Japan, the Philippines, and America. Before the tour, a London fashion designer created new stage clothes for the group, who wanted to project a more stylish and mature image, much to Brian Epstein's consternation. The tour opened on June 24 at the Circus Krone in Munich, West Germany. Following a date in Essen, the Beatles returned to Hamburg for the first time in three and a half years. Prior to their performance at the Ernst Merck Halle, the group renewed old friendships. John visited Astrid Kirchnerr, who gave him two letters written by Stuart Sutcliffe before he died. Paul looked up an old girlfriend he had dated during the Beatles' Hamburg period. McCartney and his date went to the Indra and Star clubs, and met with Dr. Bernstein, who had once been the group's physician.

En route to Japan, the Beatles spent ten hours in Anchorage, Alaska, waiting out a typhoon that was hitting the island. They arrived in Tokyo on June 29 for appearances at the Budo Kahn Hall under the threat of death from the followers of Budo, a martial art that combines judo and karate. Vic Lewis, who was then the managing director of NEMS, arrived in Japan two weeks ahead of the entourage to arrange the security.

"We had thirty-five hundred policemen for the five days that they were there," says Lewis. "The reason we had the police was that the Budo Kahn was a hall of worship and the people there said, 'If the Beatles come in, they won't come out alive!' I attended nine conferences with the police. It was just like a president of a country was coming there. We sat there with chalkboards, and on every solitary bridge on the route from the Hilton Hotel to the Budo Kahn there were machine guns, because these people threatened to shoot the Beatles. They said it was a disgrace for the Japanese government to allow pop music to take place in a hall of worship. Since then, every pop act has played there, but the Beatles were the first."

The Beatles and their entourage occupied the top floor of the Tokyo Hilton. A policeman with a gun was stationed in each bedroom, and a service elevator providing the only access to the top floor also had an armed guard on it day and night. The boys were told not to leave the hotel by themselves at any time.

The following day the group traveled by limousine to the Budo Kahn. "In the first car were the four boys," says Vic Lewis. "In the second car were Brian Epstein, Tony Barrow, and myself. Neil and Mal followed in the third car. We were off at eighty miles per hour and we never stopped until we got to the backstage of the Budo Kahn. Whichever way we went on the route, police followed our movements by electronics and walkie-talkies. It was a journey of about six miles. When we got to the other end, there were sixty policemen with rifles and bayonets as we drove into the building."

The Japanese Patriotic party, a right-wing political group, staged a demonstration outside the Budo Kahn, carrying signs that read, BEAT THE BEATLES, THE RIVERBANK BEGGARS, OUT OF JAPAN! The security precautions prevented the protesters and the followers of Budo from getting near the group.

The next stop was Manila. Despite a rapturous welcome on July 3 from 55,000 fans at the airport, the Beatles' two-day stay in the Philippines was their worst experience on tour. They were hauled off the plane by stone-faced "gorillas," their 'diplomatic bags' taken from them, and then they were taken to a boat in Manila Bay.The boys, thinking they were under arrest, were frightened that these "gorillas" would search their hand baggage and find the marijuana stashed in each piece. They were detained for nearly three hours before Brian arrived with Neil and Mal and angrily demanded that they be released. The police did not explain why they had detained the group, but allowed them to leave, without their bags, for the hotel, which was surrounded by 1,000 policemen—all with guns. John, Paul, George, and Ringo sat in their suite, still worrying that the police in Manila Bay would discover the marijuana they had smuggled into the country, but an hour later the bags were returned and nothing was said.

The following day the group performed for an audience of 100,000 in the Arenta Coliseum, which was designed to hold only 70,000. The concert went well, but when they got back to the hotel to watch the reporting on TV all they saw was Mrs. Marcos and a bunch of sad children. It seems they were expected to appear at a luncheon even though they had declined. Brian Epstein appeared on television to explain the situation, but the transmission was drowned by static. The media in Manila began reporting on how the Beatles had snubbed the president's wife. They couldn't get newspapers or room service, and on the way back to the airport got no police escort.

Neil and Mal had managed to get the Beatles and their entourage transportation to the airport, but when they arrived, no one would assist them with their luggage and equipment even though Beatlemania was still going strong. As the group entered the terminal building, angry Filipino adults shouted, spat, and cursed at them. Then the crowd became violent and began throwing things at the Beatles. John and George were roughed up against a wall; Ringo was knocked to the ground and kicked; only Paul somehow managed to escape unscathed. British Airways officials helped the boys carry their baggage, guitars, and amplifiers up a flight of stairs, but Filipino airport employees blocked their way to the reservation counter and incited the crowd to molest them.

The Beatles eventually got away from the angry mob and made their way to the airport lounge, where the "gorillas" reappeared. The police harassed the members of the entourage by pointing their fingers at them and shouting, *"Bang!"* and even hitting the Beatles' people. The plane's departure was delayed for thirty minutes by Manila authorities, who made Brian Epstein hand over half of the group's earnings from their Arenta Coliseum performance.

Beatlemania had given them some rough moments before, but never had they experienced such pure, crystallized fear. What little pleasure they still derived from their fame drained away. They wanted out.

The solitude of the Abbey Road Studios offered the Beatles an escape from the pressures of their public lives, a creative sanctuary in which they could immerse themselves in experimenting with new sounds, styles, concepts, and approaches to songwriting. It was apparent that the group had been working on a higher level of creativity when their next Parlophone LP, *Revolver*, was released in the U.K. on August 5, 1966.

The Beatles were anxious to see how their fans would react to the album, because the music was a radical departure from anything they had recorded before. *Revolver* did not attempt to cater to teenage fans' musical tastes; rather, it reflected the group's own interests and personal experiences and feelings.

New Musical Express writers Nick Logan and Bob Wolfenden called *Revolver* the Beatles' "most consistently successful album. The painstaking care granted to each track was quite unique, as was both the scope and the unimpaired brilliance of their inventiveness. It showed that touring for them had become something more than an irritating duty." With this LP, the group had progressed past the experimental phase and had committed themselves to being a studio band who would explore the spectrum of music with no regard for how it would affect their fan following.

The Downfall that the Beatles were half hoping for materialized in America shortly before the release of *Revolver*. In late March 1966, John had expressed his views on religion in an interview with Maureen Cleave, a journalist from the *London Evening Standard*. "Christianity will go. It will vanish and shrink. I needn't argue about that; I'm right and I will be proved right. We're more popular than Jesus now. I don't know which will go first, Christianity or rock 'n' roll. Jesus was all right, but his disciples were thick and ordinary. It's them twisting it that ruins it for me."

Lennon's remark hardly fazed the English public, but before the Beatles launched their final U.S. tour on August 12, the American teen magazine *Datebook* published the interview. The result was a mass movement to denounce the group and John Lennon.

The movement began in Birmingham, Alabama, when disc jockey Tommy Charles, of station WAQY, read the quote over the air and immediately announced that WAQY would ban the Beatles until a retraction was made. "I wasn't defending the church; I was defending sanity," says Charles. "Who in the hell does Lennon think he is telling me that Christianity is not as big as he is, or church is not as popular as he is, and that Christ's disciples are thick and ordinary? That's how I felt. It was offensive."

The boycott would have remained local had it not been for an Associated Press reporter driving through Birmingham listening to Charles's broadcast. He put the story over the wire: COMMENT ON JESUS SPURS A RADIO BAN AGAINST THE BEATLES! Within hours a dozen radio stations throughout America joined the boycott; others staged public bonfires and encouraged teenagers to bring symbols of the group's popularity to be burned. Published photographs showed children, too young to grasp the nature of the issue, destroying Beatles records and souvenirs.

Lennon's remark reinforced the belief of many people that there was something satanic about rock 'n' roll. But the Beatles were to be doubly feared—they were foreigners bent on the manipulation of American youth. Certainly the Beatles wanted to influence youth all over the world, but in a different manner than their detractors believed. To them, Lennon was blatantly playing the role of the antichrist, defying and challenging God Himself. Lennon's blasphemy not only infuriated the evangelists and fanatic Christians, but was perceived by millions as the height of conceit. Ironically, the Beatles had expressed much harsher views on religion to *Playboy* magazine the year before, but their remarks did not encourage any negative reactions in America.

Brian Epstein left a sickbed in London and flew to New York to try to quell the controversy. "Norman Weiss and I met Brian at the airport, and he was a very worried person," recalls Bob Bonis. "The situation was serious enough to bring him to America to talk to the press, because there was no point in having it get worse and worse." At a press conference, Brian said: "The quote that John Lennon made to a London columnist nearly three months ago has been quoted and misrepresented entirely out of context of an article that is, in fact, highly complimentary to Lennon as a person and was understood by him to be exclusive to the *London Evening Standard*. It was not anticipated that it would be displayed out of context and in such a manner as it was in an American teenage magazine. In the circumstances, John is deeply concerned and regrets that people with certain religious beliefs should have been offended in any way." When asked whether John would change his remarks, Epstein replied, "It's highly unlikely."

Despite Brian's efforts to explain John's statement, more radio stations in America and throughout the world joined the boycott. Maureen Cleave tried to explain that John had been "observing that the state of Christianity was so weak that the Beatles were better known to people," but the public did not see the statement as a commentary on the times. Each person who was offended by the remark interpreted it in a different way. Journalist Ralph Gleason, writing in the *San Francisco Chronicle*, said: "The fuss about Lennon's remark was a symptom of a sick society. No radio station that was ever a factor in the pop music field banned the Beatles disc. Only stations that didn't matter banned them. Lennon's remark has been attacked by everybody but the church, and his critics are in the interesting position of being more righteous than the religious leaders."

A concerned Brian Epstein, after telling the press that promoters of the group's fourteen-city U.S. tour were not anxious to cancel the concerts, privately asked Nathan Weiss, his American attorney, how much it would cost to cancel the tour. When Weiss told him one million dollars, Brian was willing to pay the money himself because he didn't want anything to happen to them. Epstein was told by GAC agent Norman Weiss that canceling the tour would create a bigger problem.

By the time the Beatles left Heathrow Airport for their tour, they were extremely pessimistic, particularly Lennon. "We've never left for America with this sort of feeling before," he said. "Frankly, I'm worried." The whole situation had a terrible emotional effect on John, as Tony Barrow recalls: "It was a totally different John Lennon that I certainly hadn't seen before. At the time, he was a changed person and under tremendous nervous stress because he took all this badly. A guy who normally has a very strong, very biting sense of humor was shaking physically and mentally. He was at a loss for words and didn't know how to cope with it all."

On August 12 the Beatles arrived in Chicago to begin their U.S. tour. At a press conference, John went to great lengths to explain what he'd meant—and what he had not meant. "If I had said television was more popular than Jesus, I might have gotten away with it. As I just happened to be talking with a friend, I used the word *Beatles* as a remote thing. But I'm not saying we're better or greater or comparing us with Jesus Christ as a person. I just said what I said and it was wrong, or it was taken wrong, and now there's all this . . . I never meant it as a lousy antireligious thing. From what I've read or observed, Christianity just seems to be shrinking, to be losing contact. My views on Christianity are directly influenced by a book, *The Passover Plot* by Hugh J. Schonfield. The premise in it is that Jesus' message had been garbled by his disciples and twisted for a variety of self-serving reasons by those who followed, to the point that it has lost validity for many in the modern age."

At the end of his explanation, a reporter shouted, "Okay, John, are you prepared to apologize?" In desperation Lennon said, "If it will make you all happy, I'll apologize. I'm sorry I opened my mouth. I still don't know what I've done!"

The apology was accepted by the press. The *Chicago Daily News* ran the headline LENNON FORGIVEN, BEATLES MOSEY ON RICHER THAN EVER! Even the Vatican accepted John's retraction in the *L'Observatore Romano*, one of the most influential newspapers in the world, saying, "Lennon gave Christians a well-placed kick where it was most needed!"

Throughout the tour, backlash from the statement continued to be of constant concern to the Beatles. Brian Epstein and GAC agents took every threat more seriously than before. GAC hired four ex–FBI agents, who were former presidential bodyguards, to protect the boys. It was a strange time for the Beatles—everything was so much different. They had seen an angry, almost violent reaction from a country that had once cheerfully welcomed them. Added to the anxiety and feelings of entrapment that touring had always evoked, this recalcitrant reaction stirred longtime feelings of bitterness in each of the boys, making them resentful of the road and their fans. The typical jovial press conference was now a thing of the past. The press discovered that the Fab Four were actually quite opinionated young men and began to ask them serious questions, such as how they felt about the Vietnam War, to which they replied that "war is wrong."

Lennon had added a new object of contempt to his list: America. The American press and public had forced him to eat crow for his earlier remark, and John harbored a degree of hatred for the U.S. and much of what comprised the American way of life. At a press conference in Toronto, Lennon encouraged young Americans to flee to Canada to avoid fighting in Vietnam.

On August 19, the Beatles arrived in Memphis, the heart of the Bible Belt, where criticism against the group was most fervent. Before the date, the mayor of the city had made an unsuccessful attempt to ban the group from Memphis: "We're going to protect Memphians against the Beatles' use of the public Coliseum to ridicule anyone's religion." While the Beatles performed inside, the Ku Klux Klan demonstrated outside, carrying a large wooden cross with a Beatles record affixed to it. Security was tight because of numerous death threats against John. "A firecracker went off among the crowd," says Tony Barrow, "and immediately my eyes flashed across to John, and so did [those of] the other three Beatles, to see if he was going to fall flat on the stage with a bullet in him."

After appearances in Cincinnati and St. Louis, the Beatles gave two shows at Shea Stadium. The press, noting that the stadium's 56,000 seats were only eighty-percent filled, stated

that the group's era of surefire sellouts had passed. The Beatles
did lose some fans because of John's remark, but it didn't
matter to them—they just wanted the tour to be over. Before
the group appeared onstage, the management of Shea Stadium
presented them with a large cake. Upon learning that the cake
did not contain a scantily clad woman, John said, "We don't
want any of your fuckin' cake!" and walked away.

Toward the end of the tour, John, Paul, George, and Ringo
were physically and mentally wiped out. Bob Bonis recalls:
"They were still really nice, personally, but it was becoming
too much of a chore. You could tell that they'd just about had
it, and they were happy to tell you that. Their shows were less
energetic, but the fans didn't notice. The Beatles were going to
do some new numbers and were going to rehearse, but they
never got around to it. I went out and bought some props
because they were going to do 'Yellow Submarine.' I spent five
hundred dollars on ship bells and foghorns—in fact, for years
the big ship bell that I got for them adorned George Harrison's
door. They just stuck to the old tried-and-true—the old comfortable numbers."

The Beatles gave their last concert performance at Candlestick Park in San Francisco on August 29, 1966. It was not
publicly announced as their farewell, but as Tony Barrow remembers, "There was this kind of feeling among all of us who
were around the Beatles that this might be the last concert.
They seemed to put in extra ad-lib material that they really
hadn't put in on any other occasion."

Immediately following the show at Candlestick Park, the
Beatles flew to Los Angeles and boarded another plane for the
long flight back to England. George Harrison wearily took his
seat, sipped a drink, and casually said, "Well, that's it. I'm
finished. I'm not a Beatle anymore."

13

After three and a half years of performing before thousands of hysterical fans in seventeen countries, the Beatles decided to end this aspect of their careers.

It had become obscene—a perversion of the promise of the early days when teenagers were drawn to the clubs of Liverpool and Hamburg to see and hear the Beatles. These early fans had shared an intimacy with the group unknown to the tens of thousands of Beatlemaniacs who screamed, gasped, and basked in the quartet's afterglow. The massive crowds came to witness the presence of gods, to worship their idols. Hearing the music was not necessary, or possible.

John, Paul, George, and Ringo understood to an extent why teenagers responded hysterically, but they were unable to comprehend how fame could bring so much madness and confusion into the lives of four musicians whose collective ambition was to earn a living by performing rock 'n' roll music. They could not answer this question then nor five years after the group disbanded, when each said that they could look back on their lives in the 1960s with objectivity. Remembering the touring years, John felt that the Beatles' greatest accomplishment was "remaining sane" amid "the lunacy that surrounded us."

According to Paul, the Beatles did not at the time view their fans' hysteria as "lunacy." Beatlemania was indeed an extraordinary experience—it changed the lives of all four of the Beatles and spiritually bonded them together for the rest of their lives. Yet somehow, amid the hysteria of the touring years, the public overlooked the fact that the Beatles were four human beings. As the intensity and scope of the group's popularity increased, so did the absurdities to which they were subjected. References to the Beatles as "gods" were not merely fan rhetoric: There were adults who believed that the group possessed the power to heal the sick; during the 1965 American tour, people would bring blind, crippled and deformed children to them to be healed. It's not surprising they put up a wall between themselves and the rest of the world.

After the Beatles finished their last tour of England, they were prepared to give up touring, not for musical reasons then, but because they feared for their lives. The North American tours instilled this fear in them. For instance, during the group's extensive 1964 tour, they arrived in Montreal and were informed that a death threat had been made on the life of Ringo Starr, and a policeman sat on stage to protect him. Toward the end of the tour, in Dallas, several teenage boys, jealous that their girlfriends had fallen in love with one of the Beatles, stood at the end of the runway with pistols and rifles and fired at the group's chartered American Flyers plane. Years later, the pilot of the plane told George Harrison that the tail and wings were riddled with bullet holes.

Their nerves were always taut from the pressures, particularly when John was labeled a satanist and the group toured America under the threat of violence. Following a show in the rain in Cincinnati's Crosley Field on August 20, 1966, Paul returned to the hotel and vomited from the tension and fear of being electrocuted.

On tour the group's artistic freedom and sense of performance dissolved into a stage show that, to them, was so predictable as to be monotonous. They played the same twenty-minute set show after show and started going out of their minds with boredom. John felt they lost all their skill as musicians as a result of the repetition.

Despite Lennon's harsh self-assessment, the group's music, amid the chaos of Beatlemania, *had* matured and improved. By 1966 they were no longer regarded as a social phenomenon, but were considered prolific composers and artists. Their music had become so sophisticated that they could not perform many of the songs from *Rubber Soul* or *Revolver*, especially with the orchestral and electronic scores incorporated into the arrangements. Thus, while Beatles music displayed a high level of creativity, they performed relatively sophomoric tunes onstage to please the fans. As a result, the group declared to themselves that they would never tour again, although they didn't make an official announcement at the time.

On August 31, 1966, the Beatles returned to England from America. Immediately following the tour, John, Paul, George, and Ringo went their separate ways, having decided to regroup in the recording studio in December. They would have three months to relax, collect their thoughts, and devote themselves to the interests that touring had not allowed them to fully pursue.

In mid-September, John traveled to West Germany and had his hair cut short for the role of Private Musketeer Gripweed in Dick Lester's antiwar film *How I Won the War*. It was a very positive experience for him, as he felt for the first time that he wasn't "a monkey on display." John spent a month and a half shooting in Spain, then returned home.

George devoted his three-month holiday away from the Beatles to understanding the Indian culture, which, by the fall of 1966, he no longer regarded as just a hobby. Since acquiring what he termed a "crummy" sitar, he frequently spent his time off at the Asian Music Circle in London and met with musicians who instructed him on the instrument. These sessions enabled him to play the sitar on "Norwegian Wood." In June 1966, before the Beatles embarked on their last world tour, he was introduced to Ravi Shankar by the man who directed the Asian Music Circle. Shankar taught him the basics of the sitar.

In October the spiritual refuge of Hinduism and musical

expression of India drew George to India. He took yoga lessons, studied the sitar under Ravi Shankar, and practiced every day with Shankar's students. Harrison attended an eye-opening religious festival on the banks of the Ganges River that profoundly moved him.

Ringo did not involve himself in any artistic ventures after touring. He received numerous offers to act in films but turned them down because directors wanted to exploit his name. Ringo still sought the workingman's simplicity. His desires and dreams were always humble, and he never had as many problems with his identity as the others. He found stability through his desire to keep things simple. Maureen had given birth to a son, Zak, on September 13 at Queen Charlotte's Hospital in London. After the American tour, Ringo and his family traveled to the south of France for a holiday and later to Spain, where he visited with John.

Paul McCartney had definite ideas about what he would do with his life once touring was over. He continued an on-again, off-again appreciation of classical and symphonic music; he had amassed an extensive record collection that included the works of Brahms, Bach, and Beethoven, as well as the recordings of the experimental artists Stockhausen, Cage, and Bussotti. McCartney's wealth led him to become more aristocratic than John, George, and Ringo. He dined at the finest restaurants, attended exhibitions at prominent art galleries, and was seen in the audience of major theatrical productions in the company of Jane Asher. Paul also devoted time to reading the work of leading novelists.

Absorbed in his upper-middle-class attitudes and lifestyle, McCartney was becoming a snob. He let few things interfere with the new order of his life. "Paul is now leading a very organized life," Tony Barrow said then. "The other three don't know what they are doing; they wait for the others to tell them. But Paul always knows. You ring him up and he'll say, 'No, not Thursday, I'm dining at eight. Not Friday, because I've got to see a man about a painting. But Saturday's okay.' It isn't that he's changed, but out of all of them, he has developed the most."

In October, Paul accepted the task of composing the music

for the Boulting Brothers' film *The Family Way*. One of his compositions, "Love in the Open Air," received an Ivor Novello Award in England for the best instrumental theme at the 1967–68 presentations. When his work on the film was completed, Paul went with Jane on safari in Kenya, cutting his hair short and growing a moustache so he could travel incognito. He told a reporter that his new appearance was part of breaking up the Beatles.

His remarks prompted the *London Times* to write: "Last week it emerged that the Beatle phenomenon was ending. In a sense the very best of the Beatles' music was an expression of sheer delight at being a tightly knit group of attractive young up-and-comers. Maturity, the waning of their collective narcissism and the development of separate interests was bound to kill this phenomenon."

In December 1966 the Beatles regrouped in London. Each one's outlook on life and on the future of the band had sharply changed during the months they were apart. Success and wealth had firmly locked Paul into an upper-middle-class well-organized way of life, and he was brimming with confidence in his talent as a composer and musician. The influence of spiritualism had a profound affect on George Harrison and led him to search for a purpose in life. And Ringo still maintained his simple, working-class mentality.

The most drastic change in personality and character was seen in John. The once aggressive, confident, and determined Beatle was overwhelmed by apathy about his life and the future of the group. Though each knew that public performances were over, an overwhelming feeling of insecurity gripped Lennon. It was hard for him to adjust to not being on stage anymore.

In 1966 it was unprecedented for a pop/rock group to retire from the stage for artistic reasons, or in order to escape their fame. A group simply would not have walked away from such adulation unless they were disbanding. In January 1967, when the Beatles did announce that they would not perform in public again, many people in the music industry considered this a disastrous career move that would lessen their appeal to the record-buying public. The end of touring, however, was harmful to the Beatles for a different reason. Traveling, working, and living together had kept them a close-knit group, and prevented them from developing interests that the others did not share. Now this bond was broken, and their determination to stop live performances was one of the last decisions that Lennon, McCartney, Harrison, and Starr would all agree upon without argument.

14

The Beatles were now a full-fledged studio band. Though they knew that their experimentation during the *Revolver* sessions had only scratched the surface, it revealed to John, Paul, George, and Ringo what could be accomplished in the studio when they had the time to record and create, and the results excited them. The awareness that many more musical thresholds lay before them, as well as the commercial success and critical acceptance of the album, encouraged the Beatles to be bolder and more daring with the next LP, *Sergeant Pepper's Lonely Hearts Club Band*.

Today, *Sergeant Pepper's Lonely Hearts Club Band* is regarded as the apex of rock 'n' roll, the most influential album made by a pop/rock group. However, when the LP was being recorded, it was a culmination of the influences that had been molding and directing the group's musical direction since 1965.

The Beatles always had an extensive awareness of who was

210

on the British and American charts, the style of records their contemporaries had released, and the innovations that were being introduced to pop/rock. John, Paul, George, and Ringo were influenced as much by the music they heard during the touring years as by the music they heard as teenagers growing up in Liverpool. Cognizant of their position as the world's top vocal group, one thought guided the Beatles' work habits in the studio: They were determined to be second to no one. Whenever a performer or a group was praised for their artistic achievements on vinyl, the Beatles were inspired to be more creatively brilliant and articulate when recording their next single or album. For instance, before one note of *Rubber Soul* was recorded, the group listened intently to Bob Dylan's *Highway 61 Revisited* LP. John and Paul, in particular, were impressed by the creative lyricism of Dylan's music, which had a profound influence on the compositions they wrote for *Rubber Soul*.

Before the Beatles began recording *Sergeant Pepper's Lonely Hearts Club Band*, they knew that many artists had released records that helped expand the boundaries of pop/rock music. The group believed that they *had* to issue an extraordinary follow-up album to *Revolver*, and three long-playing discs released in the summer of 1966 led them to realize the kind of album they had to record.

The first was Bob Dylan's double LP *Blonde on Blonde*. The high standard of performance and lyrical invention that Dylan maintained throughout the two-record set was considered unprecedented then. George Harrison listened incessantly to this epic LP and pestered the others to hear it.

The second was an album called *Freak Out*, released by Frank Zappa and the Mothers of Invention. It is considered to be rock's first concept album, and Paul McCartney owned a copy of it.

The Beatles' major creative rivals then were the Beach Boys, who, in the early summer of 1966, released an album called *Pet Sounds*, which set new standards in pop/rock for musical arrangement and record production. Two tracks on the LP had a significant influence on the Beatles. To Paul McCartney, the song "God Only Knows" was so beautifully written and performed that it inspired him to compose "Here,

There and Everywhere." The other track, "Good Vibrations," indicated to the Beatles that the Beach Boys were also working on a higher level of creativity. Articles in the music press had mentioned that the Beach Boys spent six months recording the three-minute, thirty-five-second song. No artist had ever in vested that much time and money to produce a single pop recording. Though *Pet Sounds* was a commercial failure, the competition the LP presented worried the Beatles.

In early December 1966, these fears and influences were present in the Abbey Road Studios when the Beatles commenced work on *Sergeant Pepper's Lonely Hearts Club Band.* By Christmastime, however, their fears had been replaced by excitement. Having by then recorded three songs for the album ("Strawberry Fields Forever," "When I'm Sixty-Four," and "Penny Lane"), the group knew that the sessions to follow were going to be special, if not magical.

Over the Christmas holidays, during which time John and Paul worked together writing additional material for the LP, EMI asked the Beatles and George Martin to prepare a single for the new year, since they had not released a record in nearly four months. The two songs selected—John's "Strawberry Fields Forever" and Paul's "Penny Lane"—gave the record-buying public and the music industry an indication of the musical direction in which the group was going.

The song titles were inspired by actual places that Lennon and McCartney had known as children. "Penny Lane," for instance, is a bus roundabout in Liverpool, but when the Beatles glamorized it on record, it became a street where one could encounter interesting people. The piccolo trumpet solo was added to the recording after Paul attended a performance of the Bach Brandenburg concertos. McCartney was impressed by the range of the instrument and felt it would give his song an unique quality.

"Strawberry Fields," a Salvation Army school where John and his childhood friends attended garden socials, acquired a mystical quality when it was immortalized on disc. The song, the first to be recorded by the Beatles after the American tour, would not have been released had it not been for the genius of producer George Martin. The first recording was too sluggish and neither John nor George Martin was pleased, so John asked Martin to do a score for it. This second version was better, but still not right. John gave Martin carte blanche to "fix it." George then reduced the speed of one version, spliced the two together—and *voilà!*

The Beatles believed then that their music and influence could change the direction of pop/rock. To further promote the change and gather the following that the group wished to have, "Penny Lane" and "Strawberry Fields Forever" were released with film clips. (The Beatles were the first to use video to promote records.) The films, which were shown on television throughout the world, showed the Beatles sporting moustaches and noncomformist, surreal clothing—a totally new image that provoked controversy among Beatles fans, many of whom dropped their allegiance to the group they had seen in *A Hard Day's Night* and *Help!*

The Beatles knew that changing their music and appearance would cause many of their fans to abandon them, but they didn't care—they no longer wanted fans, but listeners, and they wished to increase this number by teaching young listeners to appreciate the new direction of the band. They even set out deliberately to change the life-style and appearance of the youth of the world.

The only song the Beatles had recorded for their new LP was "When I'm Sixty-Four," which was written in 1962–63 by Paul, who revised and retitled the arrangement in honor of his father's sixty-fourth birthday. On February 1, 1967, the group returned to the Abbey Road Studios to record the guitar tracks for a McCartney composition called "Sergeant Pepper's Lonely Hearts Club Band," whereupon McCartney suggested to the others that they make the album as though Sergeant Pepper were real and making the record. Though George Martin was not impressed with the song, he was fascinated by the idea.

The group originally conceived *Pepper* as a live show. The album was not going to have any spiral grooves between tracks; each song was the segue into the next. Their musical approach to recording the LP was equally innovative. The Beatles were to be the Lonely Hearts Club Band, the protégés of Sergeant Pepper and the album was to be the Lonely Hearts Club Band's debut. Every aspect of the album—the music and the packaging—was going to offer something that people of all ages could enjoy. *Sergeant Pepper* was not going to be just another Beatles album.

As the sessions progressed through February and March, the Beatles and George Martin applied the most unconventional and, at times, eccentric recording techniques to achieve the sound imagery they wanted on vinyl. Aside from a variety of sound effects, ranging from audience laughter to farm animals, the recording speed was reduced or doubled, performances were played backward and dubbed onto tape. Recordings of Victorian steam organs (heard on the track "Being for the Benefit of Mr. Kite") were dubbed onto tape, cut in foot-long sections, tossed into the air, and spliced together at random. Forty-two well-disciplined musicians from the Royal Philharmonic Orchestra were instructed to perform out of sync to capture John Lennon's "end of the world" feeling for the album's climactic "A Day in the Life." Anything that was possible or impossible was tried.

Producer George Martin believed that he and the Beatles were creating pictures in sound.

George Martin's influence on the group's music was more obvious in their 1967 recordings than in their previous albums. He composed all the orchestral arrangements in the album with the exception of "She's Leaving Home," which was scored (behind Martin's back) by Mike Leander at Paul McCartney's behest. Martin was also responsible for nearly all of the surrealistic instrumentation heard on the album. Another testimony to his genius lies in the fact that *Sergeant Pepper's Lonely Hearts Club Band* was recorded on a four-track machine, a very primitive tool for such sophisticated results.

The Beatles spent an estimated 700 hours in the studio recording *Sergeant Pepper.* John, Paul, George, and Ringo usually arrived at Abbey Road at seven o'clock in the evening and recorded, with their equipment set up as though they were performing to an imaginary audience, until three in the morning. The techniques that George Martin employed to stretch his four-track machine "to the limits" required engineers to meticulously adjust and readjust the numerous microphones placed throughout the studio to achieve the proper sound levels. This painstaking process sometimes interrupted the sessions for hours. The Beatles, in the interim, either rehearsed the instrumental backing they were going to record or, since most of the songs for the album were written during the three-month recording sessions, worked on the final form of their latest composition.

The end of touring had yet to disrupt the group's work habits or the harmony of their personal relationship. But a sense of artistic dissatisfaction began to form in George's mind. He was beginning to get the impression that John and Paul considered his songwriting efforts of no consequence compared to their own, and he was annoyed by their lack of encouragement. George had in fact emerged as a creative force in the Beatles by contributing three songs to *Revolver*, but on *Sergeant Pepper* he was limited to one track. He felt that Lennon and McCartney were alienating him from the album's creative process, and could not shake the feeling that McCartney was ignoring him. There were several occasions when his suspicions were justified, such as the time he was told not to perform on a track, but to sit, watch, and wait until he was called for. Instead of voicing these suspicions to the others, George kept them to himself and quietly expressed his annoyance by not attending some of the recording sessions.

George knew that John and Paul were the creative force behind the Beatles, and though there had been a gradual deviation in their songwriting styles and musical preferences, they were both musically and personally closer to each other then than at any time since 1965. Lennon and McCartney dictated the direction of *Sergeant Pepper* and collaborated on many of the songs in a manner similar to the way they had composed as teenagers. When additional music was needed for the LP, John and Paul would meet in the afternoon at McCartney's house in St. John's Wood and each would play for the other an incomplete version of a song that he was writing.

Of the twelve compositions credited to Lennon and McCartney on *Sergeant Pepper*, four were true collaborations. The song "A Day in the Life" is an example of one of the ways Lennon and McCartney wrote together. The main body of the composition was written by John, but he was unable to think of a middle verse and brought the song to Paul for ideas or suggestions. McCartney played him a verse of an untitled song he had partially written. After a few minor alterations, Paul's tune, which he sang on the recording, became the "middle eight" of "A Day in the Life."

Lennon and McCartney composed "With a Little Help from My Friends" and "Getting Better" with the titles as their only inspiration. With Paul sitting at the piano and John strumming an acoustic guitar, they played a meaningless series of chord progressions until one developed an interesting melody. Then they took turns singing an improvised line to the other. This system usually took them a day or two to construct the music and lyrics to one song. They also wrote together a reprise to "Sergeant Pepper" to unify the theme of the album.

In March 1967 John and Paul were enjoying a close friendship, and would do so throughout the spring and summer months. They knew that fame and success had led them down different paths, and each was attempting to understand and be more tolerant of the other. Lennon, once disgusted with McCartney's highbrow attitudes, began to accept Paul's desire to lead an upper-middle-class life, while McCartney, who felt that he had lost touch with John, began making an effort to establish contact with him.

Since John and George's introduction to LSD, Paul had felt excluded from their camaraderie and somewhat jealous of the closeness they shared through their mutual experiences with the drug, especially when John jokingly taunted him for being too scared and straight to try it. But one night during a recording session in March, Lennon accidentally swallowed an LSD capsule and Paul drove him home and decided to try the drug. They sat together into the early hours of the morning riding out their first trip together. The experience made John feel much closer to Paul.

During the recording of *Sergeant Pepper*, John and George were at the height of their LSD consumption. Paul, however, after three psychedelic experiences, decided the drug was not for him; he preferred the mellowing effects of marijuana, as did Ringo. Drugs of all kinds were present in the studio.

The Beatles' drug use in the studio had little to do with providing creative inspiration. Marijuana enabled them to relax quickly during breaks, and "speedballs" gave them a temporary spurt of energy whenever they were exhausted. Since George Martin disapproved of drugs, they furtively smoked marijuana in the washroom at Abbey Road. Martin, however, knew what they were doing and noticed their changed demeanor when they resumed recording. They would often get giggly and unproductive. Martin did not know that the Beatles used LSD until the day John accidentally took it in the studio.

On April 2 the Beatles finished recording *Sergeant Pepper*. During the final session, the group spent eight hours recording two seconds of silly noises, which were preceded by a whistle that only a dog could hear, to be inserted on the groove between the record label and the last track of side two. Later, when people began playing Beatles' music backward, searching for secret messages that the group allegedly recorded, the inner track of *Pepper* supposedly was found to contain an obscene message: "We'll fuck you like Supermen."

Sergeant Pepper's Lonely Hearts Club Band was released in England on June 1, 1967, to the acclaim of music critics throughout the world. It was clear to them that the LP was an explosion of new ideas, concepts, and highly sophisticated textures in sound. No recording artist had ever conceptualized a project of this magnitude.

Even before the disc was removed from the jacket, *Sergeant Pepper's* format was striking. The album was the first to carry printed lyrics on the sleeve, and one of the first to boast an artistically extravagant cover. On the jacket is a gathering of sixty-two people—a kind of superstar celebration of the project.

Then there was the music, described as the world's first forty-one-minute single—a veritable sound track of the times. There were thirteen tracks in a synthesis of styles: traditional, classical, ragtime, Eastern, rock 'n' roll, pop, and psychedelic.

The Beatles, however, encountered stern criticism over the drug references in the album. On the cover the group is standing in front of a grave burying the "old" Beatles, and around the floral arrangement are marijuana plants. Some people pointed out that the lyrics were drug-oriented and the music hallucinatory. They even stated that the Beatles used the subtle messages in the lyrics to encourage kids to take drugs. Of the album's thirteen tracks, critics cited four as being drug-oriented: "Lucy in the Sky with Diamonds," because the lyrics were "too far out not to be" and because the initials LSD appeared in the title; "Fixing a Hole," which was interpreted as a heroin addict shooting up; the line "I get high" in "With a Little Help from My Friends"; and the verse in "A Day in the Life," which makes references to smoking and passing into a dreamlike state.

In an extraordinary exercise of poor timing, Paul inflamed the controversy by saying in an interview on June 19 that he had tried LSD and advocated the drug as a universal cure-all. McCartney's simplistic vision typified the Beatles' attitude during the *Sergeant Pepper* era. Although they were now fully aware of their overwhelming power, they had not accepted the responsibility that came with their popularity. Did Paul's display of honesty do anything to further the cause of peace and the search for truth? Or was he simply urging the youth of the world to turn on with a dangerous drug? Paul was twenty-six years old when he made the admission. He assumed that he was all-knowing, that he had the secret of the world in his mind, that the mass distribution of LSD to world leaders would make them see the error of their ways and bring paradise to the human race. This was the epitome of drug talk. The Beatles, greatly affected by their psychedelic experiences, saw themselves as the ultimate vehicle of peace and goodwill. A whole generation affected by the pacifying influences of LSD, they privately reasoned, would come to power, ending animosity that had besieged and plagued man since the beginning of time. The Beatles saw themselves as the Pepper Messiahs whose actions gave drugs new legitimacy. The results? Millions of teenagers teetering on the edge, wondering whether or not to try LSD, saw their idols use it, live to say so and praise its virtues. Fans who had already used it felt closer to the Beatles, and many decided to step up their drug use.

Although no surveys were taken to determine what percentages of drug users were inspired by the Beatles admissions, or how many drug overdoses were reported in the days following McCartney's remark, one cannot underestimate the incredible influence wielded by the Beatles then. Parents all over the world, horrified at the prospect of addicted children, were furious that drug use was being encouraged by the world's most popular foursome. Evangelist Billy Graham warned parents that Paul's admission might encourage teenagers to use LSD. "I am praying for Paul that he finds what he's looking for," said Graham. "He has reached the top of his profession and now he's searching for the true purpose of life."

John, George, Ringo, and Brian Epstein stood behind Paul by admitting that they, too, had experimented with drugs. Their loyalty to each other was admirable, but in this case misguided. That a sugar cube drenched in hallucinogens would hasten the ascent of man was the kind of thing dreams were made of in the Pepper era.

On June 25, 1967, the Beatles brought a message of peace and love to over 400 million people via the "Our World" television spectacular, which was seen in fourteen countries. Although the song they sang, "All You Need Is Love," was presented as a solution to world violence, it carried an underlying message of sarcasm directed at the American hippie movement. The Beatles had believed that young people could change the world by preaching love and understanding, but that belief was shattered when George Harrison, who provided John Lennon with the inspiration for the song, visited San Francisco's Haight-Ashbury district. He returned to England disillusioned with America's hippie movement as a result of the filth and excessive drug taking going on there, which destroyed the positive aspects of the hippie movement. George said that seeing Haight-Ashbury turned him off drugs completely.

During the spring and summer of 1967, George had immersed himself in the philosophies and teachings of the Hindu culture. By early August, Harrison, who had used LSD more than John or Paul, was sure that the drugs, rather than being the ultimate answer, were in fact a diversion from the pure spirit. Harrison's awakening to the spirit was the beginning of another direction for the group. He convinced the others that Hindu spiritualism offered a natural method of departing from their troubles. Transcendental meditation may have helped the Beatles to give up hard drugs at least. John, however, said they'd stopped taking drugs before they became involved in meditation.

Patti Harrison, whom George had married the previous year and who was initiated into transcendental meditation in February 1967, told George about an East Indian guru named Maharishi Mahesh Yogi, who was scheduled to lecture at the Hilton Hotel in London on August 24. The Harrisons persuaded John and Paul to attend the lecture with them. (Ringo did not attend because his wife had given birth to their second son, Jason.) John, Paul, and George were impressed with the Maharishi and with the advice he gave his audience, which was basically that the material things of life can't be enjoyed until the spiritual values are in place.

The next day the Beatles accompanied the Maharishi to Bangor, Wales, to attend his summer conference at the Teachers Training College and be indoctrinated in transcendental meditation. Their initiation required each of them to bring six fresh flowers, a white handkerchief, and two pieces of fruit. After one day, the Beatles believed that meditation was the new cure-all. In Bangor there was new hope; there was an incredible natural high among the boys. This *had* to be the answer to the mystery of lasting peace. Several days later, though, their euphoria suddenly vanished. The news smashed into Bangor like a fast, tragic train—Brian Epstein was dead.

15

In the year that passed between the Beatles' last stage performance and his death, Brian Epstein became a pathetic man. His five-year association with the group had made him wealthy and famous, but after the group stopped touring, life was no longer exciting or fulfilling for him. The Beatles had enlivened the otherwise miserable existence of their often manic-depressive business manager. Since 1962 his life had revolved around the group and he'd lived vicariously through them. Feelings of power, security, and self-importance filled him whenever they performed. He could be seen standing offstage, tapping his foot and swaying to the rhythm, relishing the adulation that tens of thousands of fans were lavishing on his Beatles. It was thrilling for him to know that he had introduced this show-business phenomenon to the world.

Being a shy, provincial businessman was hardly a promising background for a man who guided show business's greatest attraction, but since the early days, Brian Epstein had contributed much to the success of the Beatles. His faith in them, coupled with persistence and hard work, gained public attention for them when no one was interested in musicians from the provinces. Once that was accomplished, the boys' talents as performers and songwriters established the quartet's popularity throughout the world. But it was Epstein who made it possible by opening doors for the Beatles.

From January 1962 to August 1966, Brian Epstein was everything to the Beatles: father figure, organizer, banker, and slave. He was their whipping boy when things went wrong and their mouthpiece when they had no answers. Although his critics have said that he was not a good businessman, Epstein earned his keep by being all of the above. There was never any doubt in the minds of John, Paul, George, and Ringo about the sincerity of his devotion to them or his love for them. Knowing that Brian was looking after their interests and was always there when they needed him gave the Beatles the confidence to concentrate on their music. "Brian was always very protective of them," says Peter Brown. "He wouldn't let anyone touch them, not out of insecurity, but he had to make sure, himself, that everything was perfect. Brian was a devil for detail." Whenever one of the boys had a serious problem, they always turned to him first because there was no one they trusted more. "The success that they had and were able to sustain in his life," says former press officer Brian Sommerville, "came from that relationship between the Beatles and Brian Epstein."

In the years that followed Epstein's death, critics failed to understand why he had not been more money-hungry. But while the Beatles always joked about money being the primary motive behind their desire to be famous, they were determined not to take part in get-rich-quick schemes at the expense of their fans. In 1964, for example, they refused to allow Capitol Records to release a live album from the Hollywood Bowl concerts, which surely would have earned the group millions of dollars in royalties. Some may say their greed was curbed by the fear of bad publicity, but the boys knew how easy it was for their fans to spend money on hundreds of products that bore the group's name and likenesses, and they would not allow themselves or their fans to be excessively exploited by the crass commercialism that their fame attracted.

It was Epstein's job, of course, to make money for the Beatles, but he was cognizant of the negative reaction that would have been generated had he permitted promoters and licensed manufacturers of Beatles products to overcharge the fans, and he managed to make the boys rich without resorting to that. The Beatles' business was so new that there were no precedents for Brian to base his decisions on. "He was really moving instinctively, and his instincts made enormous fortunes for the Beatles," says Geoffrey Ellis, one of Epstein's closest friends. "It's quite easy to say now that he should have done this or he could have done that or he might have prevented this. One of the instincts under which he operated was that the Beatles were the best, therefore he was going to get the best for them."

Dealing and dickering with promoters in Merseyside for an extra pound was one thing, but dealing and dickering with the music industry's wheelers and dealers in London and America was another. After the 1964 world tour, Epstein could make outrageous demands. Before Beatlemania engulfed the world, he was so cautious with his demands that many promoters and television bookers got the Beatles at bargain prices. Epstein's naïveté about the inner workings of the music industry occasionally led him to make poor and very costly decisions. For instance, when the Beatles were booked into the Paris Olympia in January 1964, the fee he negotiated with a French promoter barely covered the cost of their hotel. "I sat in a hotel bedroom in Paris with Brian," says Brian Sommerville, "with a suitcase filled with money—literally full of cash—and had to give him comfort because he was weeping and weeping and weeping because he made such a bad deal. I don't think he was the shrewd, smart businessman that some elements of the press made him out to be. He was a very nice, charming man with a flair for business so long as things were going his way. People were making big offers and he'd recognize them and snatch them up. What Brian couldn't do was drive a hard bargain. He didn't know how; he'd back down."

The Beatles made it clear to Brian early on that his expertise was not needed in the studio. During the recording of *With the Beatles,* he mentioned to the boys that a playback of "Till There Was You" did not sound right. John immediately put him in his place: "We'll make the records; you count your percentages." Brian had little say in the creation and packaging of their records; his sole creative involvement with the group was through their world tours. "The tours were very exciting for him," says Geoffrey Ellis, "because he felt like he was a member of the group. Touring with them, seeing them perform and what he had created, was probably the greatest fulfillment of his life. He found his greatest happiness in modeling their careers and working with them."

After the 1965 tour, Brian's persistent pushing to keep them onstage eventually made the Beatles resent him. The American tour was one continuous row between the boys and Brian, mainly over Brian's insistence that they wear matching stage uniforms and maintain their image as the lovable moptops. "They argued constantly with Brian," says Bob Bonis. "They said, 'Why do we have to wear these stupid uniforms? The Stones don't wear them.' "

Touring was an obsession with Epstein, and when the Beatles gave their last concert in San Francisco, he felt they would no longer need him. He wondered what he was to do next.

The problem was that Brian, as well as a majority of their fans, had not grown with the Beatles. As the group made advancements in the studio, Brian was still living in the Cavern days. He became acutely aware that the Beatles had made *him* and that he ultimately was not responsible for their success—a fact that the boys never let him forget. After the 1966 tour, he came to the conclusion that they were right—that the end of touring was the end of an era for him and the end of his involvement with the group. This realization was so hard for Epstein to accept that he did not attend the concert at Candlestick Park. His despair was compounded by the fact that he never really came to terms with his homosexuality. In September 1966 he attempted suicide by taking an overdose of sleeping pills. Those close to him say he did this not because of the group's decision to end touring but because one of his boyfriends in Beverly Hills had stolen his briefcase full of pills and private letters and threatened to expose his secret. Brian left notes to his closest friends leaving portions of his estate to them, but doctors were able to save his life after someone rushed him to a hospital. He tried suicide again several months later, again unsuccessfully.

At the beginning of 1967, Brian continued to see the Beatles socially. He dined with George and Patti Harrison and attended concerts with John and Paul. But his relationship and credibility as a manager began to wane, particularly in Paul's eyes, after he negotiated a new recording contract that tied the Beatles to EMI for nine years. McCartney, who had taken a stronger interest in the group's business affairs, was highly critical of Epstein and became furious with him when he learned that the Rolling Stones, under the management of New York businessman Allen Klein, received a higher royalty than the Beatles. Thereafter Brian did not see or hear from the boys; they had locked themselves in the studio. He no longer felt like an integral part of their lives and careers, and believed they wanted nothing to do with him. In April Brian was hospitalized with hepatitis. An enormous floral bouquet was delivered to him with a card written by John expressing his love for Brian. Epstein, touched by Lennon's thoughtful gesture, broke down and cried.

Brian Epstein was against the *Sergeant Pepper* project because, to him, the album symbolized the end of an era in which he had shared the throne. His presentation of the Beatles to millions of fans was over; now the boys presented themselves. He was even opposed to the cover they had selected for the LP, and before embarking on a trip to America in the spring of 1967, he wrote a note to the Beatles saying, brown paper wrapper was better. When the album was critically acclaimed throughout the world, Brian sank deeper into depression. It was the first time that he had not been a part of the Beatles' success.

In his pathetic attempt to veto the cover, Brian was like a reluctantly retired admiral attempting to commandeer an ultramodern vessel he knew nothing about. For all its ups and downs, 1962 to 1966 had been a glorious time, and like so many Beatles fans, Brian clung to the past, reluctant to accept change. Brian Epstein *was* the Beatles' biggest fan, and the loss of the group was devastating.

By the summer of 1967, Brian was unable to cope with

mounting pressures and problems, and his consumption of LSD and sleeping pills increased as he sought instead to escape. In early 1967 he had brought in Australian entrepreneur Robert Stigwood to assume most of the day-to-day business responsibilities, but by June he felt Stigwood had become an albatross as he relentlessly pushed a group from his native Australia called the Bee Gees, whom he presented as "the new Beatles." Epstein's despair was compounded when his father died in July. The comfort and strength he gained from knowing that his mother needed him were outweighed by the added burden of grief.

Another source of worry was the expiration of his management contract with the Beatles on October 1, 1967, and the fear that the group would not renew with him. Brian talked to the Beatles about his contract, and the boys told him of their ideas to form a company and make a film. "In the last year of his life," says Geoffrey Ellis, "Brian may have been nervous about what the future held. He never had any hesitation in broaching these topics with them. My view is that there would have been a continuing relationship with him. There probably would not have been a full, total management involvement. But he was worried about this—very much so—because they were independent cusses, although I did know that they did feel very strongly for him. They would tease him somewhat and make Brian feel insecure, and probably deliberately. There was an element of cruelty in them and a feeling that they had done a lot for him."

Realizing that their careers had made an incredible impact on their manager, the Beatles pressured Brian to meet them in Bangor and share the inner peace and happiness they had found through meditation. But on the morning of August 27, 1967, Brian Epstein was found dead in his bedroom at his home in Belgravia, London.

That morning, when Brian's secretary, Joanne Newfield, arrived at the house, she found nothing unusual in the fact that he still had not awakened; Brian often stayed in bed until the afternoon. When he was still asleep by midafternoon, however, Joanne became concerned and called Peter Brown, who suggested she phone the doctor. When the doctor arrived, he entered Brian's bedroom and came out a few moments later, saying, "Brian's dead!" Joanne told Peter Brown, who immediately telephoned the Beatles in Wales. "I was in the country," says Brown. "By the time I got to the house in London, although no announcement was made, there were already reporters outside. I called Paul in Bangor; they didn't have a private telephone because they were living in a dormitory."

Reporter George Harrison from the *Liverpool Echo* had traveled to Bangor with the Beatles and was talking to Paul when Peter Brown called. "The telephone began to ring and it kept ringing while Paul was talking," says Harrison. "Suddenly he said, 'Oh, George, I'll have to go and see who it is.' I saw him take up the receiver and then I heard him say, 'Oh, God! No! No!' He put the receiver down and ran upstairs where John, George, and Ringo were staying. The next I heard was when he came down and said, 'Brian was found dead in his bed this morning.' I said, 'Oh, Christ! It can't be!' Paul said, 'Yes, he was due to come and join us today and he was found dead in his bed this morning. It's an overdose of sleeping pills or something. I don't know anything really, but we've got to get back to London right away."

Paul and Ringo were the first to return to London, leaving George and John behind in Wales to talk to reporters. Harrison, who by then seemed much older than the others, remarked coolly and philosophically that though Brian was dead on a physical level, his spirit was still with them. John, looking physically shaken, repeated almost hypnotically the advice the Maharishi gave them not to be overwhelmed by grief and to have only happy thoughts of Brian.

The events surrounding Brian Epstein's death remain sketchy to this day. He was described as depressed over the death of his father and as having taken a lot of sleeping pills that week. His doctor, Norman Cowan, had prescribed antidepressants and hypnotic drugs for his anxiety and depression and to help him sleep.

"The story was that he had been in the country," recalls Vic Lewis, the managing director of NEMS, "and he had a row with two or three of the boys in the organization, which Brian was apt to do at any moment—he was very temperamental. Brian went home to his house in Belgravia. He was upset and had two or three brandies; he wasn't particularly a heavy drinker, but he had two or three brandies and took two or three sleeping pills. Now the only thing we can guess is that he must've awakened in the middle of the night and couldn't get back to sleep. As far as we know, and according to Joanne, the pill bottles remained intact, capped with the cotton balls inside. If you're going to take your life, you swallow all the pills and drink a gallon of brandy. You don't take three more glasses of brandy and three more pills and put the cotton back into the bottles and seal it. As far as I feel, there was no doubt about it being accidental."

Peter Brown adds: "If you know people who take pills, you know it's a situation where they can't remember if they took them. 'Didn't I take them? I can't get to sleep; I'm sure I didn't take them.' Brian was a chronic insomniac since late 1963."

While the British press, noting Brian's despondency over the Beatles' refusal to renew their management contract with him, speculated that his death was a third, *successful*, suicide attempt, investigators led the public to believe he was the victim of foul play. Clive Epstein, Brian's brother, says the theory that his brother was murdered is "absolutely ridiculous and absurd," and those close to Brian agreed that his death was not a suicide; Brian had written a letter to Nat Weiss in New York four days before expressing his excitement about an upcoming trip to America in September.

An inquest ordered by the coroner's office ruled that Epstein's death was accidental, caused by an "incautious self-overdose of the sleeping drug Carbitol." On August 30 Brian Epstein was buried in Long Lane Cemetery in Liverpool. The Beatles visited Epstein's mother, Queenie, several days before the service to express their sympathies. They were asked not to attend the funeral so that the interment would not turn into a "circus to view the Beatles." They did attend a memorial service for Brian a week later in London.

PART FOUR

THE BREAKUP OF THE BEATLES

Circa September 1967 to April 1971

16

Brian Epstein's death was the turning point for the Beatles. Two years later the group would disband, harboring bitter feelings over what their lives had become. These two years were confusing, argumentative, and mostly unsatisfying for John, Paul, George, and Ringo. Their ever-differing individual tastes in music and their disagreements about the direction that the group should pursue gradually tore them apart.

In the week that followed Epstein's death, the Beatles held meetings to discuss their future. Peter Brown was present at these meetings and was quick to remind them that he was next in line to manage the group, but the Beatles had decided otherwise: They would manage themselves. There were several reasons for this decision. They knew they were vulnerable to anyone who wanted to take advantage of them, and with Brian dead, there was no one at NEMS whom they trusted to guide them. The group had also felt for some time that they had no control over their direction. They were tired of men in three-piece suits making decisions for them—they believed that they could do a better job of protecting themselves and handling their own business affairs.

There were officers in NEMS, however, who had their own ideas about the management of the Beatles and had not always agreed with Brian's decisions regarding the direction and exploitation of the boys. Upon his death, the struggle for power was quite evident, for although Brian rarely made note of the fact, the position of Beatles manager was one of the most powerful in the entertainment industry.

The Beatles had often been disgruntled with Brian's ideas, and also had a nasty habit of hurting him by taking him for granted. But they were very much aware of one quality Epstein had that the other NEMS officials did not have—a fierce love for and loyalty toward the Beatles. They knew that Brian had always put the Beatles' needs first—indeed, he had dedicated the last six years of his life to them.

In early September 1967, the Beatles announced that they would not replace Brian Epstein and would be their own managers, making all their own decisions.

They had formerly taken only a passive interest in the business of the group, leaving the complexities of organization to Brian. They soon discovered, however, that managing themselves would not be easy.

At this time there was a dramatic power change within the group. John Lennon had lost all confidence in his abilities as a singer and composer. From the time of the *Revolver* album, he had altered his voice with studio gimmickry to cover his apparent inadequacies as an artist. He later said a large part of his problem at the time was the belief then being promulgated by Timothy Leary and others that the ego should be destroyed. Unfortunately, John succeeded. He withdrew even further after Brian died. As far as he was concerned, the seeds of a breakup had been planted. Lennon's insecurity about his creativity, coupled with the fear that gripped him after Epstein's death, eventually led to Paul's rise to power within the Beatles.

McCartney decided that he would give the others the incentive to involve themselves as a group in creative ventures. Although Paul McCartney had never been one to shun self-glory, the remarks often made about Paul's quest for dominance over the group have been somewhat unfair. True, he seized the reins of the Beatles' direction, and largely for himself. But his desire to hold the Beatles together was motivated by fear—fear that there was nowhere else to go; that individually, none of the members of the group could possibly equal the phenomenon of the Beatles. (Ironically, McCartney would years later become the most successful of the four.) The power he tried to wield over the others was thus stimulated by an almost obsessive desire to keep the Beatles alive.

One of McCartney's ideas was a film he conceived on a flight from Los Angeles to London in April 1967. In England they had things called "mystery tours," which you went on and didn't know where you were going. So he came up with the notion of a *Magical Mystery Tour*.

Several years earlier, Paul had taken up filmmaking as a hobby to occupy his time between touring and recording sessions. He now felt that he knew enough about making movies to direct one. The Beatles originally intended *Magical Mystery Tour* to be a big-screen, feature-length film that reflected their personalities then, in contrast to *Help!*, which had made them feel like puppets.

The NEMS organization helped the group launch the production by chartering a yellow and blue bus and hiring forty actors. On September 11, the Beatles set off for the south of England on their first day of filming. "The whole idea was to take this coachload of people off round the country," says Alistair Taylor, a former NEMS executive. "Instead of saying, 'On your left is such-and-such castle,' there'd be a freak-out and something would be happening."

The production was a mystery tour even to those involved, including John, George, and Ringo because only Paul seemed to know what was going on, conceiving of the movie as a record with visuals. From day one, virtually every aspect of the production was disorganized and chaotic. Actors argued with one another and griped about their sleeping accommodations. The Beatles worked without a script or sense of direction. Paul, as the creative mind behind the movie, felt that the film should be improvised as they traveled, stopping wherever the setting was suitable for filming. He was trying to capture the spontaneity that Richard Lester brought to their first film. He told the cameramen to film anything interesting and let the actors say what they wanted. The mad chase scene, filmed at the West Mallings Air Force Base in Kent, exemplified the confusion that permeated the production. Paul had George and Ringo dressed as gangsters and pursued by a group of dwarfs; actors dressed as vicars; and mothers pushing prams.

Lennon and Harrison found themselves involved in the venture without any idea of what they were doing, or why. Aggravated by the chaos, they kept their consternation to themselves. They had decided to make a film only because they needed to do something together after Brian's death and had no plans to work on an album. They also still felt they should be doing something for the public.

After a week of filming, the *Magical Mystery Tour* bus returned to London. The Beatles had planned to complete the project in one month, spending two weeks for postproduction work and one week in the studio to record the sound track. After screening the rushes, however, Paul was dismayed to find they had shot only ten hours of footage, much of it unusable. He abandoned his plans for releasing *Magical Mystery Tour* as a feature-length film and had the production edited to one hour. This process took nearly three months, and still there was not enough suitable footage, particularly for a song that McCartney wrote called "The Fool on the Hill." He decided to fly to the south of France in early November and use the countryside outside of Nice as a scenic backdrop for the segment. At Le Bourget Airport in Paris, customs officials detained him for several hours because he had left his passport in London and had to have it flown over. Then a hotel in Nice refused to accept his credit when he discovered that his wallet was at home as well.

Magical Mystery Tour was finally completed in mid-November at a cost of £40,000, twice the amount the Beatles had wanted to spend. The whole experience made the boys realize how much Brian Epstein had done for them. Paul, who had been more critical of Brian than the others, felt increasingly respectful after encountering the hazards of management himself.

On November 24, the Beatles issued their sixteenth British

single, "Hello, Goodbye" b/w "I Am the Walrus." The B-side was composed by John one day while he was at home in Weybridge and heard a police siren blaring near his house. The intonation of the siren inspired the melody, and Lewis Carroll's poem "The Walrus and the Carpenter" provided the inspiration for the lyrics. John and George felt that "I Am the Walrus" was the better of the two tracks, but George Martin persuaded them to release Paul's paradoxical "Hello, Goodbye" as the A-side. He considered "I Am the Walrus" too bizarre for the singles market.

"I Am the Walrus" appeared with five other songs on a double EP called *Magical Mystery Tour* released in December 1967. Paul composed the title track plus "Your Mother Should Know" and "The Fool on the Hill," in which he plays all the flutes and recorders. George wrote "Blue Jay Way" while staying at a house in Los Angeles on a street by that name. The song, East Indian in texture, reflects his dreary mood while awaiting the arrival of Derek Taylor. The EP featured the Beatles' first instrumental track, "Flying," on which all four collaborated as composers. The recording also introduced the mellotron, a new instrument for them which was played by John. *Magical Mystery Tour* ended the group's highly imaginative and sophisticated studio period.

In December 1967 the Beatles decided to enter the business world by forming a multifaceted company named Apple. The idea had been conceived by Paul that spring and the name was inspired by a René Magritte painting that Paul had bought during his culture kick. Paul had talked briefly with Brian Epstein about Apple Corps Ltd. during discussions about the extent of Brian's future involvement, but the Robert Stigwood crisis at NEMS did not give Epstein the time to fully develop the concept.

The first Apple venture was a retail store. They had investigated several types of businesses, including a messenger service for London, before they decided on opening the store. The Beatles then invested $250,000 in a clothing store called the Apple Boutique, for which they purchased a building at 94 Baker Street in Marylebone, London. They tried to run the shop on a humanistic basis and not be "nasty business people." The Apple Boutique stocked clothes created by a Dutch fashion team known as the Fool. They had designed the clothes for the Beatles' appearance on the "Our World" broadcast and the costumes for *Magical Mystery Tour*. The boys, still absorbed in the psychedelic period, decided to invest their money in the Fool's clothing designs. The opening of the shop on December 4 was grandiose. The Fool commissioned a group of art students to paint a psychedelic mural on the outside of the building to let London know that the Apple boutique was extraordinary.

The next Apple unveiling was the film *Magical Mystery Tour*. The BBC had purchased the screen rights, sight unseen, for £20,000 and televised the special to 13 million viewers on December 26. The following day, the press slaughtered the film, calling it "tasteless nonsense" and "blatant rubbish." The *Daily Mirror* said scornfully, "If it were not the Beatles, the BBC would not have fallen for it." The Beatles had failed for the first time—and in the eyes of the British public, they failed on a monumental scale. Once American television networks saw the reaction to *Magical Mystery Tour*, they dropped their bids to purchase the rights.

Paul was deeply affected by the criticism, saying that the movie was badly received because people were looking for a plot and there wasn't one. "*Magical Mystery Tour* is really a teaching film," says Victor Spinetti, who appeared in the film, "and should be shown at universities and colleges because of what it teaches—to celebrate the fact that you are alive. . . . It is like a Roman Catholic Mass—you celebrate every day that you are alive. And that was *their* celebration, and that's what *Magical Mystery Tour* is about. We were all on a mystery trip. We don't know where we are, and the journey is to find out who it is, what is this thing, and how much love we can give."

Paul blamed *Magical Mystery Tour*'s failure on the fact that the BBC presented the film in black and white, rather than the color it was filmed in, and that it went on at Christmas time, when everyone was expecting more normal fare.

The directions that the Beatles were taking with *Magical Mystery Tour*, Apple, and other ideas reflected yet another phase in their extraordinary lives. While on one hand Brian

Epstein's aristocratic touch was sorely missed, the group used their newfound autonomy to seek a new level of satisfaction after his death. Restlessness and anger at established doctrines in the arts and in the entertainment world spurred them into a new realm of wild experimentation with sights, colors, and opportunities that had never been available before. They were excited by the belief that anything was possible, and bewildered when the public reaction to *Mystery Tour* indicated that the world did not share their optimisim, or even comprehend it.

One thing was definite, however—there would be no return to touring. In mid-October the band rejected a million-dollar offer from American promoter Sid Bernstein for one concert at Shea Stadium. Money was no longer a motivation for the Beatles, a fact that would have significant impact on the outcome of the Apple projects.

Throughout this period, with its new emphasis on individual artistic freedom, each of the Beatles began to slowly withdraw from the group image. Ringo, interested in films, accepted the role of Emmanuel, the Mexican gardner, in the film *Candy* (with Marlon Brando and Richard Burton), and flew to Rome for two weeks in December for the shooting. George took off for New Delhi for ten days in early January 1968 to score the sound track of the feature film *Wonderwall*.

About this time, too, John's father surfaced after an absence of more than two decades. John was bitter about what his father had done to him and his mother, as well as bitter that his father waited till he was rich and famous to reappear and involve himself in John's life. The press sort of blackmailed John into seeing him, accusing him of being heartless while his own flesh-and-blood father washed dishes for a living. They then had a relationship of sorts until Fred died of cancer.

In February 1968 the Beatles announced that they were leaving for India to study transcendental meditation. The two days that they had spent in Wales convinced them that meditation was the road to inner peace, and they decided to follow the Maharishi to his Himalayan retreat in Reshikesh, India. Their comments then conveyed a sense of satisfaction they

had not felt since childhood, but the British press was convinced that the Beatles were seeking publicity. The boys were
genuinely intrigued, however. Success, wealth, and fame had
jaded them and distorted their concept of reality. They felt a
need now to understand the true purpose of life.

John and Cynthia and George and Patti Boyd (whom he'd
finally married in January, 1966) were the first to arrive in
Reshikesh. Paul, Jane Asher, and Ringo and his wife followed
several days later. At the ashram they met people from all over
the world who, like the Beatles, were seeking inner peace.
Among these people were actress Mia Farrow and her sisters
Jennifer and Prudence, folk singer Donovan Leitch, and Mike
Love of the Beach Boys. (Prudence and Jennifer were the in-
spirations for John's "Dear Prudence" and Donovan's "Jennifer
Juniper.")

Camp life in Reshikesh was primitive. There were no modern conveniences such as hot running water, and the students
had to cleanse themselves in the cold water of the Ganges
River. Their day began at seven in the morning with breakfast
outdoors under a canopy; then all the students gathered in a
lecture hall to hear the Maharishi's philosophy of life and
love. The Beatles spent a half-hour a day in meditation, and
the rest of their time relaxing, sunbathing, or writing songs.
(They composed twenty songs in Reshikesh.) John, Paul,
George, and Ringo were the Maharishi's prize students, and he
did his best to make their stay comfortable. In return, they
promised him that they would build an academy in London to
further his teachings once their three-month course was completed. The Maharishi sent the other students to meditate for
ten to fifteen hours a day while he counseled the Beatles on
meditation and the *Bhagavad Gītā.*

Before long, though, the novelty of camp life began to wear
thin. After ten days, Ringo and Maureen found the diet of rice
and vegetables too spicy and the insects intolerable. The
Maharishi told him that if he concentrated more on meditation, he would not notice the flies. Paul and Jane left several
days later, unable to cope with the primitive existence or to
comprehend the teachings of the guru. John and George,
though, had found contentment through their meditation exer-
cises and stayed for another month.

It was during this phase that John began to view George in a different light. Of the four Beatles, Harrison had changed the most, and John began to look upon him as an intellectual equal. They seemed to be on the same wavelength and shared an interest in the pursuit of spirituality. John also began to see Paul differently, feeling that now he hardly knew McCartney, who was absorbed in his upper-middle-class life-style and values. Paul, for instance, was actually proud of his MBE honor, while Lennon was embarrassed by his.

John and George's own disillusionment with the Maharishi crept in when a traveling companion, Alexis Mardas, accused the guru of attempting to seduce Mia Farrow. Mardas, a Greek electronics wizard, had impressed the Beatles months earlier with his inventions, and they had promised to finance his work. But the group's promise to build an academy for the Maharishi in London made Alexis fearful that this would interfere with his funding. So he concocted the story about the guru and Mia Farrow and told it to John and George.

Lennon and Harrison were saddened, having placed their complete faith and trust in the Maharishi. But meditation had made them both acutely sensitive, and they confessed that doubts about the guru had been building since their arrival in Reshikesh. For one thing, they'd wondered why the camp, supposedly built for peace and freedom, was guarded and surrounded by barbed wire; and why His Holiness, Maharishi Mahesh Yogi, who described himself as a simple and holy man, lived in relative comfort in a brick house while his fellow holy men of the Swarag Ashram religious settlement lived in poverty; and why Maharishi called all wars "a nuisance" but defended the draft laws. These things struck George and John as strangely out of character.

The Maharishi was upset by the Beatles' defection, but he had gained enormous publicity for his spiritual-regeneration movement from his involvement with them. Leading magazines from all over the world focused their attention on him after the Bangor conference. Soon after the Beatles ended their association with him, he latched on to the Beach Boys, touring with them in 1968.

The Maharishi was somewhat misunderstood. His "purpose" was to create a new history for mankind by teaching it to realize its full potential through transcendental meditation. He was in the final year of his three-year plan for saving humanity, after which he planned to revert to silence. Yet once he gained international notoriety, he craved publicity as few men of humility ever had.

"Maharishi was pushing the Beatles to do this ABC Television special, which just wasn't possible," says Peter Brown. "They didn't do things like that. He kept on negotiating with ABC about it. The Beatles sent me to Sweden, which was where Maharishi was at the time. I spent five days trying to explain to him that it just couldn't happen. He couldn't understand it. I had to go back and say, 'I couldn't make sense to him; I couldn't get through.' He was on a different wavelength; whether or not it was on purpose, I don't know. When you'd say, 'It can't be done,' he would talk about it actually being done. George and Paul returned with me to Sweden and they tried to convince him, but he continued talking as though we hadn't spoken!" The Maharishi persisted until executives from ABC asked the Beatles when the special was to take place and were told that it was not.

John wrote a song about Maharishi called "Sexy Sadie," saying he'd "made a fool of everyone." The Beatles felt that the Maharishi had taken advantage of their trusting natures and made them look like fools. In their disgust, however, all four of them overlooked the fact that through this guru and meditation, they had learned that drugs were not the answer to their problems.

The Beatles had been seeking someone on whom they could depend, a human being in whom they could place their faith. But that person was dead. It was Brian Epstein who had carried an unconditional love and admiration for them collectively and individually. Despite the merits and tranquillity of meditation, the group discovered that no gods walked the earth—that no one person or a group of people had all the answers.

There had been too many would-be solutions that had turned out not to be the solution: the end of touring; drugs; isolation; and now Maharishi. But the Beatles kept looking, and there would be one last attempt to search for self-worth. They would try their luck at being businessmen.

17

While the Beatles were in Reshikesh, Neil Aspinall commuted between London and India to keep them abreast on the development of Apple. They had decided to use their influence and collective wealth to help struggling artists, composers, and filmmakers break into show business without experiencing the disappointing and discouraging routine of repeated rejections. The Beatles invested $2 million in an organization that promised to be one of the most extraordinary ideas in the entertainment industry and one that they envisioned to be a vast empire of talent and creativity.

Apple was divided into six divisions: electronics, films, merchandising, music publishing, records, and retailing. The company would manage eighty percent of the group's partnership contract, signed in April 1967, and collect their royalties from records and films, while each of the Beatles retained a five-percent interest. To manage the company, the Beatles surrounded themselves with such old and reliable friends as Neil

Aspinall, Mal Evans, Alistair Taylor, and Peter Brown, and hired experienced people to administer the various divisions.

"The structure of Apple was brilliant and it was brilliantly conceived," says Peter Brown, "not only the idea, but the administrative machinery we set up. We took in as the heads of the various divisions of Apple the best possible people. It was a marvelous concept and it was being operated by very clever people who knew what they were doing. The structure was based on the fact that Apple would be totally owned by these shareholders—the Beatles—so that John, Paul, George, and Ringo would own all their enterprises. They would totally own and be the masters of their destiny."

In April 1968 the Beatles unveiled Apple with the promise of fulfilling the dreams of would-be entertainers. Full-page advertisements, conceived by Paul, were placed in Britain's music papers with a picture of Alistair Taylor dressed as a street entertainer with the caption:

> THIS MAN HAS TALENT!
> One day he sang his songs to a tape recorder (borrowed from the man next door). In his neatest handwriting he wrote an explanatory note (giving his name and address) and remembering to enclose a picture of himself, sent the tape, letter and photograph to APPLE MUSIC, 94 BAKER STREET, LONDON W1. If you were thinking of doing the same thing yourself—DO IT NOW! This man now owns a Bentley!

They wanted to help other people without acting like big wheeler-dealer businessmen and without degrading the artists.

John and Paul flew to New York in May to announce Apple. During a four-day stay, they talked to the press and held the first American board meeting on a Chinese junk sailing around the Statue of Liberty in New York Harbor. They then appeared on "The Tonight Show," playing down the Maharishi and playing up their new company. Actress Tallulah Bankhead, another guest on the show, did not enjoy being upstaged by the two young entertainers and threw cutting remarks at John and Paul throughout their interview. But the promise of Apple reached millions of struggling American artists.

The Beatles' idealism brought hundreds of dreamers and schemers knocking on the door at 95 Wigmore Street in London, Apple's first corporate location, all hoping to get a slice of the pie. People who claimed to be talented crawled out of the woodwork asking to be discovered or bankrolled. A few days after the announcement, the Apple Music Publishing Office, located at 94 Baker Street, was inundated with cassette tapes, nearly all of which were ignored.

The principal source of Apple's income was to have been derived from the record label. During the summer, Apple was busy signing artists to the company. Paul would produce a record for the Black Mills Dyke Band and an eighteen-year-old Welsh folk singer named Mary Hopkin, who was brought to McCartney's attention by Twiggy after Hopkin won a talent contest on the television program "Opportunity Knocks." George was set to produce Jackie Lomax, an old Liverpool friend of the Beatles', who played in a group called the Undertakers; and Mal Evans discovered a northern group called the Iveys (later Badfinger), who impressed John and George.

There was no question that Apple was Paul's pride and joy. He devoted more time and effort to the company during its infancy than the others did. In June, he flew to Hollywood and spoke at the Capitol Records convention to personally announce that "all future Beatle recordings will be issued on the Apple label." The Beatles launched Apple in the belief that the venture would give them greater artistic freedom, and, indeed Apple had every possibility of becoming a prosperous company. There were, in the hierarchy of the company, qualified people capable of directing it to success, but the Beatles' naïveté, unorthodox business methods, and constant interference with people they'd hired to administer the company's day-to-day affairs threw Apple into chaos and brought about its demise. The Beatles never made an important decision without consulting the I Ching, or until Caleb, an astrologer, told them whether or not the stars were in their favor. John, Paul, George, and Ringo were not qualified businessmen and made most unbusinesslike decisions. They did not see the need to work with contracts or keep track of finances. They believed that the "Beatle magic" would rub off on anything they touched.

* * *

On his return from America, Paul began to step up his role as self-appointed manager of the Beatles. "There were several reasons for that," says Peter Brown. "John was going through the latter stages of an unsuccessful marriage and was genuinely not very excited about his life, which was one of the reasons, I suppose, he grabbed on to the Maharishi. John lost interest in most things, and Paul grabbed the reins." One of the things Lennon lost interest in was the Beatles. His attention was diverted from the group by the presence of a new woman in his life—Yoko Ono.

Yoko Ono was born in Tokyo on February 18, 1934, to an affluent Japanese family. Otherwise, her childhood closely paralleled John's. She did not have a close relationship with her parents (she was required to make an appointment whenever she wanted to talk to her father) and grew up to be self-reliant. At a young age, she developed an interest in music, playing the piano as well as composing songs and illustrating them with artwork, but her parents did not encourage her artistic interests. When Yoko was eighteen, her family immigrated to America and settled in Scarsdale, New York. She was sent to study philosophy and music at Sarah Lawrence College in nearby Bronxville, where she encountered prejudice from schoolmates because of her nationality and spent many lonely hours playing the piano, writing music and poetry. After three years, she left Sarah Lawrence and in 1964 married a Japanese musician named Toshi Ischiyanagi. Her parents disapproved and subsequently broke off relations with their daughter. Yoko and Toshi divorced later that year.

Throughout the mid-1960s, Yoko drifted around the New York underground art scene in Greenwich Village. Her tastes in music ranged from Japanese folk music to the works of the experimental composers such as John Cage and Karlheinz Stockhausen. She was a strong-willed, determined artist and her forceful nature and intelligence intimidated many men. She remarried later in 1964 to filmmaker Tony Cox, who fathered their only child, Kyoko. But Yoko's feisty independence and determination to have things done her way led to many arguments with Cox, and their marriage ended in 1967.

During her New York period, Yoko was involved with a

group called Fluxus, whose members were experimental artists, filmmakers, and composers. It was here that she developed most of her attitudes about art before setting off on her own. Yoko's conceptual art—or "events," as she described them—often left people scratching their heads in bewilderment, and her desire to remain true to her art made her a depressed and lonely woman. Once she tried to commit suicide after a Japanese newspaper gave one of her Tokyo exhibitions a negative review.

Yoko arrived in London in mid-1966 and found the art movement compatible to her work. She impressed critics and gallery promoters with her conceptual events, one of the first of which was the Trafalgar Square Wrapping Event, where she wrapped a white tarpaulin over one of Landseer's stone lions.

John and Yoko met for the first time in November 1966 at the Indica, a West End art gallery run by John Dunbar, a friend of the Beatles. Yoko had an exhibit full of strange conceptual pieces, such as a few nails or an apple on a stand—for a few hundred dollars. John immediately thought it was a con, until he came across something called "Hammer-a-Nail," a board with a chain and a hammer hanging on it and some nails. Yoko charged him five shillings to hammer one nail in. John then offered an imaginary five shillings to hammer an imaginary nail. John's remark told Yoko that they were on the same wavelength.

In the year that followed their first meeting, they met two more times and did a show together. John found himself alternately excited and irked by Yoko's work, especially by her book *Grapefruit*, which had sayings like "Paint until you die."

During the two months he spent in Reshikesh, John began to wonder if he was in love with Yoko, and she would write him extraordinary, fascinating letters. Lennon was fascinated by Yoko Ono because she was so different from any woman he had ever known. He'd never had an intense relationship with a woman before; his marriage to Cynthia had been one of necessity rather than love.

When he returned from India, John discreetly kept in touch with Yoko by writing letters and talking over the telephone. After his trip to America in May 1968, they spent the night together. John called her to come over, played her all his tapes;

they then made one themselves (*Two Virgins*), after which they made love.

The British press became aware of the liaison between John and his Japanese artist friend and on June 18 launched an attack on them. The occasion was the opening of the stage adaptation of *In His Own Write* at the Old Vic Theatre in London. The press, waiting for John's arrival, was prepared with baited questions that drew the response they wanted. "Where's your wife, John?" asked a reporter. "I don't know!" snapped Lennon.

At the opening of his art exhibition at the Robert Fraser Gallery, John declared his love for Yoko, dedicating the show "To Yoko, from John, with Love." Paul, George, and Ringo were equally bewildered by John and his new love. As Yoko recalled, they were always present in spirit.

Since late 1966 an animated film based on the song "Yellow Submarine" had been in preproduction in America and London. Filmmaker Al Brodax, who had successfully produced a Beatles cartoon series for ABC Television in America, obtained Brian Epstein's approval to make a film. "It was due to the success of the cartoon series that Brian Epstein allowed the feature," says Brodax. "He was a difficult man. I had many versions of the film written, and he would turn them down because he didn't like the color of the cover. He didn't like purple, so that script was out. Some very good stories went down the drain. In the end, it just became a matter of wearing him down. He did like the notion of the title, *Yellow Submarine*, but he died before the script was finished."

The Beatles initially were not interested in the movie, particularly after the failure of *Magical Mystery Tour*, but Brodax sold them on the idea by telling them they did not have to do anything for the film except sign a piece of paper and write four original songs. Brodax said that he would do all the work, and at the same time they could fulfill their three-picture commitment to United Artists.

Brodax, working with then Yale professor Erich Segal (who later wrote *Love Story*) and Jack Mendelsohn, took songs from the *Rubber Soul*, *Revolver*, and *Sergeant Pepper* albums and stitched them into a love-conquers-all theme. The animated feature cost $1 million to produce. At the height of production, over 130 artists worked on the animation, producing nearly 250,000 original drawings.

When the Beatles returned from India, the film was not completed, but what they saw persuaded them to become involved in the production. "They loved what we had done, especially John and Ringo," says Brodax. "They'd come down to the studio and horse around and make comments. Ringo said, 'My nose isn't big enough.' They were in the picture at the end. That wasn't my idea; they wanted to be in it. I thought they were going to stay in India for some time. The whole idea was that they didn't want to do any work, so I never expected it. But they were hanging around and said, 'How can we get into this?'"

Brodax remembers receiving a telephone call from John Lennon at three o'clock one morning. "Wouldn't it be great if Ringo was followed down the street by a yellow submarine?" said John, and hung up. Brodax used the idea in the picture. "I liked them very much, and somehow we got along very well," he says. "They all had their individual schticks. Ringo was just lovable and funny; Paul was a wise-ass PR sort of guy; John was very moody, brilliant—he could be very pleasant or standoffish; and George was always very decent." About Yoko, Brodax remembers: "It was a very testy time and they were all feeling their egos, and she came in and stirred it up. But she's gotten a bum rap over breaking up the Beatles."

The world premiere of Yellow Submarine on July 17, 1968, at the London Pavilion was attended by John and Yoko, Paul and Jane, and George and Patti. The opening sparked the last massive demonstration of Beatlemania, with 10,000 fans jamming Piccadilly Circus.

Apple now had a second office, at 3 Savile Row in the tailoring district of London. The purchase and renovation of the Georgian building cost the Beatles £500,000. In July they decided to close the Apple Boutique after suffering considerable losses. Since its opening, employees had stolen almost £125 a week from the cash register. The shop had been so mismanaged that the Beatles were too embarrassed to consider legal action. The closing resulted in a massive two-day give-way of £24,000 worth of merchandise. Paul concealed the group's embarrassment by saying that the decision to close the boutique was to get the Beatles out of the retail business, saying it was becoming too ordinary.

The Beatles concentrated on launching the record label, which they hoped would recoup the losses that the company had suffered. In August, Apple debuted its first releases with a self-proclaimed National Apple Week and a promotional package of singles called "Our First Four," containing Mary Hopkin's "Those Were the Days," Jackie Lomax's "Sour Milk Sea" (composed by George), the Black Mills Dyke Band's "Thingumybob" (composed by John and Paul), and the Beatles' first Apple release, "Hey Jude" b/w "Revolution."

"Revolution" was John Lennon's boldest statement as a songwriter about social change and was directed at the activists of the world who sought to overthrow governments by violence. Since 1965 Lennon had been writing songs that carried weight, and now his lyrics were blunt and to the point. "Hey Jude," composed by Paul McCartney, was the Beatles' longest track to date, with a three-minute fade-out.

One night Paul and a few friends slipped into the vacant Apple Boutique and painted HEY JUDE on the window with whitewash to promote the single, but it was interpreted by some as an anti-Semitic saying.

John interpreted "Hey Jude" as Paul's way of saying that it was all right for him to have Yoko, but others saw the song as McCartney consoling himself after his relationship with Jane Asher ended. In August Jane appeared on a television program called "Dee Time" and announced that she and Paul had split up.

The couple had had a rocky five-year relationship, during which they were rumored to be married or getting married. But Jane's involvement with Paul overshadowed her acting career, and she became known to the public as Paul McCartney's girlfriend. Six months after Paul and Jane announced their engagement, it was broken off. He had pressured her to give up her acting career to become a housewife and mother, which she was not prepared to do. London gossip columnists believed the split was temporary, even though Paul was seen in nightclubs with several women, one named Francie

Schwartz. When his affair with her ended, Paul went to Sardinia with a woman named Maggie McGivern, but this romance lasted only a short time. In October 1968 another woman began to figure prominently in McCartney's life—Linda Eastman.

Born on September 24, 1941, Linda Eastman came from a prominent and affluent New York family. Her parents, Lee and Louise, were loving and attentive to Linda and her brother, John, providing them with the best education and what are usually termed "the finer things in life." Lee Eastman had a successful law practice in Manhattan and represented clients from the entertainment industry. (The Eastmans' original family surname was Epstein, and they are not related to George Eastman, founder of Kodak, as has been reported.) The family had an apartment on Park Avenue and a home in Scarsdale, where Yoko Ono lived (though its unlikely that the Eastmans and Onos ever met). When she was eighteen, Linda, like Yoko, entered Sarah Lawrence College, and that same year her mother died in a plane crash. Two years later, in 1960, Linda married a geologist named John See, and in December 1962 she gave birth to a daughter, Heather. The marriage ended several years later. After her divorce, Linda moved to Tucson, Arizona, with Heather, and enrolled in college to study photography. When she returned to New York, she found work as a photographer for *Town & Country* magazine. Her first major assignment was a cover story on the Rolling Stones, which gave her notoriety on the New York rock scene. Linda began working as a free-lance photographer, concentrating on rock 'n' roll stars and anyone else who excited her.

She met Paul for the first time at a press reception hosted by Brian Epstein in May 1967 for *Sergeant Pepper's Lonely Hearts Club Band*. They talked briefly during the reception, but nothing happened between them. In London weeks later on an assignment with the group Traffic, she saw Paul again at a club called the Bag O' Nails.

When Paul came to America to unveil Apple, he met Linda again at a press conference at the Americana Hotel, and they spent time together throughout his stay. He returned to America in June to see Linda once again, and together they went to Hollywood. She came to England in August, during the final days of a Beatles recording session at Abbey Road, and in October moved in with Paul at his home on Cavendish Avenue.

Two strong-willed and determined women now made their presence felt among the Beatles.

During his divorce proceedings, John and Yoko lived in a flat on Montague Square in London. On October 18, they were awakened from an afternoon nap by the police pounding on the door. When they entered, they began searching throughout the apartment and claimed to have found cannabis resin. John and Yoko were taken to the Paddington Green Station and charged with possession of drugs and obstruction of justice. The following day, policemen escorted them into the Marylebone Magistrates Court Building, where John and Yoko appeared before a judge. Lennon pleaded guilty to the charges.

John believed that the bust was set up by Detective Norman Pilcher of the Scotland Yard drug squad. The press were there at the bust, and John had even been warned by a reporter named Don Short. John claimed he cleaned the house and only pleaded guilty to prevent the government from expelling Yoko.

The press escalated its attack on Lennon and Ono after the drug bust. John couldn't understand why everyone was against him loving Yoko.

It has been said that Lennon was overreacting to the criticism flung at him and Ono by the press. But there was no doubt that a subtle trace of racism underlay the attacks. The fact was that the Beatles were British, and many felt that the U.K. had an unwritten claim on John, Paul, George, and Ringo. That John had left a respectable English girl for a strange Oriental woman left many Britishers feeling somewhat betrayed. This wounded John deeply, but he was even more hurt when he sensed a different kind of resentment toward Yoko from Paul and George. They seemed unable to accept his falling in love.

By autumn 1968, Apple's record division was flourishing. "Hey Jude" topped the singles charts in America and Britain, and Mary Hopkin's "Those Were the Days" was also a hit; both discs had sold nearly 15 million copies combined worldwide. The group's first Apple album was released in late November, a thirty-track double LP called The Beatles. The plain white cover was in striking contrast to the ornate Sergeant Pepper's; the music was a return to rock 'n' roll. Reviewers felt that the Beatles should have released only the best tracks on one disc, which George Martin had tried to persuade them to do, but the group was anxious to fulfill their contractual obligation of recording seventy sides for EMI. (During the eighteen-month period following the signing of their new EMI record contract, they had recorded fifty-six songs.)

The Beatles spent five months working on the "White Album," during which a clash of egos surfaced among them. They argued with one another constantly, and at one point Ringo walked out during a session, fed up with Paul's criticism that his drumming was "redundant."

Ringo's first composition, "Don't Pass Me By," which he had written five months earlier, was featured on the "White Album." The album featured four of George Harrison's songs, including "While My Guitar Gently Weeps," for which Harrison brought in Eric Clapton to play lead guitar.

Yoko was with John throughout the "White Album" sessions, and her presence contributed to the tension. She never left John's side for a moment, even followed him to the bathroom.

The press maintained its attack on the couple, particularly during John and Cynthia's divorce proceedings and after his drug bust. But the ultimate shock came with the release of their first album, Unfinished Music No. 1/Two Virgins, which displayed John and Yoko in the nude on the front and back cover. The album was a collection of avant-garde electronic music, bird calls, and gastric noises. EMI and Capitol refused to issue the record, and all the British music publications refused to print advertisements for it. Two Virgins was finally distributed in England by Track Records and in America by Tetragrammation Records. Reviewers did not think much of the solo effort, saying that the album would become the first million-seller that nobody listened to.

The British public was outraged by what they considered an obscene gesture, which increased the disgust and contempt they already felt for John. Some support for the album came from the British Naturist Association, who thought it was splendid. According to John, however, Paul and his henchmen did everything they could to kill *Two Virgins*. John believed they, like the press, couldn't accept people's bodies and lovemaking.

Toward the end of 1968, Steve Maltz, an accountant at Apple, sent each of the Beatles a letter stating that they were in a precarious financial situation. The realization that he was on the verge of bankruptcy was stimulus enough for John Lennon to take a renewed interest in Apple and the Beatles. He was fed up with all the people taking advantage of them and spending all their money. The Beatles discovered, among other things, that Apple had purchased two cars and a house that they did not remember buying.

Since April the day-to-day affairs at Apple had become one continuous party. Not content with a sandwich from home and a pint of beer, employees had Apple's cordon bleu chefs prepare lavish meals of roast beef, which they washed down with expensive wines, such as Napoleon's Chateau Malmaison or Château d'If. When the pubs closed in the afternoon, executives from other music companies would head for Apple for a drink. Number 3 Savile Row played host also to a variety of people who were not connected to Apple or the music business. The Hell's Angels, welcomed by George Harrison, made Savile Row their home for several weeks; and a family of six from California, en route to the Fiji Islands, was allowed to live in the office for a time.

Although Lennon was quick to blame the downfall of Apple on all the "beggars and lepers" of the world, it was the Beatles' incompetence as administrators that threw Apple into near-bankruptcy. "The four people became individuals," says Peter Brown, "and therefore had different interests. That's when they stopped agreeing. And part of it was Paul taking over and creating Apple, and John waking up one day and saying, 'Hey, what is this?' " The Beatles had tried abandoning conventional business practices, but they began to realize that business was best handled by experienced people.

That the Beatles were not savvy businessmen came as no

surprise to anyone else. Their lives had been very much a fantasy, their experiences unreal. Apple had been a whim motivated by two somewhat naïve desires—to become the saviors of talent and to kick the traditional entertainment industry in the butt. They were shocked to find that Apple was attracting parasites from several continents, and that while the enterprise did pave the way for such talents as Mary Hopkin, James Taylor, Badfinger and Billy Preston, 3 Savile Row was mostly occupied by untalented moochers.

From the opening of the Apple Boutique, with its designer group appropriately known as the Fool, the corporate haven was already lost. But while the Beatles had learned something about their limitations, they were bolstered by those around them who either fed the group's self-image of infallibility or, fearing the loss of a good thing, continued to keep quiet about the insanity of it all.

18

At the outset of 1969, the Beatles were scheduled to begin work on a one-hour film special for the BBC. For months they had planned to stage a concert at the Royal Albert Hall, their first in over two years, based on the songs from the "White Album." "We tried to arrange one last concert," says Peter Brown, "but it just wasn't practical; there were too many obstacles." Paul McCartney, though, persuaded the others to produce a movie of their own. He wanted to film the group at work in the recording studio, a documentary of how the Beatles made a record. Instead, the film *Let It Be* became a documentary of how the Beatles broke up.

On January 1, 1969, the production of *Let It Be* began at the Twickenham Film Studios. After the confusion that surrounded *Magical Mystery Tour*, John, George, and Ringo were not enthusiastic about the project. Paul's idea was to film the band while they rehearsed, but after twenty years, rehearsal was the last thing the rest of them wanted to do.

The tension that was prevalent during the recording of the

"White Album" carried over into the *Let It Be* sessions—but now it had reached an even higher level. As Paul tried to keep the others involved in the film, his dominance and over-bearingness annoyed John, George, and Ringo, who began to feel like McCartney's backup group. Paul and director Michael Lindsay Hogg approached them with the idea of performing in a Tunisian coliseum, which was dismissed as impractical. Then McCartney had an idea of recording the album on an ocean liner at sea, which was equally impractical. The filming of *Let It Be*, according to George Harrison, washed away any last shreds of enjoyment he had playing with the Beatles. In his determination to have things his way, Paul needled George about his guitar playing, even as they were filming, until eventually George walked out. The others talked him into returning. Throughout, Paul was disturbed by the others' lack of enthusiasm.

During the filming, John Lennon predicted the financial collapse of Apple, saying, "Apple is losing money. If it carries on like this, we'll be broke." Since December 1968 the Beatles had been looking for someone to manage the company. John and Paul met with several leading business consultants in London to discuss this, but the people they talked to either were not suitable for the job or turned it down. Lee Eastman had been trying to sort out the chaos at Apple, but John, George, and Ringo were uncomfortable about his close relationship to Paul, whom they believed was trying to take over the Beatles and Apple. Lennon's announcement brought a new figure into the Beatles' camp—Allen Klein.

Klein had a reputation in the music industry as being one of the toughest wheeler-dealers in the business. His New York–based company, ABKCO Industries, had managed the Rolling Stones, and Klein's name had been linked to the Beatles earlier when a newspaper reported in late 1966 that he was approached by two members of the Beatles about management. These rumors were denied by Brian Epstein and the group, but the Beatles' situation changed drastically with Epstein's death. Upon hearing of Epstein's death, Klein was certain he would become the Beatles' manager, as in his opinion there was no one else qualified.

Nearly a year and a half passed after Brian Epstein's death

before Allen Klein made contact with the Beatles. "He kept calling me because he wanted to speak to John," says Peter Brown. "Klein wanted me to set up a meeting with the Beatles, and I just dismissed it as another fan who wanted an audience. I never returned his calls, ever. Klein had a contact through the Rolling Stones, who was a friend of Derek Taylor's, and he said, 'Get Peter Brown to return his calls.' Derek said to me, 'Why aren't you returning his calls?' and I said, 'I don't want to speak to him.' Derek said, 'Well, do us a favor. It'll be easier if you return his calls and get me off the hook with this guy.' So I returned the call and I set up a meeting with John and Yoko. It was the worst thing I ever did."

John was willing to talk to anyone who could save him from bankruptcy. In January 1969 he met Allen Klein at the Dorchester Hotel. Lennon briefed Klein about the situation at Apple, telling him that Lee and John Eastman were trying to make sense of the chaos, and that he was interested only in someone looking into his finances.

John was impressed with Allen Klein and asked him to look into his affairs. To show that he was not pushy, Klein did not ask for a contract, though Lennon made it easier for him to make inquiries by providing letters of authorization that said, "Allen Klein and ABKCO Industries are working on behalf of John Lennon." The following morning, John telephoned the people who were to receive the letters so they would not be surprised.

On the set of Twickenham, Paul, George, and Ringo learned of Klein's involvement when an Apple employee asked John during lunch if the rumor he had heard from an EMI executive was true, that Allen Klein worked on his behalf. John, without missing a sip of his soup, said, "He does." Linda Eastman, who was sitting with Paul, said, "Oh, shit!" Lennon arranged for the others to meet and talk with Allen Klein that day to hear how he could help them. John Eastman was also invited to attend the meeting because an impending deal he was working on (buying NEMS) was to be discussed.

After the meeting, George and Ringo talked with Allen and asked him what he was doing for John. When he explained, they asked him if he would look into their business affairs, too, and Klein agreed. Lee Eastman came scurrying back to England once Allen Klein had arrived. John, George, and Ringo, still harboring some reservations about Klein, were prepared to sign with the Eastmans, but a confrontation, initiated by Lee Eastman, finally sold them on Klein. Eastman ranted that Klein was no good, a strategy that backfired. The Beatles were not impressed with his behavior.

On February 3, 1969, Allen Klein was officially appointed business manager to the Beatles, with the provision that he would generate income for the group. John, George, and Ringo signed a three-year contract with ABKCO Industries, which any of the parties could terminate at the end of each year. A similar announcement was made the following day naming the law firm of Eastman & Eastman as legal counsel to Apple.

Klein's reputation preceded him wherever he went, and his presence instilled terror in the staff at Apple. He initiated a corporate shake-up, terminating anyone who was not essential to the company. When he fired Ron Kass, the head of Apple Records, shocked employees were convinced that anyone was expendable. Neil Aspinall was demoted from president of the company to literally an office boy.

One of Klein's first steps as manager was to regain the group's fortune by purchasing Northern Songs. The deal was designed primarily for John and Paul, who did not control the rights to their songs. Collectively, Lennon and McCartney owned thirty percent of Northern Songs, but unknown to them, Dick James had sold his thirty-seven-percent interest in the company to Sir Lew Grade of Associated Television (ATV). The Beatles regarded this as a betrayal, but according to Dick James, he had given John and Paul ample warning about the sale.

"After Brian died, I put forward a very tremendous concept," says James. "I had daily meetings with lawyers, accountants, with the boys and their advisers, including George Martin as well, to make a complete conglomerate of the Dick James Organization as it was then, including Northern Songs, but using Northern Songs as the platform. [I wanted to] bring Apple into it, to bring George Martin and his independent production company into it. I almost got it together, but there were too many people pulling in too many different directions for me to finally clinch it. It was a tremendous concept, everybody felt it was a great idea, and I believe we would have built perhaps the greatest creative business entity within the entertainment industry. But it wasn't quite to happen. I did predict that if we didn't get closer together, it was inevitable that we'd get farther apart."

By the beginning of March, the Klein-Eastman power struggle for control of the Beatles had gained momentum. When it became clear to them that they were losing the Beatles, the Eastmans went to extremes to make life difficult for Allen Klein, instead of working for the good of the group and Apple. They ran an ad in *Billboard* saying Eastman had taken control of the Beatles operations.

On March 12, Paul solidified his ties with the Eastmans by marrying Linda at the Marylebone Registry Office in London. Their marriage was hastened by the news that Linda was four months pregnant. (Their child, Mary, was born in August 1969 in a London nursing home.) The arrangements for the wedding were made the day before, including Paul's purchase of a ring that cost £12. The simple service was attended by Paul's brother as best man, Peter Brown, and Mal Evans. After the ceremony the McCartneys had their marriage blessed in an Anglican church in St. John's Wood, London. Immediately following a reception at the Ritz Hotel, Paul returned to the recording studios and spent his wedding night completing work on Jackie Lomax's album.

George Harrison was in the studio on Paul's wedding day when he received a frantic telephone call from his wife, telling him that Scotland Yard had raided their home in Esher. When George arrived, both he and Patti were arrested for possession of cannabis, which was found in a tin box in the living room. Detectives said that there was enough of the illicit substance to make 100 marijuana cigarettes. The Harrisons appeared in court the next day and were each fined £500.

On March 20, John and Yoko were married in Gibralter. In "The Ballad of John and Yoko," John told of the difficult time they had finding a place where they could exchange vows.

From Gibraltar, where they finally were able to get married,

John and Yoko flew to Amsterdam and began the first of a series of peace events. This one was called a Bed-In for Peace, which John described as a commercial for peace. The couple stayed in bed and chatted with people who came to call.

Wherever John and Yoko traveled, the press eagerly greeted them because their "events" and statements were controversial, humorous news. For instance, the Lennons suggested that world leaders should conduct peace talks around a table inside a giant bag, and that all soldiers should be required to remove their trousers before going into battle. At the end of March, the Lennons flew to Vienna to attend the television premier of a movie they produced called *Rape*, an avant-garde message film that showed the psychological violence that stems from invading one's privacy. The star (victim) of the movie was a young Hungarian woman named Eva Majlath, who was selected at random and filmed by strangers everywhere she went.

The film premiered at the Sacher Hotel, where John and Yoko conducted a press conference from inside a white bag. However silly or ridiculous the public found their eccentric behavior, John's life-style with Yoko helped ease the pain he felt about the attacks on his relationship with his wife. Yoko opened the door to a different world and made him feel alive. He could deal with the financial situation at Apple because he knew things would improve, but going back to the Beatles was a living nightmare for him—he could not cope with Paul's and George's contempt for the woman he loved. The near-bankrupt condition of Apple forced Lennon to return to work with the Beatles.

In April the Beatles issued "Get Back" b/w "Don't Let Me Down." The A-side was composed by Paul and featured a keyboard player named Billy Preston, whom the boys were thinking of adding to the group and whose name appears conspicuously on the single's label. John always felt that when Paul sang "Get Back" he was referring to Yoko. John's confidence in his talents as a musician and composer had been restored by this time, as was evident in "Get Back," for which he played lead guitar. The change in Lennon's feelings about himself and life grew out of his love for Yoko, who inspired him to write "Don't Let Me Down."

On June 1 the Lennons took their peace campaign to Canada, where they staged a Bed-In for Peace at the Hotel La Reine Elizabeth in Montreal. (They tried to stage a Bed-In in America, but immigration officials refused to allow them into the country because of John's drug conviction.) The song "Give Peace a Chance" was recorded in the Lennons' hotel room and released as a single on July 4. John's composition gave the American peace movement an anthem.

In the summer of 1969, John and Yoko announced the formation of the Plastic Ono Band, which was Yoko's idea of a conceptual group. The press was invited to a reception for the release of "Give Peace a Chance" to meet "the band," but John and Yoko were involved in an automobile accident in Scotland and could not attend. Reporters, expecting to meet musicians, were greeted by a robot pointing a camera at them that projected their images on a television screen, and a sign that read YOU ARE THE PLASTIC ONO BAND.

The press did not understand the concept behind the Plastic Ono Band, and believed it meant the Beatles were breaking up. Instead, the Plastic Ono Band became a new vehicle for John to record and release his songs, for there was too much material to release on Beatles albums alone.

John had several other reasons for favoring the Plastic Ono Band. The avant-garde world to which Yoko had introduced him fascinated him. Moreover, he derived more pleasure from working with her than with the Beatles on creative ventures. He deeply resented the fact that since 1966, most of the songs on the Beatle's albums were written by Paul, forgetting that his own compositions had dominated the group's long-playing discs before that time. He'd been unable to persuade the others to release his "I Am the Walrus" and "Revolution" as A-side singles. Now he could not get the Beatles to even record some of his songs, such as "Cold Turkey," a song for which they had absolutely no enthusiasm, so he recorded it himself and released it as a Plastic Ono Band single.

For nearly three years John had kept his feelings of dissatisfaction to himself and had allowed the bitterness to build inside. After the group completed work on the *Abbey Road* album in midsummer, Lennon had aired his grievances during a group meeting at Apple. Directing his outbursts at Paul

McCartney, he complained about the maneuvering and game-playing that seemed necessary in order to get space on an album. The others felt that John was mourning his own loss of power within the group. Lennon recalled that he had given up his right to demand three or four tracks on an album and had left it to the others to "invite" him to write or perform on their records. But he made it clear he wanted to put four of his own songs on the album.

Part of the resentment that John harbored about Paul's domination of the albums—a feeling also shared by George—stemmed from having to record songs that McCartney wrote and that the others disliked, such as "Maxwell's Silver Hammer" and "Ob-La-Di, Ob-La-Da," wasting space that could have been used for their songs.

George Harrison was feeling resentful, too: He had to contend not only with Paul's superior attitude toward him but with McCartney's and Lennon's domination of the Beatle albums and singles. He also resented their lack of encouragement, even for an excellent song like "While My Guitar Gently Weeps." Harrison voiced his grievances to the group, mostly to McCartney, saying he felt he had the right to more space on an album and also wanted a chance at earning more money by having more tracks on the discs.

Feelings of dissatisfaction ʳⁿd artistic repression ran deep in John and George. Ringo was caught in the middle of these rows. He was not concerned about sharing space on the albums, because he didn't take his songwriting as seriously as the others, but he could no longer tolerate McCartney's domination.

The fight for equal time and space heralded the ultimate demise of the group musically. There was no longer enough room in the Beatles machine for each of its members. After the group meeting at Apple the Beatles never again returned to the studio to make a record together.

By the summer of 1969, John was beginning to have his doubts about Allen Klein. When he became their manager, Klein had told the Beatles all the things he would do for them—buying NEMS and Northern Songs—but he had yet to produce real results. True, Apple was operating more smoothly now, and for the first time the group knew where their money was going. But Klein's business deals had fallen through, and he didn't seem to be making any money for the Beatles. Klein saved his reputation by negotiating a new recording contract for the group with EMI in September 1969. The contract they had signed two years earlier tied the Beatles to EMI for nine years and promised seventy recordings (or sides), but the group had misunderstood the agreement, thinking instead that they owed EMI seventy sides or nine years. Because they had already done seventy sides, they could have not done another song for the period of the contract. But if they didn't work for EMI, they couldn't work for anyone else either. So Klein worked out a new contract awarding the boys increased royalties and, more important, ownership of their work in America. Even Paul, who had openly opposed Allen Klein and was still trying to convince the others that his in-laws could do a better job, eagerly signed his name to the new agreement.

That September, a telephone call from Toronto brought the group closer to its demise. John Brower, a Canadian promoter who had organized a rock 'n' roll revival show in Toronto, invited Lennon to attend the event as a special guest. Before Brower could outline the acts on the bill, Lennon agreed to come—but only if the Plastic Ono Band could perform. The demand came as a surprise to Bower, but he eagerly assured John that he would take care of all the arrangements and accommodations for his group.

There was only one problem: There was no "group." The show was scheduled for the following day, and John had a name but no band, so he quickly got Eric Clapton, Klaus Voorman to play bass, and a studio musician named Alan White to play drums. They had no repertoire and they could only rehearse on the plane with electric guitars—they didn't have acoustic—so they had no idea how they sounded. John didn't even know the words to many of the songs, some of which he hadn't played since the early Cavern days.

Before the Plastic Ono Band appeared onstage at the Varsity Stadium, Lennon, nervous about performing, vomited from the tension. But as soon as the group began to play, his apprehension dissappeared. The audience—100,000 curious and enthusiastic fans—gave the Plastic Ono Band a standing ovation. The Plastic Ono Band's performance was recorded and released as an album called *Live Peace in Toronto*.

Moreover, the rock 'n' roll revival show gave John the courage to make an important decision—to break away from the Beatles, a decision he made on the plane flight back to England. It wasn't announced then because Klein convinced John there were too many business reasons not to.

19

The Beatles' last gasp was in fact one of their finest albums, *Abbey Road*, released in late September. George Martin—who, since *Sergeant Pepper*, had become less of a producer and more of a technical adviser—was at first reluctant to work with them on the album because "they were always fighting with one another." It turned out to be, however, a very happy album in Martin's estimation, although John didn't think much of it.

Paul's songs dominate the album: "Maxwell's Silver Hammer," "Oh! Darling," "Mean Mr. Mustard," "She Came in through the Bathroom Window," "Golden Slumbers," "Carry That Weight," "The End," "Her Majesty," and "You Never Give Me Your Money," a song that reflected the financial problems at Apple. John's songs included "Come Together," "I Want You" (a bluesy love song to Yoko), "Because," and "Polythene Pam." Ringo's contribution to the album was a song called "Octopus's Garden," which he wrote during the *Let It Be* sessions with George's help. *Abbey Road* featured two compositions by George Harrison: "Here Comes the Sun," which he wrote while sitting in Eric Clapton's garden, and "Something," which John considered to be the best track on the album. The song, inspired by James Taylor's "Something in the Way She Moves," was written about George's wife, Patti, and became Harrison's first A-side single when it was released with "Come Together."

In October, John and the Plastic Ono Band released "Cold Turkey" on a single coupled with Yoko's "Don't Worry, Kyoko." Lennon's composition related his feelings and experiences while withdrawing from heroin, which he says he sniffed but had not injected. He blamed the Beatles for his and Yoko's use of it. "Cold Turkey"—which featured Eric Clapton on lead guitar, Klaus Voorman on bass, and Alan White on drums—was banned in England by the BBC because it was considered to advocate drugs.

The Beatles had reached the point where they were barely speaking to one another. The pressure was too great for Lennon, and at the beginning of October he had a confrontation with Paul upstairs at Apple during a business meeting. During the meeting, McCartney tried to persuade the others to go on the road. Paul believed that performing as the Beatles would help the group musically. They would make surprise visits at small clubs. Lennon could no longer keep his feelings to himself and told Paul he was quitting the group.

When Paul left the Savile Row offices after the meeting, he went home, sat in his garden, and cried. He felt depressed and useless. He could no longer record with John, George, or Ringo because of personal and musical differences, and the idea of going solo had yet to form in his mind. He had a difficult time accepting the fact that the Beatles were finished as a group. Since Brian's death, he had struggled to keep the group from falling apart by trying to give them a sense of direction. His whole existence had revolved around the band. Now he was on his own, without a career.

In October he and Linda fled to their farm in Scotland and retreated so completely that a rumor circulated claiming McCartney was dead. After the release of Abbey Road, an American college student wrote a thesis stating that Paul had died on a rainy night in November 1966 in an automobile accident and that the other Beatles had replaced him with a talented look-alike who'd had plastic surgery. The evidence, drawn from album covers and songs, seemed so convincing that a Detroit disc jockey perpetuated the rumor until the national press picked up on the story and gave it credibility. Fans pored over album covers and dissected Beatle recordings, looking for proof, and concluded that Paul McCartney was indeed dead.

Inundated with telephone calls from fans and reporters all over the world, the Apple press office repeatedly denied the rumor, saying, "Someone has started something very stupid!" Paul himself, however, was unaware of what was happening but when he was informed he told everyone to relax, the publicity was good.

At this time John began the process of divesting himself of his Beatle image. He traveled to Dorset, England, to visit his aunt Mimi, and retrieved his MBE medal, which had rested on top of the television set since 1965. On November 25 John enraged the English establishment by returning his honor to the queen in a brown envelope with a note that read:

> Your Majesty,
>   I am returning my M.B.E. in protest against Britain's involvement in the Nigeria-Biafra thing, against our support of America in Vietnam, and against "Cold Turkey" slipping down the charts.
>
> With love,
> John Lennon of Bag.

Bill Oakes, an employee of Apple Corps at the time, typed the letter for John and tried to talk him out of mentioning "Cold Turkey" but John was furious the record wasn't a hit. Lennon's protest created even more fury in England than when he had accepted the medal.

A week before Christmas, John and Yoko launched another phase of their peace campaign by erecting billboards in twelve major cities proclaiming: WAR IS OVER—IF YOU WANT IT. HAPPY

CHRISTMAS, JOHN & YOKO. They arranged to have the billboards displayed in prominent locations where the message would have the most impact, such as near army recruiting centers. John and Yoko received thousands of letters from young men saying that they were not going to join the army and would grow their hair long.

The Lennons initiated the "War is over" peace campaign by playing a concert at the Lyceum Theatre in London billed as "Peace for Christmas" and donating the proceeds to the United Nations Children's Fund. The band, which called itself the Plastic Ono Super Group, featured George Harrison, Eric Clapton, Delaney and Bonnie, Billy Preston, and Keith Moon.

From September 1969 to early 1970, John, George, and Ringo worked in the studio on solo recordings. On February 6, John released a single produced by Phil Spector called "Instant Karma!" coupled with Yoko's "Who Has Seen the Wind?"

"Instant Karma" was written, recorded, and released in four days.

On March 27, 1970, Ringo's first solo album was released, *Sentimental Journey*, which he had recorded in September 1969 with George Martin. Ringo had planned to make a country-and-western album first, but decided to record old standards that his mother and stepfather liked. The tracks were arranged by Richard Perry, Maurice Gibb, Paul McCartney, and Quincy Jones. The reviewers were disappointed with Ringo's first album, criticizing his vocals and the sentimental theme. The album sold a half-million copies in two weeks.

On April 10, more than five months after John's still-secret divorce decree from the Beatles, the breakup was made public and official when Paul suddenly announced that he had left the group. The announcement was tied to the release of his first solo album, *McCartney*. Apple press officer Derek Taylor explained to the media that Paul's decision to leave the Beatles did not mean that the group had disbanded, just that they wanted to pursue their own projects. The day before McCartney's announcement, he spoke to John Lennon over the phone and told him he was doing what John and Yoko were doing.

John had agreed not to turn his departure from the Beatles

into an event, and when he heard what Paul had done, Lennon was furious, with himself and with Paul, because it now appeared that McCartney was the only dissatisfied member of the Beatles. All issued statements saying the Beatles were still around *sans* Paul.

Paul had begun recording the *McCartney* album in November 1969 at home, using a four-track machine and one microphone, and playing all the instruments. He produced the LP hastily, and when it was issued on April 17, critics slaughtered it, comparing it to John and Yoko's first three efforts. Out of fifteen songs, only three were considered worth listening to: "Every Night," "Teddy Boy," and "Maybe I'm Amazed," which was the strongest cut. Although *McCartney* was poorly received by the music press, the LP sold 1 million copies in four weeks.

The release date of Paul's first solo album was close to that set for the Beatles last album, *Let It Be,* and as a result, complications arose. Paul told the *London Evening Standard* at the time, "We all have to ask each other's permission before any of us does anything without the other three. My own record nearly didn't come out because Klein and some of the others thought it would be too near the date of the next Beatle album. I had to get George, who's a director of Apple, to authorize its release. We're all talking about peace and love, but really we're not feeling peaceful at all."

Ringo met with Paul to persuade him to postpone the release of his album until *Let It Be* was issued. Paul told him that since there was no definite date set for the release of the film and the album, he was releasing *McCartney* as planned. Ringo told him that a date had indeed been set for the Beatles album. To Ringo's surprise, Paul started shouting at him and told him to get out. Depressed and shaken by the incident, Ringo called Allen Klein that night and told him to give Paul what he wanted.

That the Beatles took to attacking each other over matters that weren't important in the past was symptomatic of their rebellion against the Beatles image. John, Paul, George, and Ringo were becoming more and more aware that they no longer wished to belong to the Beatles, yet each of them resented the others for the new influences they'd chosen for their lives. George was resented because he was going eastern and because he nagged to show more of his wares on Beatles discs. John was begrudged his preoccupation with Yoko and the peace movement. Paul was resented for his aristocratic pursuits and his alliance with the Eastmans. And Ringo drew wrath when he picked sides—any sides. The struggle to let go or not to let go gnawed at the boys.

Lennon showed courage in proclaiming his "divorce." It was a grueling and soul-wrenching decision that crushed Paul; and yet it was the first step toward the final act. Though the scene was to become uglier by the moment, it had to be played out. The Beatles were through.

The release of the *Let It Be* album was withheld until early May 1970. Throughout the previous year, engineer Glyn Johns had worked on the recordings without the assistance of the Beatles, for they didn't want to know about the album or have anything to do with one another. Allen Klein was not satisfied with the quality of the recordings, and in January 1970 he brought in producer Phil Spector to salvage the tapes for an album.

Spector edited the twenty-nine hours of tape and pro-grammed a twelve-track LP that included "I Me Mine" and "For You Blue," written by George; "Across the Universe" by John; and "One after 909," one of the first songs composed by John and Paul when they were teenagers. Tracks written by Paul were "Let It Be," "The Long and Winding Road," and "Get Back." McCartney objected to Spector's arrangement of strings and chorus on "The Long and Winding Road" and said that he was not given approval over the final mix.

Record reviewers in England did not think much of the album. In America, though, *Let It Be* had avance sales of nearly 4 million copies and grossed $26 million, the largest initial sale in the history of the U.S. record industry.

Other solo projects followed in quick succession. On September 25, Ringo released his second album, *Beaucoups of Blues*, a collection of country-and-western songs. The album was recorded in Nashville in three days and featured musicians such as Charlie Daniels and Jerry Reed. Brilliant steel guitarist Pete Drake produced, to good result.

On November 27 George Harrison released perhaps the

best solo effort by any Beatle up to that time, *All Things Must Pass*. The album consisted of twenty-three tracks on three long-playing discs, and featured such musicians as Ringo Starr, Eric Clapton, Dave Mason, Alan White, Klaus Voorman, Billy Preston, Gary Wright, and the group Badfinger. George had composed most of the songs on the album during the "White Album," *Let It Be*, and *Abbey Road* sessions and had written several more since. Working with other musicians who liked his material did much to boost Harrison's confidence as a songwriter. Outstanding tracks on the LP included "I'd Have You Anytime," which he co-wrote with Bob Dylon; "Wah-Wah," written during the filming of *Let It Be*; "Isn't It a Pity"; "What Is Life?"; "Beware of Darkness"; "All Things Must Pass"; and "Art of Dying," which was written during the recording of the *Revolver* album. George remembers John as highly negative.

On December 11 John released his first credible album, *John Lennon/Plastic Ono Band*. The LP was highly personalized—the songs were inspired by the primal-therapy sessions with psychologist Arthur Janov that John and Yoko had participated in during the spring. Phil Spector and John shared the production credits on the album.

The solo recordings released by John Lennon, Paul McCartney, George Harrison, and Ringo Starr throughout 1970 were proof of the musical diversity that had existed among them since 1967. Going solo gave each of the four what he wanted: the chance to showcase his talents. They each found that being on their own gave them an artistic freedom that being with the Beatles had not.

20

Throughout 1970 Paul McCartney relentlessly sought both his release from the Beatles partnership and the dissolution of Apple Corps Ltd. McCartney endeavored to gain his freedom from the partnership agreement through amicable means, but without success. In midsummer 1970, John Eastman wrote to Allen Klein asking for Paul's release and was refused for tax reasons.

Paul wrote to John Lennon and asked for his release, but Lennon told him to get George's and Ringo's signatures first, then he'd think about it. In late October, Paul and George met by coincidence in New York, but the meeting failed to produce any positive results for McCartney.

Around Christmastime 1970, Paul and his family retreated to their farm in Campbelltown, Scotland. It was not the happiest Christmas for the McCartneys. John Eastman, who joined them to discuss the situation, had been preparing a case to take Apple to court, but was waiting for Paul to give him the go-ahead. During a walk though the loch country with his brother-in-law, Paul made the decision to sue.

On December 31, 1970, Paul launched a lawsuit against Apple Corps Ltd., seeking the dissolution of the Beatles' partnership. Paul's action left John, George, and Ringo stunned and sad. But something serious had happened. The British Inland Revenue Department began making inquiries about the Beatles' earnings, information that Paul did not have because Allen Klein had not provided financial statements. In early December the Inland Revenue Department served a writ against the Beatles for failing to file information about their income. This left Paul with no other alternatives but to initiate a lawsuit. Earlier he had seen his artistic freedom obstructed when Klein and the others tried to postpone the release of the *McCartney* album. The tax writ would have left him bankrupt.

On January 19, 1971, the case of *McCartney* v. *Lennon, Harrison, Starkey, and Apple Corps Ltd.* came to trial. The case focused on the business differences between Paul and the others and on the integrity of Allen Klein. Justice Stamp, who presided over the trial, was told, "He is a man of bad commercial reputation. Mr. McCartney has never either accepted him as manager or trusted him. And on evidence, his attitude has been fully justified." The attack on Allen Klein set the tone for the trial.

The case dragged through an English court for nearly four months. John, George, and Ringo did not appear in court but leveled attacks against Paul through affidavits, calling him a "spoiled child," telling of the rows that had been commonplace among the Beatles since their early days in Liverpool, and explaining their reasons for appointing Allen Klein in the face of Paul's opposition. "I wanted him as my manager," said John. "I introduced him to the other three. But if Paul is trying to suggest that I was rushing them and pushing him down their throats, this is a wrong impression. . . .

Ringo stated in his affidavit that they'd chosen Allen Klein over John Eastman because Eastman "did not seem to me to be cut out to enjoy the dealing with the hurly-burly of business life or to relish the pretty tough world of the music scene. Klein impressed me straightaway. He took the trouble to find out what he could do about our problem." John added: "We all knew of Paul's friendship with the family, and it was in March 1969 that Paul and Linda Eastman were married. I was against the idea of having as manager anyone in such a close relationship with any particular Beatle, but apart from that, they did not strike me as having the right experience or knowledge for the job that had to be done."

According to Lennon, he, George, and Ringo wanted Klein's appointment to have the unanimous approval of the Beatles, but McCartney kept making excuses for not signing his name to Klein's managerial contract, and his procrastination eventually forced the others to outvote him and sign the agreement.

Justice Stamp, however, ruled in Paul's favor, saying, "The appointment of ABKCO without the concurrence of the plaintiff was, in my judgment, a breach of the terms of the partnership deed." The judge ignored the musical disputes and did not dwell on the Eastmans' interference with Allen Klein's business deals. The point he thought more important was the financial state of Apple. On March 10 Stamp ruled:

> I am satisfied, on the evidence of the accountants and the accounts to which I am referred, that the financial situation is confused, uncertain and confusing. A receiver is, in my judgment, needed not merely to secure the assets, but so that there may be a firm hand to manage the business fairly between the partners and produce order. I have no doubt that a receiver and manager ought to be appointed.

John, George, and Ringo filed an appeal, but on April 26, 1971, they abandoned their fight and Apple was placed in the hands of a court-appointed receiver.

PART FIVE

LIFE AFTER THE BEATLES

Circa May 1971 to 1983

21

During a press conference in 1964, a reporter asked the Beatles how long they expected the group to remain together. John Lennon, whose off-the-cuff remarks were ironically more accurate than his well-thought-out prophecies, casually replied, "Five years." The last song that the Beatles recorded was "Come Together"—five years after that press conference.

Brian Epstein had maintained a balance of power within the Beatles, had kept them thinking as a group, and was able to settle their personal disputes to everyone's satisfaction. The Beatles lost that balance and sense of oneness and harmony when Brian died. Tension, bitterness, discontent, and misunderstandings among the four began to grow with Paul's rise to power in the group and the appearance of Yoko Ono, until the Beatles were finally divided by Klein and Eastman.

The problem was complicated by their musical differences. Although the Beatles had gained the artistic freedom to do almost anything, they found that there was little individual freedom within the band because Beatles music was limited to a certain style. For instance, the group would not have recorded either the music that appeared on the *Plastic Ono Band* album (as shown by their lack of interest in Lennons' "Cold Turkey") or George's songs praising the Lord Sri Krishna.

It is ironic that four individuals who once believed that they had the potential of becoming an extraordinary communications vehicle were unable to communicate with each other. By the time they finally voiced their grievances, they were too far apart for reconciliation. John Lennon, Paul McCartney, George Harrison, and Ringo Starr would never again share a close personal relationship.

During the year that followed the appointment of a receiver, Paul made little effort to reconcile his differences with the others. For instance, when George was organizing a benefit concert for the relief of Bangladesh and invited Paul to play, McCartney said, "Sure, I'll come, if you dissolve the partnership." His response saddened and disgusted Harrison, but Paul was equally irked that George would act as though nothing had happened between them.

The Bangladesh concert did not improve George's relationship with Lennon, either. John and Yoko arrived in New York two days before the event and met with Harrison at his hotel. Lennon was eager to perform in the concert, but was put off when George told him he didn't want Yoko to perform. After arguing with George for a while, John remembered some pressing business he had to attend to back in London. Only Ringo agreed to perform in the concert, which the press called "the greatest rock show on earth."

Throughout 1971 and 1972, the four of them saw no point in sitting down to settle their differences peacefully. McCartney's determination to have things done his way, even after the breakup, created a wider rift between him and the others, though their anger was tempered with love for the man. John and Paul occasionally spoke to each other on the telephone, but their conversations ended in heated arguments. In May 1971, two months after Apple was placed in receivership, Paul and Ringo met en route to Mick Jagger's wedding party in St. Tropez, but did not say a word to each other while traveling.

Ringo, who had once said that meeting the other Beatles was like finding his three lost brothers, was affected most by the bitterness that broke up the group. He recalled his face-to-face meeting with McCartney for a journalist from *Playboy* who was interviewing Allen Klein. When Ringo finished, his eyes were filled with tears.

Ringo's feelings about the breakup, which he expressed in the song "Early 1970" (the B-side of "It Don't Come Easy"), were intensified by his memories of all the good times he and the others had shared. If meeting John, Paul, and George was like finding three brothers, then the breakup was like losing them.

The bitterness between McCartney and Lennon escalated when Paul released his second album, *Ram*, in May 1971. John believed that one of the songs, "Too Many People," was directed at him, and he also interpreted the line "We believe that we can't be wrong" from "The Back Seat of My Car" as McCartney's opinion about the lawsuit. Paul says that the only reference to John on the album was the line "Too many people preaching practices."

As subtle as Paul's lyrics were, Lennon did not mince words in his reply, which appeared in the *Imagine* album in September 1971. The song "How Do You Sleep?" was a harsh, straightforward attack designed to shatter McCartney's ego. George Harrison's presence on the track gave additional credibility to "How Do You Sleep?" and the song initially had the desired effect on McCartney. Lennon later said neither of them took it seriously.

The attack on Paul continued in March 1972 when Ringo Starr released a single called "Back Off Boogaloo," which George Harrison produced with himself on lead guitar. The meaning of the song eluded the public, but McCartney knew it was directed at him. "Boogaloo" was a code name for Paul that John, George, and Ringo used whenever they wanted to speak to him on the telephone.

John's and Paul's war of words was waged in the press from 1970 to 1972. In late 1970 *Rolling Stone* conducted a penetrating interview with John, later published as a book called *Lennon Remembers*. John unleashed the full fury of his wrath and resentment in the article, telling the world that the

Beatles were not the "cute" and "lovable" mop-tops that everyone thought them to be and making it perfectly clear that he felt it was Paul who broke up the group. During the court action to dissolve the partnership, the public learned of the heated rows that had been commonplace among the Beatles since their earliest days in Liverpool and of the displays of temperament that led to numerous walkouts.

Following the litigation, Paul told his side of the story to *Life* magazine and blamed Allen Klein for the breakup of the group. Klein, vowing to "roast McCartney's fuckin' ass," was interviewed by *Playboy* in late 1971. He blamed Paul and his in-laws for the breakup, making them all look like spoiled children. George and Ringo refrained from attacking Paul in the press, but the affidavits they submitted to the High Court confirmed what John had said about Paul.

McCartney, of course, was deeply hurt by John's claim that he was responsible for the breakup of the group. McCartney believed he had kept the Beatles going after Brian Epstein's death by giving them a direction while John walked around in a daze for nearly a year. Paul found it hard to understand how Lennon, who had sung about his desire for honesty in "Gimme Some Truth" (on the *Imagine* LP), could say such harsh things about him.

Over the next two years, John, George, and Ringo's rage kept them from believing anything that Paul said. They were convinced that he had tried to take over the Beatles and Apple, and that his warnings to them about Allen Klein's reputation was solely for the purpose of installing the Eastmans as the group's managers, thus giving him complete control. In the spring of 1973, however, John, George, and Ringo terminated their contract with Klein. Finally heeding Paul's advice, the three had begun to question Klein's trustworthiness.

Paradoxically, tensions eased among the four when Klein launched a lawsuit against Apple. Paul McCartney was elated. During one of their telephone conversations, Lennon admitted to McCartney that he was right about Allen Klein. Another topic of discussion among John, Paul, and George was Ringo, whose career had been one of their concerns when the Beatles broke up. Although the music world did not expect as much from Starr as it did from the others, John, Paul, and George decided to give Ringo the incentive to record an album, something he had not done since 1970, by offering to work with him.

The recording sessions for the *Ringo* album began in mid-1973 in Los Angeles. George Harrison contributed a song called "Sunshine Life for Me," collaborated with Ringo on another called "Photograph," and performed on both tracks. On July 10, 1973, John, George, and Ringo recorded a Lennon composition called "I'm the Greatest." The session, which started at eight at night and finished at three in the morning, included John on piano and harmonies, George on guitar, Klaus Voorman on bass, Billy Preston on keyboards, and Ringo on drums. Ringo felt it was a "good experience," their getting together again in the recording studio.

Paul wanted to participate in the recording of "I'm the Greatest," but was unable to obtain a visa to work in America because of his 1972 drug conviction. When the recording sessions moved to London, Paul began working on the album with Ringo. McCartney contributed a song called "Six O'Clock," in which he performed and sang backup vocals with Linda. He also played the kazoo and sang backup vocals with Harry Nilsson in "You're Sixteen." The *Ringo* album, which was the closest the former Beatles ever came to a reunion, gave Ringo his biggest-selling LP and produced two hit singles: "You're Sixteen" and "Photograph."

Beatles reunion rumors gained momentum in March 1974 when John, George, and Ringo met in Los Angeles to discuss a financial settlement of Apple. (Paul, who had been granted an entry visa in December 1973 to work in America, was supposed to meet them in Los Angeles but at the last moment decided not to come.) The royalties they had earned since 1970 from individual record sales were being held in a joint escrow account that had accumulated nearly $15 million after taxes. It was arranged that all moneys go into four individual accounts.

Throughout the Seventies, there were countless rumors, confirmations, and denials that the Beatles were reuniting, as well as dozens of offers by promoters, none of which was ever taken seriously by the former members of the group despite the incentive of huge sums of money. A year after the release of *Ringo*, John and Paul at one point said they would work together, but when their excitement wore thin, they changed their minds. Although they never ruled out the possibility of working together again, none of the former Beatles wanted to regroup on a permanent basis—and in fact there were numerous obstacles that made a reunion impossible. John Lennon, for example, was unable to leave America in 1973 during his deportation trial for fear of being refused reentry, and Paul could not enter the country until December. On the other hand, that same year all four enjoyed their greatest commercial successes since leaving the Beatles with their albums *Mind Games, Band on the Run, Living in the Material World,* and *Ringo.*

In 1974, George Harrison publicly voiced his opposition to a reunion, saying he could never play with Paul for musical reasons, thus effectively putting an end to any reunion rumors.

In November 1974, George became the first ex-Beatle to embark on a concert tour of North America. At a press conference, he expressed his desire to live in the present and not in the past. The following year, 1975, was a happy one for Lennon. The U.S. government dropped its deportation case against him (granting him citizenship in 1976); and Yoko, having suffered two miscarriages, gave birth to their only child, Sean, on October 9. John decided to retire from the music business to take care of Yoko during her pregnancy and raise his son. His retirement, however, was not revealed to the public.

Post-Beatle hysteria peaked in 1976. It was believed in the music industry that a reunion would take place after the Beatles' contract with EMI Records expired in January. Bill Sargent, a West Coast entrepreneur raised the public's hopes by offering John, Paul, George, and Ringo $30 million for one show, and then increasing it a month later to $50 million for a July 5 concert at Olympia Park in Montreal. After that, a British newspaper quoted George Harrison's father as saying that the group had decided to get together. Ringo, however, says they never had any plan to reunite and only spoke to say they wouldn't do it for any amount of money.

The group's popularity with the record-buying public was as strong as ever—the Beatles had accounted for nearly sixty percent of Capitol's profits throughout the Seventies. In May 1976 EMI reissued twenty-three Beatles singles, including "Yesterday," which made the Top Ten in the *New Musical Express;* the other twenty-two registered throughout the Top 100. When asked what he thought about the repackaging of their work and the resurgence of Beatlemania, John said that he "loved the idea." Paul told a journalist that Wings was not going to release a new single during the "Beatles blitz on the charts," as the press described it. "Just imagine if it's a hit," said Paul, "but is kept out of the number one spot by 'Love Me Do.'" Capitol Records released a compilation album called *Rock 'n' Roll Music,* which entered the Top Ten, and a single, "Got to Get You into My life," which became number one.

In the spring of 1976, Paul McCartney embarked on a concert tour of North America. Instead of denying his past, as George Harrison had done, Paul accommodated those who still believed in it by performing five classic Beatles songs, including "Yesterday." The Wings tour attracted mammoth media attention because again hopes of a reunion were raised: John Lennon had requested two tickets for the New York show; many expected him to appear onstage. But the only reunion on the tour took place at the Los Angeles Forum when Ringo joined Paul onstage to say hello and present McCartney with a bouquet of flowers.

The most absurd reunion offer—George termed it "sick"— came in September 1976 from New York promoter Sid Bernstein, who had promoted the Beatles' dates at Carnegie Hall in February 1964 and the two Shea Stadium dates in 1965 and 1966. In a full-page open letter to the Beatles in the *New York Times,* Bernstein encouraged them to reunite to save humanity:

Dear George, John, Paul and Ringo,

You made the world a happier place to live in. Your music has found its way into the hearts of millions of people in every corner of the world. For almost ten years now, your dedicated old friends and countless new friends have hoped—have waited, and patiently watched for a signal from you—that you might play on one stage just one more time, individually or together.

In a world that seems so hopelessly divided, engaged in

civil war, scarred by earthquakes, and too often in fear of tomorrow's encores of tragic headlines—more than ever, we need a symbol of hope for the future. Simply by showing the world that people can get it together.

Let the world smile for one day. Let us change the headlines from gloom and hopelessness to music and life and a worldwide message of peace. You are among the very few who are in a position to make the dream of a better world come together in the hearts of millions in just one day.

The burden of the world is not on your shoulders—we all share that responsibility. This proposal is made for your consideration—only if you can find the time—and the strength to put it together.

We out there would welcome your return.

The last attempt to reunite the Beatles was made by United Nations Secretary General Kurt Waldheim in the autumn of 1979. Waldheim asked Paul McCartney if he could persuade the others to play a charity concert for the refugees, or boat people, of South Vietnam. Paul, George, and Ringo expressed an interest so long as the press did not know about it, but John refused, saying, "Charity begins at home."

On May 19, 1979, Paul, George, and Ringo attended a party in England celebrating Eric Clapton's marriage to Patti Harrison (the Harrisons were divorced in the mid-Seventies). During the course of the celebration, the three former Beatles appeared together on a makeshift stage and performed several old Beatles songs. Paul said it felt great and wanted to do it again—but with John along as well.

Domestic life was affording John a long sought-after tranquillity. Touring, making political statements, and making music—the hallmarks of Lennon's life—could not compare with the pleasure of watching Sean grow. John acted as both father and mother, and it was a responsibility that filled him with a simple joy that had never been present in his chaotic life. Baking bread, changing diapers, giving baths, and singing childhood lullabies seemed to restore Lennon, giving him a new strength, until he felt ready to slowly reemerge.

In the autumn of 1980, John began working in the recording studio on an album with Yoko. On October 24, Geffen

Records released the single "Starting Over," and a month later issued the *Double Fantasy* album. By the time of the album's release, Lennon had reached another phase in his life. He was now wiser, stronger, more alert, and more at peace with himself and the world. After a long absence, he reappeared at his best: tranquil, patient, optimistic—happy.

Rumors of a Beatles reunion started up again now that John was returning to the studio. But on December 8, 1980, John Lennon was murdered outside his New York City home.

Ringo Starr, vacationing in the Bahamas with his fiancée, Barbara Bach, immediately flew to New York to be at Yoko's side.

Paul McCartney said, "I have hidden myself in my work today. But it keeps flashing in my mind. I feel shattered, angry and very, very sad."

George Harrison canceled his recording sessions and went into seclusion. He issued a statement the following day: "After all we went through together, I had and still have great love and respect for John. To rob someone of life is the ultimate crime."

In May 1981, Paul and Ringo performed on George Harrison's single "All Those Years Ago," a tribute to John. Paul, who had initially appeared the least affected by the news of Lennon's death, expressed his love for his friend in the song "Here Today" from his *Tug of War* album.

To at least one generation, the music of any Beatles song triggers the replays of a memory tape in the mind, stirring up images of innocence and optimism, love and beauty, wild and spirited good fun. The Beatles machine was maintained partly by myth—the substance of the group was not always as solid as people were led to believe. But the Beatles served a purpose that will never be undermined. More than any other pop or rock phenomenon, they brought us almost a decade of consistently fine music, and, through that, constructed a kind of pipeline to trends in style and philosophy. It is strange that the group was most effective in this conduit when they weren't trying so hard to convince the public that individuality mattered most.

The Beatles first symbolized the tremendous power of fun.

And because this was so appealing to us, we stayed on, even as the group became more serious, even when an air of gloom overshadowed their presence. The Beatles phenomenon had become the well of our dreams, and we fed off their combined talents long after they had ceased wanting to give. When they tried to tell us it was over, we argued that it was only another phase of their changing lives. We were reluctant to face their dissolution because they were comforting heroes. Their breakup was one of many disappointments that characterize the end of one era and the beginning of another.

The Beatles will never share the same stage again. We're left with the only real thing we can keep, unconditionally. We're left with memories.

SOURCES

Davies, Hunter. *The Beatles.* New York: McGraw-Hill, 1978 (rev. ed.).

Fawcett, Anthony. *One Day at a Time.* New York: Grove Press, 1981.

Gambaccini, Paul. *Paul McCartney: In His Own Words.* New York: Quick Fox, 1981.

Harrison, George. *I, Me, Mine.* New York: Simon & Schuster, 1981.

Lennon, Cynthia. *A Twist of Lennon.* New York: Avon, 1975.

McCartney, Mike. *The Macs: The McCartney Family Album.* New York: Delilah Books, 1981.

Martin, George and Jeremy Hornsby. *All You Need Is Ears.* New York: St. Martin's, 1980.

Miles, Barry. *The Beatles: In Their Own Words.* New York: Quick Fox, 1978.

Miles, Barry. *John Lennon: In His Own Words.* New York: Quick Fox, 1981.

Playboy magazine. February 1965, November 1971, November 1980.

Tramlett, George. *The Paul McCartney Story.* New York: Popular Library, 1975.

Wenner, Jann. *Lennon Remembers.* San Francisco: Straight Arrow Books, 1972.

Williams, Alan. *The Man Who Gave the Beatles Away.* New York: Ballantine, 1975.